AF608156

Transforming Monkey

Transforming Monkey

ADAPTATION AND REPRESENTATION OF A CHINESE EPIC

Hongmei Sun

UNIVERSITY OF WASHINGTON PRESS
Seattle

THIS BOOK IS MADE POSSIBLE BY A COLLABORATIVE GRANT FROM THE ANDREW W. MELLON FOUNDATION.

Copyright © 2018 by the University of Washington Press

Printed and bound in the United States of America

22 21 20 19 18 5 4 3 2 1

All rights reserved. No part of this publication may be reproduced or transmitted in any form or by any means, electronic or mechanical, including photocopy, recording, or any information storage or retrieval system, without permission in writing from the publisher.

University of Washington Press
www.washington.edu/uwpress

Cataloging-in-Publication Data available from the Library of Congress.

ISBN (hardcover): 978-0-295-74318-9
ISBN (paperback): 978-0-295-74319-6
ISBN (ebook): 978-0-295-74320-2

To my parents.
With you there, I will never feel lost.

To my three sisters.
We do not mention the love between us, only because we know it is always there.

CONTENTS

ACKNOWLEDGMENTS

The writing of this book is a journey that can be compared to the journey of Monkey, one that has crossed many borders, lasted many years, and encountered many demons (obstacles). Along the journey I have been indebted to many whose guidance, support, and generosity have helped me getting started and moving forward. My deepest gratitude to my teachers, mentors, and friends, who have inspired, encouraged, and challenged me during the earlier stages of writing: Elizabeth Petroff, William Moebius, Edwin Gentzler, Enhua Zhang, Floyd Cheung, Paola Zamperini, Maria Tymoczko, Jules Chametzky, and Jonathan Lipman. Without you, this book would not exist. Many thanks to all my friends who have shared with me your laughter and dragged me along through the most difficult days, especially Kanchuka Dharmasiri, Swati Burla, Srinivas Lankala, Antonia Carcelen Estrada, Nicole Calandra, and Bunkong Tuon.

I am grateful to my mentors, colleagues, and friends at George Mason University and other places and institutions, with whose help and encouragement I was able to give the book its needed transformations, especially Carma Hinton, Rei Berroa, Karl Zhang, John Foster, Briankle Chang, John Crespi, and Jane Larson. My special appreciation goes to Douglas Eyman, who has been my many-time first reader and most reliable supporter.

I would like to thank the two anonymous reviewers of the manuscript, whose insights have been essential for helping me realize its final form. I owe special thanks to my editors at University of Washington Press, Lorri Hagman and Niccole Coggins, for their passion and patience. Many thanks to Susan Murray for her diligent work as copy editor.

An earlier version of my discussion of *Lost Empire* and *The Forbidden Kingdom* appeared in *Asia Pacific Translation and Intercultural Studies*, 3:2 (2016): 175–87.

Transforming Monkey

Introduction

Sun Wukong, known as the Monkey King in English, is the protagonist of the Ming dynasty novel *Journey to the West* (Xiyou ji). He is famous for his ability to shape-shift and ride the clouds, his size-changing magic rod, and his love of playing tricks. The longevity of his story reflects his popularity in Chinese culture: the "Journey to the West" narrative is among the most malleable and long-lasting in Chinese literary history. With the repeated adaptations of the narrative over the centuries, the image of the protean monkey character has evolved into the Monkey King we know today.

Journey to the West is a one-hundred-chapter novel published in the sixteenth century during the late-Ming period. It is considered one of the four masterworks of the Ming novel, along with *Water Margin* (Shuihu zhuan), *Romance of the Three Kingdoms* (Sanguo yanyi), and *The Plum in the Golden Vase* (Jinping mei).[1] Loosely based on the historical journey of the famous monk Xuanzang (602–664), who traveled in the Tang dynasty from China to India in search of Buddhist scriptures, the story experienced a series of adaptations over hundreds of years before it was developed into the full-length novel, which recounts a mythological pilgrimage of the monk Tripitaka (the fictional Xuanzang), accompanied by three disciples and protectors he converts along the way: Sun Wukong (aka the Monkey King, or Monkey), Zhu Bajie (aka Zhu Wuneng, Pigsy, or Pig), and Sha Wujing (aka Sha Seng, Sha Heshang, Friar Sand, or Sandy). These disciples, as well as a dragon prince who transforms into a white horse as Tripitaka's steed, are demons or animal spirits who have sinned and who agree to accompany Tripitaka as atonement. Along the way, the group encounters and overcomes eighty-one tests, most of which involve demons and spirits who want to capture Tripitaka and eat his flesh in order to gain immortality.

The history of *Journey to the West* represents a process of continuous adaptations of Xuanzang's story. The historical trip becomes a mythological journey in a world full of demons, spirits, Taoist gods, and Buddhist celestials. At some point—the actual origin and provenance remain unclear—the monkey follower of Xuanzang was added to a retelling of the story. Once included, the monkey figure grew in popularity until he replaced the monk as the main character and protagonist. It is owing to the long process of adaptation that today the Monkey King remains popular globally.

In 2013, Lincoln Center in New York City presented *Monkey: Journey to the West* as "China's greatest story retold for the 21st century," a theatrical piece coproduced by Chinese director Chen Shi-zheng, British musician Damon Albarn, and British artist Jamie Hewlett, combining music, animation, singing, and acrobatic and martial art performances. Before appearing in this venue, it had been performed around the world, following a 2007 premiere in Manchester, England. In contrast, the competition for mascot for the 2008 Beijing Olympic and Paralympic Games was a story of failure for Sun Wukong. Many applications featured him, reflecting his popular status in Chinese culture as a beloved figure for both adults and children. However, the monkey lost the competition precisely because of this popularity—so many registered brands featuring him existed throughout Asia that crafting a unique image with the Olympic theme was deemed difficult.[2]

In more recent years, new films of the Monkey King have been created and consumed annually: *Journey to the West: Conquering the Demons* (Xiyou: Xiangmo pian) produced and directed by Stephen Chow (2013); *The Monkey King* (Xiyou ji: Da'nao tian'gong) starring Donnie Yen and Chow Yun-fat, which was primarily a Hollywood production (2014); the animated film *Monkey King: Hero Is Back* (Xiyou ji zhi dasheng guilai), which was lauded as a breakthrough in Chinese animation (2015); *The Monkey King 2* (Xiyou ji zhi Sun Wukong sanda Baigu Jing) and *A Chinese Odyssey: Part Three* (Dahua Xiyou 3), both sequels of successful earlier installments (2016); and the list goes on. The uneven quality of these films seems to have little effect on their commercial success: the popularity of the

Monkey King's image alone serves as rich cultural capital that can be repeatedly reused.

The 2016 Year of the Monkey in the Chinese lunar calendar was a time when the Sun Wukong theme was particularly welcomed, especially during the New Year holiday period. One of the two 2016 Monkey King movies, *The Monkey King 2*, was released in China on February 8, the first day of the lunar New Year. There had been much speculation about which Monkey King would appear on the televised Chinese New Year gala (*chunwan*), a must-watch for many Chinese viewers. Many were disappointed to discover that Zhang Jinlai, known as Liu Xiao Ling Tong for his acting of the Monkey King in the 1986 CCTV television series *Journey to the West*, and considered by many to be the quintessential Monkey King actor in China, was not invited by CCTV to perform at the gala. Many fans posted their opinions online, urging CCTV to include Zhang in their program, since they couldn't imagine a gala for the Year of Monkey without him.[3] This anecdote reveals several key points about the Monkey King and *Journey to the West*: the influence and popularity of the 1984 television series as an adaptation of the classical novel; acceptance of the image of Zhang Jinlai as the classic Monkey King, just as the television series has established itself as a classic for many audiences; and the position of the *Journey to the West* television series and Zhang's Monkey King in the collective memory of the generation of Chinese people who grew up watching the show. In short, it demonstrates how influential a literary classic can be, and how, via adaptation, the classics exercise such influence.

Much of the existing scholarly research on this classic story is focused on the authorship and formative history of the sixteenth-century novel and on the originality and development of the main characters. Literary analyses of the text have taken diverse and heterogeneous approaches but have predominantly focused on the religious and allegorical meanings of the tales.[4] Little has been written about the Monkey King image in contemporary settings from the approach of adaptation, despite the obvious importance of this approach for *Journey to the West*, which is the product of repeated adaptations and maintains its influence in popular culture through ongoing adaptation today. *Journey to the West* is an accretive text, shaped by many hands at many times, and through interactions with many audiences. Although current readers tend to think of contemporary adaptations as "adaptations only" and the sixteenth-century version as "the original text," the latter itself falls in the middle of a long chain of adaptations and exists in multiple forms, so one must gather an idea of the "original" from among the variations, inasmuch as this "original" is derivable. One topic of controversy surrounds the relationship between the Shidetang edition of *Journey to the West* and the two shorter versions of the novel, *A Chronicle of Tang Sanzang's Journey to the West and Deliverance from the Ordeals* (Tang Sanzang xiyou shi'e zhuan) by Zhu Dingchen and *Story of the Journey to the West* (Xiyou ji zhuan) by Yang Zhihe.[5] Scholars have debated which of the three was published first and which were adaptations, but for lack of new data and more convincing interpretation, the Shidetang edition printed in 1592 is generally considered the "original." Although it is now generally accepted that Wu Cheng'en (ca. 1500–ca. 1582) is the author of the Shidetang edition of *Journey to the West*, this position is supported only by the lack of better candidates and more convincing evidence.[6] Furthermore, the origin of the Monkey King character remains unclear.[7]

Adaptation is a subject of increasing interest among scholars. Within adaptation studies, areas of focus include the cultural, social, and intertextual significations of adaptations.[8] Classicists have long scrutinized modern adaptations,[9] but in the field of Asian studies, despite much excellent work on the authorship of *Journey to the West*, history of the narrative, character development, and the meaning of the pilgrimage story, little attention has been given to the work's popularity today and its contemporary adaptations. Through hundreds of years the Monkey King figure has shown amazing adaptability. His story appears in various forms in all media, crossing borders of culture and time, and his image has been frequently used in racial and political representations with social and political impact. Sun Wukong's changes throughout modern history, intertwined with the construction and representation of Chinese identity, require a thorough examination.

My focus on Monkey as the protagonist does not mean that there exists a consensus that Sun Wukong is the most important character of *Journey to the West*. Given the complex nature of the text and the varied approaches of criticism, Sun Wukong is often not singled out as the chief protagonist in both traditional and contemporary studies. Recent Monkey criticism attempts either to uncover Monkey's origins by linking him to various other monkey figures in literary and cultural history or to view Monkey as a religious figure embodying a religious vision.[10] This volume instead focuses on Monkey's influence on contemporary Chinese culture: today's adaptations do not care about Monkey's "origin," when Monkey himself has become more famous and influential than the other monkeys in Chinese culture that might have influenced him. And although religious messages may well be embedded in the novel for its writer and for its readers near the author's time, today's much enlarged readership, which has experienced *Journey to the West* on screen and stage and in graphics and games, is less interested in religious exegesis than in how they relate personally to the character of the Monkey. In the field of translation studies, translation and adaptation are seen as closely interrelated processes. The examples presented here are mostly loose adaptations, keeping only the basic characters and theme of *Journey to the West*. This type of adaptation is essentially a form of what translation theorist André Lefevere calls "rewriting," which encompasses translation, historiography, anthologization, criticism, and editing. The importance of rewritings should not be neglected, since their influence and impact are often greater than that of the original texts.[11] Scholars in translation studies have called for a broad understanding of translation, which can be seen as writing inspired by the encounter with other tongues, and translation study is thus viewed as an increasingly transdisciplinary and open-ended field.[12] In the case of *Journey to the West*, each adaptation is a translation across time and, in many cases, across language and culture. Although *Journey to the West* is a well-known classical title in China, it is through these contemporary rewritings inspired by cross-cultural encounters that the classic work continues to gain influence among broader audiences, and a study of these popular versions offers new perspectives for understanding the classic.

My intention is not to find the origin of the Monkey King figure, or to trace a genealogy for Sun Wukong, or to provide a linear development of the evolution of the story. Instead, I acknowledge the dispersion of the adaptations and deal with only a selection of the most prominent rewritings of the Monkey King myth. It is precisely the differences apparent in these rewritings and the seeming disconnectedness of these characters that is of interest. In many of these cases, the image of Sun Wukong is used as self-representation, and accordingly the monkey's story is revised and the image changed or even manipulated to satisfy the political agenda of the adaptors. A study of the changes that the Monkey King image has undergone is therefore closely related to the issues of domestic and transnational Chineseness, the politics of representation and self-representation, and the politics of cross-cultural translation.

EDITIONS AND TRANSLATIONS

Among the versions of complete and abridged English translations of *Journey to the West*, Arthur Waley's abridged translation *Monkey: Folk Novel of China* (1942) is probably the most influential. Although it includes only thirty chapters out of one hundred and has left out all poetic segments and revised prose sections, it is the most popular and accessible version. Waley's translation of the character names—Monkey, Tripitaka, Pigsy, and Sandy—reappear in countless later rewritings and are hence known by many readers. Anthony C. Yu's multivolume complete translation, *The Journey to the West* (1977–83), is the most authoritative version, with extensive scholarly introduction and notes. An abridged version was published under the title *The Monkey and the Monk* (2006), in which Yu's original romanization of Chinese terms according to the outdated Wade-Giles system was converted to the globally accepted Hanyu Pinyin system. In 2012 a revised edition of the complete translation was published, with the Pinyin romanization and updated scholarly annotations. In this volume, when referring to *The Journey to the West*, I use Yu's 1977–83 translation, since this version had been widely used for some thirty years before the more recent one was published. Since Pinyin is used throughout this volume, I have changed the Wade-Giles forms into Pinyin for consistency.

William John Francis Jenner's translation *Journey to the West* (1982–84) offers a more readable translation for general readers. It is a complete translation with no scholarly notes. In 2003, a six-volume bilingual edition was published, with Chinese and English on facing pages. This edition is welcomed by readers who are less scholarly oriented but are nonetheless interested in understanding a text that is as close to the "original" as possible with the assistance of the translation, and possibly also the interactions between the two languages.

In contrast to the sixteenth-century novel, I use "Journey to the West"—in quotation marks—to refer to the narrative, which has a longer history than the novel. For the convenience of discussion and comparison, I refer to the 1592 edition of *Journey to the West* as the "original," based on which, either directly or indirectly, contemporary adaptations have been produced. Although in this particular case study of adaptations there is really no original, for quotation I use the Chinese edition published by Renmin Wenxue Chubanshe (1980), and Yu's English translation *The Journey to the West* (1977–83). Yu's translation is based on the version published by Zuojia Chubanshe in 1954, which is essentially the same as the Renmin Wenxue edition.[13] Based closely on the 1592 edition of *Journey to the West*, the Zuojia/Renmin Wenxue edition added a chapter about Tripitaka's birth and life that exists in other editions but is not included in the 1592 version. Thus, editing and publication have also actively shaped (or adapted) the novel.

Tracing further back from "Journey to the West," two major sources for the narrative have been found: the historical journey of Xuanzang and the mythical figure of the Monkey King. Although the historical event clearly refers to the journey to India that the monk Xuanzang undertook in the seventh century, and the historical figure Xuanzang is accepted almost unanimously by scholars as the source of the character Tripitaka in the novel, the source of the Monkey King is unclear. Multiple figures may have influenced the image of the Monkey King, including Hanuman in the Indian tradition and monkey lore in the Chinese tradition.[14] Each of these two major narrative lines revolves around one protagonist, who together become the two major characters in *Journey to the West*. Although the Monkey King figure was adopted into the narrative of the journey to India as only a helper of the monk, in later versions of the story the monkey becomes the protagonist, as becomes evident in *Journey to the West*, and more obviously in contemporary adaptations in China, where the Monkey King becomes the central figure with whom the audience identifies, and Tripitaka is portrayed with more negative features.[15] In order to understand this "special effect" by means of adaptation, an outline of the central characteristic of the Monkey King is necessary. Why is it that Sun Wukong has been enjoying a long-lasting popular life in China and many other Asian countries, and what is it in the Monkey King character that attracts so many people of diverse cultural backgrounds to write about it and to make use of the image to express something as important as their own identity? In many of the influential texts adapted from the Monkey King story, the adapted plot bears scarce resemblance to that of the original. In these cases, what is it in the Monkey King character that enables the audience to still recognize him as Sun Wukong and to what extent is this variation from the original acceptable?

TWO MONKEYS

At first glance the theme of this project bears much similarity to that of literary critic Henry Louis Gates Jr.'s *The Signifying Monkey: A Theory of Afro-American Literary Criticism.* Both are about a trickster monkey who plays an important role in an ethnic culture in the United States; both are related to a translator/interpreter; and signification/revision is a major focus of both studies. The monkeys from the two cultures almost resemble each other too much. However, even as both monkeys are central tropes for their respective projects, each of the tropes works in a distinct way.

Gates argues that the Signifying Monkey stands as the rhetorical principle in Afro-American vernacular discourse. He uses the figure of this monkey as the trope of literary revision and develops a theory of literary criticism for African American literature. Signifyin(g) is used as a concept to analyze the intertextuality between works of prominent African American writers, specifically Richard Wright, Ralph Ellison, Zora Neale Hurston, and Ishmael Reed. Basing his criticism on a monkey figure, he first argues for the kinship between the Signifying Monkey and Esu-Elegbara because of "their functional equivalence as figures of rhetorical strategies and of interpretation," and then the central status of the Signifying Monkey as a trope of Signifyin(g) in African American literature.[16]

There is a curious comparability between the Signifying Monkey and Sun Wukong as translators. Both Esu and the Signifying Monkey play the role of interpreter in the myths in which they are characters. Esu is the interpreter of the god Ifa, and the central figure of the Ifa system of interpretation. The Signifying Monkey, Esu's Pan-African kinsman, "stands for the rhetorical strategies of which each literary text consists."[17] Their trickster characteristic is represented by Esu's two mouths (double voice) and the Signifying Monkey's playing with double registers in the rhetorical strategies he uses.

As Gates admits, "All texts Signify upon other texts, in motivated and unmotivated ways."[18] That is to say, Signifyin(g), as a "metaphor for textual revision," is not something that is limited to Afro-American literature.[19] The Monkey King serves as a trope of revision, like that of the Signifying Monkey, but in his own ways. Although Sun Wukong is the first disciple of Tripitaka/Monk Xuanzang, the great translator of Buddhist texts, and the "Journey to the West" story itself is about a journey to fetch texts to be translated, translation itself is not a major theme in the story. In fact, "Journey to the West" mostly neglects the impact of language, even though the journey is through numerous countries and the travelers no doubt have to deal with language differences as a result. Nevertheless, the "Journey to the West" narrative, and especially the Monkey King, can serve as a trope for revision/adaptation: not only has the story been through adaptations both before and after the sixteenth-century classic *Journey to the West,* but the transformability of Monkey is frequently used in recent examples to illustrate the experience of adapting and adjusting. The aspect of the Monkey King that is interesting for the adaptations lies in the image, not in the voice. If one were to narrow the rich meaning of the Monkey King image down to a trope, it would lie in the tension between the monkey, the human, and the god that coexists in the Monkey King. Because the tension exists in something as important and personal as the body itself, the image of Sun Wukong is therefore being used in varied situations representing the struggles in identity. What the Monkey King can contribute to the issue of Asian American identity is the metaphor of transformation, the freedom one can attain in one's body, and by extension in aspects of one's social life.

This project is also informed by the significance of the Monkey King in my own life. Growing up in a working-class family in China shortly after the Cultural Revolution, as I watched this figure in the Peking Opera, animated film, movie, and Web versions of the story that still move me to tears, I had no doubt that the hero was Chinese and that he belonged to me. Coming to the United States in 2001, I was astounded to see the Monkey King playing a significant role in Asian American cultural texts. In 2003, while doing research on one such text, Maxine Hong Kingston's *Tripmaster Monkey,* I came across a Monkey King who was entirely new to me, at moderntales.com, in a webcomic by Gene Luen Yang, then titled *American Born Chinese: Reflections on the Chinese American Experience.* This online comic would grow to become a popular and critical success, be published as a graphic novel that was nominated for the National Book Award, and win the Michael L. Printz Award, among others. Although portions of the main plot of *Journey to the West* are still recognizable, this graphic story abounds with references to the lives of Chinese Americans. The front cover of Yang's original, self-published print publication of *American Born Chinese* speaks volumes: Three main characters stand close together at the middle of the page: a boy with an Asian appearance, the Monkey King, and a figure

Figure I.1. Book cover showing the three main characters standing together. From *American Born Chinese* © 2002 by Gene Luen Yang. All Rights Reserved.

that resembles the living stereotypes of the Chinese in the United States. This cover image indicates the three interconnected themes of the book and raises questions about how Monkey fits in a story about a Chinese American boy and in relation to the evil figure looming at his back. Such creative adaptations invite us to address rewritings comparatively by examining how new stories based on *Journey to the West* differ widely from each other yet make complete sense in their own historical and cultural settings.

The chapters that follow not only focus on the crossing over of the story and image of Sun Wukong from one time/space to new cultural and political environments, but they also bring together different types of disciplinary research. While the texts themselves cross the Pacific Ocean, bridging the gaps between historicity and modernity, and between cultures, languages, and media, a study of these texts brings together the Asian and the Asian American, the premodern and the contemporary, as well as the literary and the visual. We begin with an introduction to the novel *Journey to the West* and its influence, followed by an analysis of the characteristics of the protagonist Sun Wukong. Because of the fundamental multivalence in this figure, various political and ethnic groups use him as a representative to tell their own stories. The following chapters examine five stages of Monkey's adaptations. Historically speaking, "Journey to the West" is a product of adaptation. When the image of the Monkey King is added to the narrative and gradually takes the shape of Sun Wukong in *Journey to the West*, the influence of antecedents and the interlacing traditions of popular and elite culture together shape what we know as the protagonist of the sixteenth-century novel. A major transformation takes place in the mid-twentieth century during the reign of Mao Zedong, when the trickster monkey is collectively recast as a revolutionary hero. This heroic image remains the mainstream view until a new change is initiated by a Stephen Chow film, *A Chinese Odyssey* (1995), after which the image of Monkey takes a postsocialist turn. While the new transformation of the Monkey King as a hero is ongoing in China, in American popular media the Monkey image is adapted in a different manner, representing a mythical and antiprogressive oriental. Asian American adaptations, on the other hand, use the image of the Monkey King to illustrate the struggles of ethnic minorities in the United States, racial stereotypes, and ethnic identity. Monkey continues to shape-shift in new places and times, and each new Monkey collectively enriches our understanding of his image.

CHAPTER 1

Who Is Sun Wukong?

The Image of the Monkey King in Journey to the West

At the beginning of the hundred-chapter novel *Journey to the West,* a monkey is born from a primeval stone egg. This uncommon birth makes it impossible to place him into a distinct taxonomic category. "Born of the essences of Heaven and Earth," he is nonetheless still one of the "creatures from the world below."[1] While the Monkey King belongs to both heaven and earth, his legendary birthplace is not easily locatable in either. According to the Buddhist cosmology introduced to the reader at the beginning of the first chapter, the Flower-Fruit Mountain (Huaguo Shan) appears to be located on the East Purvavideha Continent (Dong Shengshen Zhou), one of the four continents of the world. However, its geographic location relative to heaven and earth, or to the other continents that the monkey traverses in his journey, is never accounted for. To some extent the ambiguous birth and birthplace of the monkey contribute to his multivalent character.

At home on the Flower-Fruit Mountain, the monkey soon declares himself the Monkey King after demonstrating his prowess by crossing a waterfall and discovering a new territory, the Water-Curtain Cave, on behalf of the entire monkey kingdom. It is the first breakthrough in his life and is accomplished through crossing boundaries. Soon thereafter, and having become dissatisfied with a mortality that, by necessity, would subject him to the border between life and death, the self-proclaimed king sets off on a raft in search of a teacher who might guide him toward immortality. This journey brings him from the East Purvavideha Continent to the West Aparagodaniya Continent (Xi Niuhe Zhou), where he finds a master in the Patriarch Subhūti (Xuputi Zushi) on Lingtai Mountain. In chapter 1 the monkey has already accomplished a "journey to the west" on a smaller scale, a journey for himself. Of no small significance, the master, one of the ten disciples of the Buddha, is described here as one who finds harmony among Buddhism, Taoism, and Confucianism.[2] By means of this physical and spiritual journey from east to west, the monkey has acquired a name, Sun Wukong (Awaking to Emptiness), together with esoteric techniques enabling him to wield magical powers.

After returning to the Flower-Fruit Mountain, Sun Wukong successfully defends the subjects of his monkey kingdom by defeating a demon foe and thereby creating a name for himself among the demon kings. In addition, he befriends a number of immortal beings who occupy neighboring lands, one of whom is the Bull Demon King (Niumo Wang), who later becomes an antagonist of the pilgrims. By becoming brothers with these demons on earth, Sun Wukong posits himself as one of them. He tests his power in the water realms and convinces the dragon kings there to present him with their treasured magic iron, which becomes his famous iron rod. He also creates turmoil in hell when he deletes the names of his monkey tribe from the Register of Life and Death, hence attaining immortality, although unofficially. The sphere in which he can be active is thus enlarged to include the earth, the sea, and the underworld.

Heaven, having learned of the monkey's mischievous behavior, appoints him as Supervisor of the Imperial Stables (Bimawen), in an effort to co-opt him. His territory is thus further enlarged to include heaven. This is an important step in his life since he is now recognized as a deity within the heavenly hierarchical system rather than an outsider demon. When Sun Wukong recognizes his low position in the celestial hierarchy, he returns to his mountain and lays claim to the title "Great Sage, Equal to Heaven," essentially declaring himself the strongest demon in the world in possession of an outlaw power on a par with heaven's. Dissatisfied with marginalization within one system, he simply chooses to create a parallel system and names himself its head. And when heaven is unable to take him by force, it once again must reabsorb the monkey peacefully by reaccepting him into the heavenly fold. Despite being officially recognized as the Great Sage, the Monkey King still constantly breaks rules in heaven, and ultimately creates havoc when he learns he is not invited to the Peach Banquet. The disgruntled monkey breaks off yet again from heaven, this time demanding that he replace the Jade Emperor himself. Significantly, the domains that Sun Wukong has so far tested and conquered include the earth, water, hell, and the Taoist heaven. Being active in all levels of the mythic cosmos enables him to enjoy immense growth in his realm—but more importantly, he becomes effectively limitless.

Sun Wukong's rebellion comes to an end when he meets the Buddha. He accepts the wager the Buddha has proposed, which is to jump out from the Buddha's palm. Failing to do so, since the Buddha's palm can grow as fast as Wukong can jump, he is subsequently imprisoned under the Five Phases Mountain for five hundred years, which functions as a turning point in Monkey's life and an intermission in the narrative. What Monkey goes through during this period is completely omitted by the narrative, which simply switches to the story of Tripitaka and the beginning of the journey. When the Monkey King reappears in the story, his life starts anew on a very different track.

The monkey is in due course released by the traveling monk Tripitaka, who becomes his master and gives him the name Pilgrim (Xingzhe). At the beginning the master is shocked by Wukong's demonic behavior and worried that the monkey might be out of control. The Bodhisattva Guanyin responds by setting a fillet on the monkey's head. The tightening of this band—in response to Tripitaka's recitation of the Tight-Fillet Spell (Jingu Zhou)—enables Tripitaka to control the monkey's actions. Henceforth Sun Wukong serves as Tripitaka's protector and as leader of the other disciples. He becomes the monk's most reliable defense against demons and monsters on their way to the West. In the following eighty-seven chapters, which are primarily a long series of captures and releases of the pilgrims by monsters, demons, animal spirits, and gods in disguise, Sun Wukong either defeats the adversaries himself or finds a natural or sociopolitical conqueror of the enemy to ensure victory.

In *Journey to the West,* Monkey's life can be summarized as composed of two parts, with the Five Phases Mountain as the watershed.[3] Before his subjugation by the Buddha under the Five Phases Mountain, his life can also be divided into several phases, each phase with a different name and identity:

I: Before Subjugation:

- a. The nameless stone monkey
- b. The Handsome Monkey King (Mei Houwang)
- c. Sun Wukong (name given by Subhūti)
- d. The Supervisor of the Imperial Stables (Bimawen)

e. The Great Sage, Equal to Heaven (Qitian Dasheng)
Intermission: 500 years under the Five Phases Mountain
II: After Subjugation
Pilgrim (Xingzhe)

The five phases of the monkey's life before his subjugation by the Buddha demonstrate the innate drive of the monkey to test every limit that defines his sphere. With each step the monkey takes in his life, there is a transformation, a breakthrough, and his magic skills allow him to transgress limits. Step by step he broadens his sphere, challenging every authority, until he is facing the greatest cosmic power (who is, interestingly, the foreign Buddha from the West, invited by the indigenous god, the Jade Emperor). It is the spirit that challenges all limits that identifies him as a demon, one of those who dwell outside of the space of heavenly order. Since hierarchical control is about keeping boundaries and maintaining order, this kind of nonstop challenge cannot be accepted. Monkey therefore has to be either considered as a challenge from the outside (a demon) or changed and coopted within the system.

The narrative does not address the meaning of Monkey's imprisonment; the five hundred years of his life under the mountain are left undiscussed. The narrative simply branches off to other story lines, instead providing information about the Buddha's intention to impart Buddhist canons to China, family stories of Tripitaka, the journey of the Tang emperor to the underworld, and the commission of Tripitaka as the scripture-seeking pilgrim after the epiphany of Guanyin. Five hundred years later, when Tripitaka comes to the Five Phases Mountain and releases Monkey, Wukong is very eager to accept his task as a disciple of the monk. The five hundred years serve as a narrative gutter,[4] before which Monkey strives to surpass all boundaries—the patriarch of all beings—while after it the monkey becomes a servant, a pilgrim following the orders of a monk, confined by the magic headband. Before the gutter, he was a demon himself; after the gutter, he becomes a demon-subjugator and a demon killer. When encountering and fighting antagonist demons, the pilgrim monkey continually boasts to them about his glorious past as a demon monkey but then kills or subjugates them by himself or with celestial help. In this sense, the journey of the pilgrims is at the same time a story of demon-conquering and an account of the subjugation of the monkey himself. The eighty-seven chapters of the pilgrimage story continually replay self-contradictory anecdotes. He is simultaneously the one and the other, dual contradictions within one body.

But this is not only a journey from China to India.[5] The Monkey King's journey, far from unidirectional, is also full of upward and downward movement—he bounces between the heavenly gods and the demons and monsters on earth both before and after his submission. The nature of these trips does, however, change after his imprisonment. In the early phases of his life, the journeys up and down are carried out via his free will, whereas the later ups and downs as a pilgrim are mostly arranged by Guanyin and other gods, as part of the trials of the journey. Just as his somersault never enables him to jump out of the hand of Buddha, his somersaulting up and down during the pilgrimage never gets him out of the determined trajectory of his life. He is only fulfilling his task, the mission of a pilgrim who works as a mediator.

The character of the Monkey King is fundamentally self-contradictory. In the earlier stage of his life, he is a self-important heroic rebel, but later he transforms into a loyal disciple of the monk master and a pious believer in Buddhist thought. Monkey does go through some transitional periods during the journey, including a few incidents in which he is in disagreement with, yet has to obey, Tripitaka, but later in the journey the narrative demonstrates that his understanding of the Heart Sutra often even surpasses that of Tripitaka. For instance, when the group of five leave the Dharma-Destroying Kingdom (Mie Fa Guo), Tripitaka feels disturbed when seeing another evil-looking mountain in front of them on their way. Wukong reminds him of the gatha that the Crow's Nest Zen Master taught him: "Seek not afar for Buddha on Spirit Mount; Mount Spirit lives only in your mind. There's in each man a Spirit Mount stupa; Beneath there the Great Art must be refined." He even gives Tripitaka instructions: "Maintain your vigilance with the utmost sincerity, and the Thunderclap will be right before your eyes. But when you afflict yourself like that with fears and troubled thoughts, then the Great Way and, indeed, Thunderclap will seem far away. Let's stop all these wild guesses. Follow me." Upon hearing Monkey's words, Tripitaka feels "his mind and spirit immediately cheered up as all worries subsided."[6]

The multivalence of the Monkey King is reflected in his multiple names and titles, each related to one of his multiple identities. The narrative refers to him as the monkey or the stone monkey (before he gains any title), (Handsome) Monkey King, (Sun) Wukong, or the Great Sage in the earlier stages of his life. The title that is used most often by the narrative voice is Pilgrim, and following that, the Great Sage. All of these names and titles are frequently used by other characters in addressing or referring to him in the story, but "Wukong" or "Monkey King" is almost never used by the narrative.[7] Paradoxically, although the Monkey King wants to be the most powerful and most highly respected during his expanding phases, once he acquires the family name "Sun," he never minds being referred to as a monkey and in fact often calls himself "Old Monkey" (Lao Sun), which can be seen as an indicator of the self-contradictory nature of Sun Wukong's character. Sun is a family name given to him by Master Subhūti, because, as he explained, it comes from the character *sun* (monkey), but without the accompanying animal radical, it "accords with the Doctrine of Baby" since its compounds *zi* and *xi* means respectively "boy" and "baby."[8] *Lao* means old, but it is also often included in an appellation, especially for an elder, to show respect. Sun Wukong explained the meaning of *lao* quite well himself when responding to an enemy king: "[When] I caused great disturbance in the Celestial Palace five hundred years ago, all those divine warriors of the Ninefold Heaven wouldn't have dared address me without the word 'Venerable' when they saw me."[9] In this quote, "venerable" is an accurate translation of *lao*. *Lao* and *sun* together, therefore, form a name that is an oxymoron. The translation "Old Monkey" is a choice made based on the sacrifice of the other meanings of both *sun* and *lao*, and understandably so, owing to the lack of corresponding expressions in English. But without the meaning of "venerable" and "baby," the nature of the oxymoron in the name is lost. "Old Monkey" can also mean "Old Baby" or "Venerable Monkey," which reveal more of the ambivalent nature of the Monkey King. Among his titles, Wukong's favorite is "Great Sage, Equal to Heaven" (Qitian Dasheng), or simply "Great Sage," a title reminding him of a glorious past when he was the bravest of demons creating upheaval in the heavenly court. This title, although self-granted at the beginning, is later recognized by the Jade Emperor and thus describes the monkey as both a demon and a god. In contrast, the title "Supervisor of the Imperial Stables" is least favored by the monkey—probably not only because it is a position of low rank but more importantly because it tacitly indicates Monkey's once eagerness to yield to heaven and constrain his rebellious spirit.

Reflected by his names and titles, Sun Wukong juggles his multiple identities, some of which are sharply opposed to each other. Although Sun Wukong as Pilgrim has turned from a demon into a demon-terminator, he always proudly announces himself as the Monkey King and the Great Sage who once instigated havoc in heaven. In chapter 17, for instance, when he fights a demon for the first time in his pilgrimage, he gives a thirty-two-couplet-long self-introduction, a quite detailed outline of his life, including a vivid description of his battle against the divine troops, demonstrating his pride in that history. This grandiloquent self-introduction ends with a stately exclamation: "Go and ask in the four corners of the universe: You'll learn I'm the famous ranking demon of all times!"[10] On other occasions throughout the journey when encountering demons, Monkey will boast about himself in similar ways, bragging about once having been a splendid demon monkey.

THE MONKEY KING AS A TRICKSTER

The Monkey King can be considered a Chinese trickster, a term often used in folklore and mythology studies. Anthropologist Claude Lévi-Strauss considers the trickster as a mediator, because the trickster's "mediating function occupies a position halfway between two polar terms," and he therefore retains "something of that duality—namely an ambiguous and equivocal character."[11] Lévi-Strauss's structural study of myth argues that myths can be broken down into repetitive patterns of contradictions and that the purpose of myth is to "provide a logical model capable of overcoming a contradiction."[12] In the case of the trickster of Native American mythology, the initial opposition is that between life and death. Almost always a raven or a coyote, the trickster mediates the opposition between herbivores and beasts of prey, and ultimately mediates between life and death. Although the term "trickster" was developed originally in non-Eastern mythology and folklore, it has been applied to characters from Asian mythology.[13] In the cosmic order of the Monkey King, oppositions such as life and death do not stand against each other as opposing ends. With death being presented as a realm below, the Monkey King, as well as many other celestial beings or earth-dwelling demons, crosses the border between life and death with ease. The universe of *Journey to the West* is full of oppositions between social or cosmic categories, presented as in constant negotiation. Rather than mediating between two opposite states, the Monkey King denies and deletes dualism and brings multiple and otherwise incompatible possibilities together.

Trickster figures break borders, and although tricksters are culturally specific, examples from different traditions share common characteristics that can serve as an initial guide or typology and can be used to measure their degree of "tricksterness": ambiguous and anomalous personalities; deception and trick-playing; shape-shifting; situation-inverting; serving as messengers for and sometimes imitating the gods; and a combination of sacred and lewd behavior.[14] Although at first glance aspects of the Monkey King's behavior fit this description, part of his figure falls outside of this framework.

As the primary feature, the ambiguous and anomalous in the trickster is the most fundamental.[15] The feature of ambivalence functions as the "and" between oppositions, which can be found in the other features of the trickster, all in certain ways manifestations of the first.[16] In *Journey to the West*, the mythological universe and the social structure, as well as the Monkey King character, all demonstrate ambivalence and contradictions, not out of the narrative's inability to deal with such contradictions but, rather, owing to the ambivalence and contradictions in the society that produced the narrative. Based on previous studies about the "ambiguous" and "ambivalent" feature of the trickster, I use "multivalence" instead to refer to the same feature in Sun Wukong, to better indicate his capability of mediating among contradictions as well as the denial of contradictions in one unified body.

The multivalence of the monkey character is represented by the pair of symbols that becomes crucial in representing Sun Wukong: the Tightening Fillet (Jingu) and the Golden-Hooped Rod (Jingu Bang). The fillet and the rod are themselves a pair of dialectical contradictions. The rod that can grow and shrink as wished signifies the limit-testing and boundary-breaking side of Monkey, whereas the fillet, which causes Monkey an unbearable headache whenever Tripitaka recites the Tight-Fillet Spell (Jingu Zhou), represents the limits that the monkey has to accept, however unwilling he may be. The rod indicates outward expansion, whereas the encircling fillet represents containment. Paradoxically, the boundary-breaking rod and the order-enforcing fillet do not just work against each other. When they find their position on Monkey's body, they become indispensable and complementary to each other. Significantly, the fillet stays around Monkey's head, a firm control over the "mind-monkey" (*xinyuan*), whereas the rod stays within Monkey's ear when not in use, securely hidden in his head and within the sphere of the fillet's control.

One incident that brings the complex relationship between the rod and the band into full play is the monkey's conflict with the black bull of Laozi.[17] Before the encounter with the bull, which has escaped Laozi's control and becomes an earthly demon, the monkey draws a circle on the ground to protect Tripitaka and asks him to stay within the circle while he goes in search of food. Had Tripitaka and the other two disciples followed Wukong's advice, they would not have run into the cave of the bull demon. Interestingly, this protective circle is drawn with the rod, the weapon that the monkey uses to break circles—the caves and lairs of demons, and the gourds, bags, vases, and other enveloping devices that demons use to engulf the pilgrims. In this instance, the head fillet circle controls the rod; the rod creates a protective circle for the pilgrims; the pilgrims walk out of the circle and hence fall into the demon's snare. It would then be up to Monkey to use his rod to break up the demon's den. However, Monkey finds himself powerless before the bull's Gold Steel Ring (another circle), which seizes Monkey's rod. After many battles, with celestial help sought from different sources, Monkey eventually receives aid from Laozi, who takes the bull back under his control. Consequently, Tripitaka is rescued and returned back to the protective circle of Wukong's rod, Wukong is returned to the control of the head fillet, and the band of pilgrims march on, ready to be engulfed by the circle of another demon. In one incident after another, the story is thus propelled by the intertwining pairs of rod and circle.

One detail of this incident also points out the indispensability of the one with respect to the other. It was the Gold Steel Ring (Jin Gang Zhuo) that helped to bring Monkey under heavenly control five hundred years earlier, and in fact it was the very same ring. At that time Laozi used the ring in a very different way: while viewing the battle between Monkey and the Little Sage Erlang Shen, he threw the ring from above and hit Monkey in the head. Laozi improvised this strange use of the containing device in response to Guanyin's idea of using her vase to hit Monkey over his head. Instead of using the encompassing power of their containing devices, they both only thought of using the expelling function, which was not the strongest power of their "weapons" at all. Would it not have been much easier if they simply used the ring or vase to snatch the rod from the monkey or to engulf Sun Wukong himself into their circles? The use of the containing devices to hit instead of to encircle seems to demonstrate that the circle can also function as a rod. In other words, to hit and to encircle are just two functions of the same thing. As stated in the "Original Preface" by Yu Ji attached to the Qing hundred-chapter version *Xiyou zhengdao shu* (an abridged Qing edition of *Journey to the West*), the central message of the book is about two conditions of the mind: the retrieval or the release (*shou fang xin*).[18] Since both the rod and the head fillet play crucial roles in evolving the lessons of recovering the mind and exiling the mind, we can also say the story of *Journey to the West* is a story of the rod and the fillet.

As a narrative rejecting dichotomy, *Journey to the West* clearly rejects a simple division of the story into *shouxin* (controlling the mind, retrieving of mind) and *fangxin* (letting the mind go, exile of the mind). Not only is the "mind monkey" always fond of his mischievous ways when he remains a follower of Tripitaka, in the two episodes of the "exile" of the "mind monkey", he is never totally let loose either. [19] In both cases he has asked Tripitaka or Bodhisattva to take his head fillet off, but neither of them is able to fulfill his request. Ironically, although Tripitaka "exiles" the monkey from the pilgrim group, his power over the Tightening Fillet remains. Monkey, on the other hand, is also never totally happy when being released. In the case of the first release, Bajie (Pigsy) has to resort to a stratagem to persuade the monkey to return: he lies to the monkey that the monster who has beaten the pilgrims does not take seriously of the name of Sun Wukong and his deeds in heaven five hundred years ago. It is in defense of his reputation as the "number one monster" that the monkey leaves his Flower-Fruit Mountain and returns to rejoin the band of pilgrims.

In the case of the second "exile," the episode of the "double-mind monkey" (*erxin yuan*), a fake Wukong commits a series of monstrous crimes in his name. While one "mind monkey" is staying with the Bodhisattva, the other "mind monkey" goes to strike the master Tripitaka unconscious, takes his travel documents, returns to the Flower-Fruit Mountain, and sets up another pilgrim band, ready for his own journey to the West. The resemblance of the two "mind monkeys" deceives everyone except the Buddha, who sees through the fake Wukong and recognizes him as a six-eared macaque (*liuer mihou*). The use of a double of Wukong enables the narrative to literally grant the monkey the facility to be self-contradictory, with one Monkey being a pious follower of Tripitaka, and the other a monster who is even capable of beating his master. At the culmination of this episode, Sun Wukong uses his rod to kill the six-eared macaque, despite the fact that the macaque had already been captured by Buddha's golden almsbowl—a constraining weapon—and submitted to Buddha's control, which seems out of character for the "good" Monkey. One feasible explanation would be that it is an action of eliminating the monster in him, indicating that he is getting closer to achieving Buddhahood at this point in the journey. However, this explanation does not negate another one: that he kills the six-eared macaque because the latter has copied him too closely, the best demon among the ones that Monkey has conquered. By killing his rival who resembles himself, he plays the norm of self-contradiction to an extreme.

The methods that Monkey and other gods use to conquer demons also often use a constraining circle to force the self to play against itself. One trick that the monkey loves to play is getting inside of a monster. Not only does Wukong enter the caves and tunnels of the hostile offending animals; he literally enters their stomachs many times in the book.[20] Sinologist Andrew Plaks contends that one reason these monsters must be subdued from inside is that "the secret of subduing the hostile creature lies in tricking him into identifying himself, as if, by defining its own being, the force is reduced to the vulnerable proportions of a finite self."[21] In this sense, Monkey's mischief-making in the monster's stomach functions just like the Tightening Fillet over his head. By pinning down his true form, all the false forms are taken away, so that the ambiguity of identity achieved by taking up false forms is no longer possible.

In the Black Wind Mountain episode, the trick of getting inside is directly connected to the tightening of the head fillet. Here, as Wukong and Guanyin cooperate to subdue a demon, the Black Bear, Wukong proposes that Guanyin transform herself into a demon friend of Black Bear so that she might present the demon a cinnabar pill, which is Wukong in disguise. Black Bear ingests the pill, which makes its way to his stomach. With Wukong kicking and jumping within, the bear monster immediately loses all his power and gives up, while Guanyin, to secure this victory, puts a head fillet over Black Bear's head. When Wukong emerges from Black Bear's mouth, the headband remains as an index of his finite self, preventing him from slipping away by taking up a guise of ambiguity.

Turning to the case of the submission of "mind monkey,"[22] although the method used by the Buddha is different, the logic surrounding the constraining function is the same. The wager between Buddha and the monkey about whether Monkey can jump out of Buddha's hand is actually on the limit of Monkey's self. At the very moment the actual smallness of the monkey's bloated self is demonstrated in the shadow of the Buddha's fingers, the overblown "mind monkey" is reduced to finite proportions, and his rehabilitative imprisonment under Five Phases Mountain begins. The lesson demonstrates to him that, however far the "cloud-somersault" can reach, it would also represent his own unbreakable boundary. The Buddha's fingers serve as an index, revealing to the monkey that what beats him is his own self. Later this indexing role of Buddha's hand is taken over by the Five Phases Mountain, and after that the headband. Whenever Tripitaka recites the spell, Monkey is reminded of his own limits and the impossibility of breaking them, even with his rod.

In the case of the six-eared macaque, one can reach an opposite explanation as to why Wukong chooses to kill him: to free himself. Just as in the submission of Wukong, Buddha beats the six-eared macaque at his forte. Although the fake Wukong is strong in taking forms of others and had succeeded in confusing everyone else, the Buddha is able to exactly identify this monkey's original form: someone belonging to none of the ten categories in the universe, neither the five immortals (*wu xian*) nor the five creatures (*wu chong*). There are four kinds of monkeys who "are not classified in the ten species, nor are they contained in the names between Heaven and Earth," among which was the first, "the intelligent stone monkey (*lingming shihou*), who knows transformations, recognizes the seasons, discerns the advantages of earth, and is able to alter the course of planets and stars," and the fourth, "the six-eared macaque, who has a sensitive ear, discernment of fundamental principles, knowledge of past and future, and comprehension of all things."[23] This recognition announces the six-eared macaque's failure as one who has been trying to use his disguise to erase the boundary of his self while taking up the identity of Wukong. It also announces once again the failure of Wukong, who although not belonging to any of the ten species between heaven and earth, still falls into one of the in-between types that the Buddha names: the intelligent stone monkey, indeed a peer of the six-eared macaque. Therefore by killing the six-eared macaque, Wukong not only kills a monster who has tried to cross proper borders, but he also kills a self whose boundary has just been pinned down. This action of self-annihilation is in this sense an effort in defiance of any classification.[24]

In this light, Wukong's action of extricating demons along their way, often against the wish of Tripitaka, Guanyin, and even the Buddha, cannot be simply taken as a demonstration of his commitment to the pilgrimage, nor is it just a metaphor for eradicating the inner demons on the way to self-enlightenment. It refuses to be easily categorized and put into a neat frame labeling its nature. Subjugation by the Buddha serves as a turning point in the monkey's life, and this incident can likewise be taken as a watershed of the book, with the story of the monster monkey before it, and that of the pilgrim monkey after. Another natural step following this logic allows one to say that the former part of the story is the story of the Golden-Hooped Rod, and the latter the story of the Tightening Fillet. However, this appears to be an oversimplified analysis: the whole story is not cut into two pieces, because the rod is active in the hand not only of the monster monkey but also the pilgrim monkey. A clear dichotomy does not exist in the narrative. Readers may often find it hard to tell whether the monkey is a monster or a pilgrim during any one incident: just like the rod and headband, the monster and pilgrim are indispensable sides of the character of Sun Wukong.

JOURNEY TO THE WEST: THE MULTIVALENT TEXT

The narrative of *Journey to the West* itself also has a multivalent nature. Containing and allowing for contradictions is a central message of the book. Themes and rhetoric of Buddhism, Taoism, and Confucianism all appear in every part of the work. For a story of Buddhist monks' pilgrimage for Buddhist sutras, it also bears apparent characteristics of Taoist dual cultivation. While gods of Buddhist and Taoist traditions happily coexist, a Confucian emphasis on filial piety and loyalty is also prevalent. Owing to the coexistence of heterogeneous factors, the text gives space for various interpretations of the metaphorical meaning of the book. Many scholars have addressed the allegorical meaning of *Journey to the West* from Taoist, Buddhist, neo-Confucian, as well as political points of view.[25] In this narrative there are multiple parameters for the classification and ranking of cosmic beings, among them two basic categories—the earthly demons and the heavenly gods. At first glance the two are a pair of opposing powers, one always contradicting the other. However, a closer view of the relationship between the two reveals that the boundaries between the categories and kinds in the cosmic hierarchy are not firmly fixed. There are always possibilities of crossing the boundaries; the coexistence of all these distinctive beings is already an act of the abnegation of boundaries.

Historian of Chinese religion Robert Campany visualizes the positions of these demons in the hierarchy, within which boundaries can be crossed upward or downward by means of transformation (*hua*, the phenomenon of demons assuming bodies and forms not their own), reincarnation, cultivation, conversion, or subjugation.[26] Hierarchical distinctions are thus relative, and typological divisions appear to be mere illusion, with the pilgrims and demons both functioning as antagonists and complementing one another.[27] Although demons and the pilgrims are similar in that both strive for cultivation of self, "demons have not yet realized the necessity of submitting the self to a larger Self that is the entire cosmic order."[28] This insight points to another duality that is undercut by the narrative.

This allegorical explanation—that the pilgrims, by battling against the demons, come to realize the truth of emptiness, while Wukong, as indicated by his name, has always been aware of it—however, is too neat, as the purpose of the journey allows for multiple interpretations.[29] While the pilgrims are moving toward a destination, ironic tension is apparent between the exuberant ease with which Monkey travels between different spheres and Tripitaka's extreme difficulty in moving forward on his journey on earth. Although the narrative provides as a reason that the journey has to be completed by Tripitaka, the very special human, rather than by any other demon/god, the apparent contradiction of the two kinds of journeys renders the point of the journey questionable. A few times the narrative even makes fun of the discrepancy in Monkey and Tripitaka's travel speeds by having Wukong and Bajie talk about the possibility of carrying Tripitaka on their backs.[30]

This contradiction relates again to the issue of the paradoxical narrative, the narrative that rejects dichotomy. One such narrative paradox in *Journey to the West* is the narrative realism with which the demons are portrayed coupled with the frequent explicit statements that demons are nothing more than illusory fabrications of a confused mind.[31] Because of this narrative paradox, the polarity between Good and Evil in the book is not to be found. In *Journey to the West*, the narrative rejects the kind of philosophical dualism that can often be found in Western allegorical compositions.[32] Andrew Plaks contends that the major difficulty of dealing with the allegorical dimensions of works such as *Journey to the West* is "the fact that the element of ontological disjunction at the heart of Western allegory simply does not apply in the Chinese literary system." He further argues that the characteristic Chinese solution to the problem of duality "consists in the conception of a universe with neither beginning nor end, neither eschatological nor teleological purpose, within which all of the conceivable opposites of sensory and intellectual experience are contained, such that the poles of duality emerge as complementary within the intelligibility of the whole."[33] This argument about the Chinese concept of complementary duality provides an interesting explanation for the coexistence of contradictions in the narrative. It may also count as one of the cultural situations "generative of ambivalence and contradiction" that folklorist Laura Makarius discusses.[34] The concept of complementary duality in Chinese culture certainly helps explain the fundamental ambiguity regarding the teachings in the journey, the most famous being the merging boundary between god and demon. In the Black Wind Mountain episode, when Guanyin transforms herself into a demon, the monkey comments: "Marvelous, marvelous! Is the monster the Bodhisattva, or is the Bodhisattva the monster?" The question, unmistakably challenging the division between the Bodhisattva and demon, demonstrates Wukong's inconstant attitude. The Bodhisattva's reply is quite surprising in that it actually consents to this ambivalence and backs it up with Buddhist theory: "Wukong, the Bodhisattva, and the monster—they all exist in a single thought,[35] for originally they are nothing."[36]

The comment also relates to the concept of transformation. The Bodhisattva and the demon are only two different transformations of the same thing, and one can understand this idea only when one lets go of the concept of dual contradiction. Transformation is something practiced very commonly by heavenly immortals and demons alike in *Journey to the West*. Besides crossing the boundary between the deity and demon, it also illustrates that all "forms," no matter how different they might look, are the same because they are all manifestations, or illusions. Forms are not the true nature of a being, and an important technique for a creature to attain in becoming an immortal through cultivation is the ability to transform itself, as well as the ability to see through forms. The Monkey King is among the most adept at seeing through the false forms of demons and monsters. In short, transformation, and the understanding of transformation, seem to have a crucial connection with a nondualistic (or multivalent) understanding of the universe.

There may be questions about whether the coexistence of contradictions derives from literary juxtaposition of resources from different times and lineages, or from the inherent characteristic of a trickster Monkey King. Although not enough records exist to clearly trace the historical trajectory of the formation of the hundred-chapter *Journey to the West*, and although scholars disagree on this matter and on the authorship of the book, one thing remains certain: there was a long history of version-propagation of different parts of *Journey to the West* before someone finally gathered them together. Even if the inconsistency of the Monkey King character and the ambiguity of the text are solely produced by the layers of compilation, it is ultimately the authors' and compilers' choices and readers' acceptance that determine that the hundred-chapter version should be the one that constitutes the original story. The text's multivalence has its root in its cultural and historical milieu and deserves to be accepted as an inherent feature of the fiction and its hero(es). The monkey's "tricksterness," though it is not usually so termed, has become one of his signal identifying characteristics.

THE DUCK-RABBIT AND THE MULTISTABLE MONKEY KING

The multivalence of the image of the Monkey King can be further illustrated by discussions of metapicture and the multistable by iconologist W. J. T. Mitchell, whose analysis of multistable images such as the Duck-Rabbit can throw much light on the representations, either visual, verbal, or cinematic, of the Monkey King. Mitchell's discussion of metapictures, or pictures about pictures, showcases multistability and self-reference as their common features.[37] The Duck-Rabbit exemplifies the multistable feature, since as a dialectical image its primary function is to illustrate the coexistence of different readings in a single image.[38] It can be seen either as a duck or a rabbit, so it serves as "an emblem of resistance to stable interpretation, to being taken in at a glance."[39] Readings of the image as to whether the duck and the rabbit can be seen at the same time vary: from Ernst Gombrich's negative perspective, it is not possible to see the two aspects simultaneously, whereas Ludwig Wittgenstein's more positive approach hints that it is possible for us to see the image as "the Duck-Rabbit." Mitchell takes the side of Wittgenstein, believing that the image is meant to be "a curious hybrid that looks like nothing else but itself."[40] Considering the wide interest in the Duck-Rabbit, we may summarize that the image is so popular because it not only points to the limit of human perception to be able to experience only one reading at one

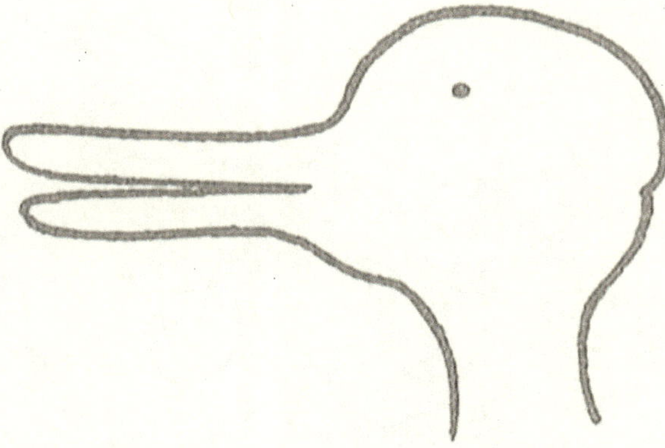

Figure 1.1. Wittgenstein's famous Duck-Rabbit, exemplifying ambiguous imagery. From Ludwig Wittgenstein, *Philosophical Investigations* (New York: Macmillan, 1953), 194.

time, but it also challenges this limit, since the Duck-Rabbit's existence as one entity can be perceived and understood after all. In various representations of the Monkey King, it is the user of the image who must either demonstrate the impossibility of perceiving the monkey as human or challenge the limit of social perception and argue for his being both a demon and a god.

Self-reference is another major feature of the metapicture. A metapicture "displays itself for inspection rather than effacing itself in the service of transparent representation of something else"; basically, "metapictures are pictures that show themselves in order to know themselves."[41] The purpose of the Duck-Rabbit is not to represent a strange creature that resembles both a duck and a rabbit; rather, it questions and confronts the viewer with the task of interpretation. In other words, the "self-reference" is an entreaty to the viewer to become the interpreter of the image, to give it meaning:

> If self-reference is elicited by the multistable image, then, it has as much to do with the self of the observer as with the metapicture itself. We might think of the multistable image as a device for educing self-knowledge, a kind of mirror for the beholder. . . . The observer's identity may emerge in a dialogue with specific cultural stereotypes . . . that carry a whole set of explicitly ideological associations. . . . If the multistable image always asks, "what am I?" or "how do I look?," the answer depends on the observer asking the same questions.[42]

Figure 1.2. Monkey in the 1962 picture-story book *Monkey Subdues the White Bone Demon*. From Zhao and Qian, illus., *Sun Wukong sanda Baigu Jing*, iii.

It is probably because of its self-reference as well as its invitation to viewer involvement that the Monkey King, like the Duck-Rabbit, has enjoyed so much attention and given rise to so many adaptations. In a certain sense, each time an artist, psychologist, or philosopher uses this image, it undergoes a rewriting. The Monkey King loudly raises the question about who he is for the reader/viewer, inviting the reader/viewer to enter into a dialogue with the image and to arrive at an analogy between the sociopolitical environment of the Monkey King and that of the reader/viewer. The Monkey King's question of "Who am I?" becomes a discussion of the identity of the adaptor of a new Monkey King story, leading to a new round of "Who am I?"

Figure 1.3. Monkey (Zhang Jinlai) in *Journey to the West*, a 1986 TV series directed by Yang Jie.

The image of the Monkey King as a multistable picture also operates via a particular dialectical feature: both the story and the representations of his image in popular culture indicate that the Monkey King can be iconized by the ring and the rod. The ring, a headband that reminds him of the limits within which he must be bound, shares a conflicting yet dialectical relationship with the rod, the weapon with which he breaks boundaries and opens up new spaces. Beyond this layer of the multistable relationship, the monkey's eyes looking at the viewer create the "This is not a pipe" effect, activating infinite reverie, such as, "This is a monkey," but then immediately, "No, but this is not a monkey; he is a human." Supported by the density of the

Figure 1.4. Monkey (Stephen Chow) in *A Chinese Odyssey*, a 1995 film directed by Jeffrey Lau.

legend of the Monkey King, the initial contradictory interpretations would become a recognition of the similarity of the Monkey King's story with a human being's story: "OK, he was born as a monkey, but that can only be an analogy. See how he acts like a human, and his story is so typical of one of us, growing up from being young and fearless to mature, tame, and realistic. How heartbreaking that even such a figure has to accept the terms of Buddha. So, yes, he is a monkey after all—but, no, he eventually finds his way to move on. Isn't his story about the human condition, always about breaking boundaries and accepting limits? Isn't this story about me?"

This monologue is only a simplified example of various ways a reader/audience might react to the image and story of the Monkey King, involving abundant contradictions, assessments, and deliberation generated by the multistable connection between the ring/rod collaborating with that of the monkey/human. So, beyond the effect of reveries and challenges engendered by the pipe and the Duck-Rabbit, the Monkey King activates an identification effect, soliciting the viewer/reader to relate their own experience of subject/subjectivity with Sun Wukong. This may explain why the adaptations and rewritings of the Monkey King story are often self-portraits of the artists/writers. Interestingly, the artists who create their own Monkey King do not always try to represent both sides of the dialectical relations, as in *American Born Chinese*. Instead, they sometimes put more emphasis on the monkey or the human side of the character, so much so that the figure of the Monkey King is reshaped, or even manipulated, to reflect their particular political agenda.

The multistable image of the Monkey King thus serves as a hypericon. The seemingly simple factors of the image, a monkey in human clothes with a head ring and an iron rod, together encapsulate a whole bundle of meanings, an entire episteme. It can be used as a decoration, and it can also be used to speak to power, knowledge, and representation. It is fascinating that it continues over centuries to appeal to readers/audiences of various social orders and successfully transforms them into creators of new images.

CHAPTER 2

The Transmutable Monkey

Between Theater and Fiction in Traditional China

The 1592 version of *Journey to the West* was not created by the author from whole cloth but instead was based on a variety of different, previously crafted sources. The characters in the story were formulated through gradual adaptations rather than being products of a single original source written by a single individual writer. Furthermore, in the continuing adaptation of *Journey to the West*, the image of the Monkey King does not grow into the Sun Wukong that appears in the 1592 work and then stabilize; it continues to change and grow, reflecting the cultural and sociopolitical history through which it travels, which in turn affects the ways people appreciate the character. The creators of subsequent adaptations then create new classical and influential images of Sun Wukong, and each of these writers makes his or her contribution to the monkey image on the basis of what they draw from the antecedents as well as the popular culture around them. It is this process that renders a Monkey that is transmutable and pertinent in many different social and political milieu.

Before the *Journey to the West* novel, the story of the pilgrims had gone through a long history of evolution: the historical records of the monk Xuanzang's trip to India were gradually transformed, via oral, performative, and written traditions, into a collection of fantastic stories of religious, mythical, and legendary imagination. Although there is a large and growing body of scholarship on the development of the "Journey to the West" story and its characters (particularly Sun Wukong) prior to the emergence of the hundred-chapter novel, a clear chronology has yet to be clearly defined. The present-day student of *Journey to the West* who seeks the answer to questions regarding the development of the "Journey to the West" narrative as well as the figure of Sun Wukong is still faced, as sinologist Glen Dudbridge put it, with "numbers of conflicting theories, opinions and speculations, often also with apparent discrepancies in the stated facts."[1] Despite the apparent popularity of Tripitaka's pilgrimage stories in oral and performative traditions, the shortage of records makes the exact process of their development difficult to ascertain. Of interest here is not which texts are the exact bases for the 1592 *Journey to the West*, or the precise genealogy of the Monkey King, but the features of pilgrimage stories that circulated before or around the same time of the first novelization of *Journey to the West.* Since the novel is an amalgamation of other sources with the author's master revision, it can be considered as an adaptation of the texts available in its cultural context. In the long chain of adaptations, it is the 1592 *Journey to the West* that stands out as a classic and has been considered as the "original" source for later adaptations. But what gives this version its long life, and what gives this version of Sun Wukong its special popularity?

There are two major antecedents of *Journey to the West* that, unlike most other works, have survived in their more or less complete forms: first, *Tale of the Grand Tang Sanzang Seeking Buddhist Sutra* (Da Tang Sanzang qujing shihua; hereafter *Shihua*), a poetic tale that possibly served as a script for storytellers in the thirteenth century; and second, a later *zaju* drama version of the story also titled *Journey to the West*, often referred to as *The Journey to the West as Zaju* (Zaju Xiyou ji; hereafter *Zaju*), attributed to the late Yuan/early Ming period writer Yang Jingxian.[2] The term "shihua" indicates a form of storytelling that contains both poetry and prose in the text and is performed through both speech and song, and *Shihua* is the first extant fictional story of Tripitaka's journey. Although it is a poetic tale that covers the entire journey in seventeen sections, it is the first in which a monkey figure appears as the assistant of the monk Tripitaka (Sanzang) and plays an essential role in the journey. *Zaju* is possibly an antecedent of the 1592 *Journey to the West* wherein the Monkey King bears the same name, Sun Wukong. This twenty-four-act *zaju* drama includes much more detailed accounts of the pilgrims and the journey than does *Shihua*, and it follows a similar trajectory to that of the novel, introducing many episodes expanded in later versions. Although there is no evidence that either of the two texts has served directly as a blueprint for the novel, there is no doubt that they both have influenced the large body of Tripitaka literature of their respective times.[3] It is generally accepted that both texts, as well as the 1592 version, are amalgamations drawn together by the hand of a single author. The change of the monkey image in the three texts reveals not only information about the authors but also what adaptations of a popular image like the Monkey King needed to consider, namely, the changing needs of the audience over time. The Monkey King's evolution into the Sun Wukong of the 1592 novel points to a tendency of a certain type of character that was made popular during the Ming dynasty. The image of Sun Wukong is the result of the mutual influence of both high and low culture, with most sources coming from popular culture. This chapter calls attention to the interrelation between the equally important elite texts and popular culture.

The link between the novel and the theater is indicative of an important historical and literary context for reading Chinese classical novels such as *Water Margin* and *Journey to the West*: the cultural fascination with and imagination of theater among Ming and Qing writers and readers.[4] While Mei's concept of "the theatrical" provides an analysis of some sequences in *Journey to the West* by understanding them as theatrical scenes, the reading is mainly focused on the novel itself. My analysis of the *Journey to the West* as a contextual adaptation of earlier and contemporary texts compares the storytelling text, the drama, and the novel, pointing to the possible intertextual links from the point of view of adaptation.

MONKEY AS GOD: THE "MONKEY ACOLYTE" IN *DA TANG SANZANG QUJING SHIHUA*

The question of the dating of *Da Tang Sanzang qujing shihua*, or the versions from the Kozanji monastery in Japan, has not yet been settled, although many celebrated scholars have studied this question and offered their theories.[5] Wang Guowei first suggested that *Shihua* may have been printed in the Song era (thirteenth century), and this history had been widely accepted.[6] More recently, scholars such as Li Shiren and Cai Jinghao conducted further studies examining the language, format, and content of the text, proposing that the text must have been written during the time of the late Tang and Five dynasties (in or before the tenth century).[7] They argued that *Shihua* is a book for Buddhist storytelling (*sujiang*) performed by temples at the time of Late Tang and Five dynasties. It is possible that the monk storytellers also refer to pictures or murals in the temple while telling the story.[8]

As a result of further discussion, Li and Cai set the date back to the end of the Northern Song era (late eleventh early twelfth centuries).[9]

Shihua is the first fictional account of Xuanzang's journey in which the monk acquires a monkey attendant who functions as his guide and protector. Following his introduction, the monkey figure enjoyed growing popularity in subsequent fictional retellings of the story, until in the hundred-chapter novel *Journey to the West* he becomes the protagonist of the story, overshadowing his master, Tripitaka (the monk character based on Xuanzang). Compared to Xuanzang's historical journey, *Shihua* introduces two major changes to the nature of the journey that are carried through later adaptations of the story. In the first, the monk's individual religious pursuit, a brave act that breaches the law of Tang and puts his own life at risk, is transformed into the performance of a decreed commission from the Tang emperor.[10] Although the imperial decree seems to have given Tripitaka a more celebrated status, his choice to defy the legal order in order to undertake his religious pilgrimage is taken away from the monk. Second, realistic challenges the monk had to face are replaced by obstacles deployed by demons and deities, which Tripitaka relies on the monkey to conquer. These two changes set the stage for a transformation of the story about Tripitaka into a story about the monkey.

Buddhist themes and elements in the story are obvious, but there is no monopoly of Buddhist themes; instead, a variety of traditions and cults are present in the text, with popular tradition being blended into the orthodox religious material.[11] In this sense, *Shihua* already begins to show what is masterfully realized in the hundred-chapter version *Journey to the West*: the encyclopedic coexistence of different and conflicting cultures and traditions. According to *Shihua*'s account, the monk is on his way to acquire scriptures because he has received an imperial commission. On his way he meets the monkey figure, Hou Xingzhe (Monkey Acolyte), who becomes his guide and assistant. This story is filled with praises of the religious pilgrimage, paying its respects to Buddha and Buddhist teaching and eulogizing the peaceful places near the Western Heaven. Unlike the later versions, it is clear in the story that the success of the pilgrimage is based on Tripitaka's deep understanding of Buddhist texts and great strength in his belief. The Tripitaka in later versions will rely on the assistance of Sun Wukong and gods from all parts of the universe to complete his journey.

Additionally, it is noteworthy that Tripitaka's protector here is the Mahabrahma Devarāja, not the Goddess Guanyin as in the later versions. The merging of Mahabrahma and Vaisravana into one in this story is one of the examples that indicate this text is influenced, as Glen Dudbridge notes, by "a great mythological complex originating in the Buddhist countries of Central Asia."[12] Zhang Chengjian takes note of the presence of Vaisravana in the story, as well as other factors that point to the Tantric tradition, and argues that the Tripitaka of the Kozanji version is not based on the monk Xuanzang of the seventh century but on the monk Bukong of the eighth century.[13] According to this finding, many of the stories in the Kozanji version might be serious preaching, not storytelling for entertainment. Whatever theory we choose to follow, the monk is a Chinese monk, while the Indian influence seems to be reflected more in the monkey figure.

There is little evidence to show where the monkey figure originated, but scholars have discussed the possible connections between Hou Xingzhe and the carved monkey figures at the Kaiyuan Temple in Quanzhou Prefecture, Fujian; monkey stories in Buddhist texts; and Hanuman of the *Ramayana*. Discussion about Hanuman as the influence or origin of Sun Wukong can be traced to Hu Shih's 1923 article "Textual Criticism of *Journey to the West*" (Xiyou ji kaozheng), but at about the same time Lu Xun, in his *Brief History of Chinese Novel* (Zhongguo xiaoshuo shilue), disagreed, connecting Sun Wukong with the ape-shaped Chinese mythical figure Wuzhiqi.[14] The two scholars who built the foundation of modern Chinese literary study thus began a long-running argument in *Journey to the West* scholarship about the origination of Sun Wukong. Even today, the problem of the origin of the Chinese Monkey King is unresolved. For, in addition to these two sources, there are other possible origins or influences, such as the influence of Buddhist texts; the figure of Shi Pantuo, a disciple of Xuanzang at the beginning stages of his trip; the Monk Wukong of the Tang; tales about a white ape who abducts women; and the Fujian cult of Qitian Dasheng or Tongtian Dasheng.[15] Many recognize the possible influences from multiple sources; in fact, most theories about the origin of Sun Wukong do not and cannot exclude influences from other sources. Regarding the origination of Hou Xingzhe, Zhang Chengjian's findings generally support the notion of a greater influence from India than from indigenous myths, and in particular the influence of Hanuman or the ape-shaped guardian general in the Tantric tradition. A major problem with the argument about Sun Wukong having originated from Hanuman is that scholars who support this view have not been able to provide a convincing theory about the paths of transmission of the Hanuman story. It would seem that the *Ramayana* may have been transmitted to and spread in China via the Silk Road, the marine Silk Road, or the path via Sichuan and Yunnan; however, these paths do not correspond with the appearance of Hou Xingzhe and the transmission of Hanuman to China in either time or place[16] Taking into consideration the new dating of *Shihua* to the late Tang, a fourth path for the transmission of Hanuman could be the Musk Road via Tibet, as the Tantric tradition reflected in *Shihua* and the spread of Tantric Buddhism at the time from India through Tibet to China demonstrates a connection between Hanuman and Hou Xingzhe.[17] It is worth noting here, though, that the necessary link between the transmission of Tantric Buddhism and the story of Hanuman is yet to be found. Nonetheless, the image of Hou Xingzhe in *Shihua* reminds us more of Hanuman and the images of the monkey protector figures found in mural paintings in Dunhuang and the stone relief in Kaiyuan Temple—these serious and godlike images bear very little resemblance to the trickster that the monkey would become in later versions.[18]

The role that Hou Xingzhe plays is Tripitaka's guide throughout the journey. Although Xingzhe calls Tripitaka "my master" (*wo shi*), he is the one who gives advice, and Tripitaka always follows it. He takes Tripitaka to the palace of Mahabrahma Devarāja, who becomes Tripitaka's protector god during the journey. Xingzhe, who already knows the way, introduces Tripitaka to the various places and cultures, answers his questions, and offers him help and advice (for example, with the three gifts from Devarāja, Hou Xingzhe helps Tripitaka to subdue demons). The descriptions of Hou Xingzhe's battle with the demons showcase his remarkable power rather than presenting his victories as mischievous tricks, as is often the case in the later versions.

Hou Xingzhe is introduced as a monkey only at the beginning of the book. Although the word "monkey" (*hou*) is part of his name, neither his appearance nor his behavior show resemblance to that of a monkey or ape. In section 2, Tripitaka and his team set off on their journey, and one day at around noon they see someone in white (or plain) clothes (*baiyi xiucai*) approaching from the east, who introduces himself: "I am none other than the king of 84,000 bronze-headed, iron-browed monkeys of Purple-Cloud Cave on Flower-Fruit

Mountain. I come now to help you to fetch the scriptures."[19] In fact at many places in the story the word *hou* is omitted, leaving the word *xingzhe* as the king of monkeys' name. The self-introduction of Xingzhe is the only place that mentions his title as king of the monkeys, and we are left to deduce from this title that he himself is or should be a monkey.

Hou Xingzhe's white/plain clothing (*baiyi xiucai*) conceals his identity as a monkey. Although *xiucai* refers to those who passed the imperial examination at the county level in the Ming and Qing dynasties, during the time of late Tang, the term was used generally to refer to scholars. Dudbridge points out that *xiucai* in plain clothes is in subsequent Chinese fiction a common disguise-motif associated with both humans and supernatural beings.[20] The white/plain clothing points to the lack of official status, in contrast to official clothing. Since the scholarly career is almost always respectable in Chinese tradition, carrying with it the possibility of attaining political importance enabled by the imperial examination, the plain clothing of a scholar suggests someone of anonymous but honorable social standing.

Hou Xingzhe's behavior does not reveal him as either a monkey or a trickster. He is serious in conversation and in action alike. The only episode in the story that tells what is later reported as a humorous tale about the monkey is narrated by Hou Xingzhe himself, and in a rather solemn tone. In section 11, Tripitaka and Xingzhe arrive at the Pool of the Queen of the West (Wangmu Chi), and Xingzhe is asked whether he has ever been to the Pool:

> Xingzhe responded: "When I was eight hundred years old I came here and stole some peaches to eat. Twenty-seven thousand years have passed since then, and I have not returned until now." The Master said: "I hope that today the peaches could bear fruit, and then we could steal a few to eat." Xingzhe said: "It was because I stole ten peaches when I was eight hundred years old that I was seized by the Queen and sentenced to eight hundred strokes from an iron cudgel on my left side and three thousand on the right, then banished to Purple-Cloud Cave on Flower-Fruit Mountain. It still hurts down my side even now. I definitely do not dare to steal today." The Master said: "This Xingzhe is indeed a god from the Taoist heaven *Daluo tian*. He told us earlier that he had seen the Yellow River clear nine times, and I thought he was lying. Today he said he had come here to steal peaches when he was young, then it must be true." . . . The Master asked, "Are these the peach trees?" Xingzhe said, "Speak softly, and do not raise your voice. After I stole here at my young age, I am

> afraid of this place even today." The Master said, "Why don't you go steal one?"[21]

This episode is an example of the localization of the Indian monkey figure, locating the foreign monkey god in an indigenous theological system. Both the Queen from the West and the *Daluo tian* originate from Chinese tradition. The story of the theft of the Queen's peaches has a well-known precedent in the legend of Dongfang Shuo (2nd–1st century BCE) recorded in *Stories of Emperor Hanwu* (Hanwu gushi) of the pre-Tang era. In this case, Dongfang Shuo stole divine peaches from the Queen of the West on three occasions and was thence banished to the secular world.[22] This story, in its later versions, becomes one of the trademarks of the "Journey to the West" stories.

Two points stand out in our discussion of this particular stage in the development of the Monkey King character in the context of adaptation: the use of humor, and the transposition of different religious traditions within a single text. The embarrassing history of Dongfang Shuo stealing peaches reflects his humorous and mischievous personality and at the same time gives him the touch of an immortal. Likewise, in *Shihua*, after hearing Hou Xingzhe's story, Tripitaka is convinced that the monkey is indeed a god. But Hou Xingzhe narrates the otherwise lighthearted story in a serious way. Just as he acts seriously, he takes his lesson solemnly and refuses to steal peaches anymore; it is Tripitaka who urges Xingzhe to try again. As a result, the humorous effect in this version is achieved from the interaction of the two: Tripitaka's repeated encouragement of Hou Xingzhe to steal, and the latter's solemn and repeated rejections. In other words, in this version Hou Xingzhe is not yet a funny character.

The other point is about the transplanting of the Monkey King story: the twig of an Indian monkey deity is grafted onto a Taoist trunk. When Tripitaka recognizes Hou Xingzhe as a god, he beholds him as a Taoist god "from the Taoist heaven." In Xingzhe's introductory appearance, he is in the guise of a *xiucai*, introducing himself as from Purple-Cloud Cave, which is later connected with the Queen of the West. If the claims of the Tantric origin of Tripitaka's monkey companion are indeed reliable, then *Shihua* demonstrates the conversion of a Tantric deity into the Taoist tradition, in contrast to later versions of the story that underline the conversion of the Monkey King and other demons to Buddhism. Indeed, as in the case with a graft, it is not easy to determine at this stage whether Hou Xingzhe is a Chinese character or an Indian god, prefiguring the characteristics of the trickster into which this character later grows.

The "Land of Women" (Nüren guo) in section 10 is another episode that enjoys much rewriting in later stages of *Journey to the West*. In this account, Tripitaka is tested by Manjusri Bodhisattva and Samantabhadra Bodhisattva, as indicated in the poem at the end of the section. Yet the description is focused on illustrating the culture and the women of the place rather than continuing the story of the pilgrims. When the Queen of the Land of Women tries to persuade Tripitaka to stay and inherit the sovereignty, Tripitaka simply "rejected [the Queen's request] once and again, then bid farewell."[23] There is no mention of any reaction from Hou Xingzhe at all. This forms a sharp contrast to the later versions, which contain extensive interactions between the women and the pilgrims.

To summarize briefly, although Hou Xingzhe appears as a clearly synthesized figure in *Shihua*, bearing influences from both Indian and Chinese cultures, he is mostly an honorable and capable godlike figure. Negative features have yet to be developed in this character.

MONKEY AS CLOWN: TONGTIAN DASHENG IN *ZAJU XIYOU JI*

The six-part, twenty-four-act *Zaju Xiyou ji* is attributed to the fourteenth-century playwright Yang Jingxian, who lived during the late Yuan and early Ming periods. In the few hundred years between *Shihua* and *Zaju*, the story of "Journey to the West" is not only more expanded, containing many of the stories that can be found later in *Journey to the West*, but the monkey figure in *Zaju* has grown into a character strikingly different from Hou Xingzhe.[24] If Hou Xingzhe in *Shihua* is depicted as an advisor for Tripitaka, a respectable albeit mysterious deity, and a brave fighter, the monkey in *Zaju* is pictured more as a rowdy clown, an untamed demon and ill-qualified Buddhist disciple.

The monkey's name in *Zaju* now is almost the same as in the sixteenth-century fiction *Journey to the West*. He refers to himself as "Tongtian Dasheng" (Great Sage Reaching Heaven), only one word's difference from "Qitian Dasheng," the title Sun Wukong receives from the Taoist heaven in the sixteenth-century book. In some versions of the Monkey King story, including the *Zaju*, Qitian Dasheng and Tongtian Dasheng are brothers, so this replacement of name may be the result of confusion at a certain stage of the promulgation of the story. Although Tongtian Dasheng is the monkey's title, in the drama everyone calls him "the monkey" (*husun*), including Guanyin, even though she is the person who gave him the names Sun Wukong and Sun Xingzhe (Acolyte). When Guanyin presents Sun Xingzhe to Tripitaka as his disciple, she gives the monkey an iron fillet, a cassock, and a knife.[25] Although the headband is similar to the Tightening Fillet that the later Sun Wukong wears, the knife is a departure from his famous weapon, the gold-banded iron rod. The monkey image has yet to develop into the well-balanced figure between the binding hoop and the breaking rod as represented in the 1592 novel. Even with the headband's control, Tongtian Dasheng's behavior and language indicate that his mind remains that of an irreverent demon.

As in the *zaju* theater tradition, Sun Xingzhe introduces himself to the audience with a poem at his first appearance. Vaunting his celestial birth, his power, and the troubles he could create, in colloquial expression rather than elegant traditional terms as others' opening poems, the monkey's poem describes him as a celebrated ape demon, referring to himself as the King of a Hundred Thousand Demons.[26] In the following statement he introduces himself and his four siblings as his demon family: His elder brother Qitian Dasheng, a younger brother Shuashua Sanlang, and two sisters, Lishan Laomu and Wu Zhiqi Shengmu. This genealogy of the monkey shows that the Sun Xingzhe in *Zaju* is already much more localized, settled into the local religious/cult culture. Unlike the monkey in other versions, this one has a wife, the abducted princess of the Country of the Golden Cauldron. He also proudly reports to the audience his famous misdeeds, which is also the reason that heaven is after him: he has stolen the Jade Emperor's celestial wine, Laozi's golden elixir, and the Queen of the West's (Xichi Wangmu) peaches and fairy clothes. He also makes upfront ribald references about himself in this very first speech.[27] The monkey's demonic heart is indicated by his intention to eat Tripitaka immediately after Tripitaka rescues him from beneath the mountain.[28] He never shows any seriousness about the business of pilgrimage, and his behavior does not improve during the journey. When the team arrives in India, he uses crude language in a conversation with an old lady about Buddhist ideas of the "heart."

The monkey's names in *Zaju* indicate his unimportant social standing. While the introductory notes of the play refer to the monkey as Sun Xingzhe, he refers to himself in more modest terms as Little Sage

(Xiaosheng). He is a monkey (*husun*) to everyone in the play, although they may address him as Xingzhe. After becoming a disciple of Tripitaka (named Tangseng in this text), he always introduces himself as Sun Wukong the first disciple of Tripitaka. In scene 14, when he meets the woman taken by Pigsy and is addressed as "Respected Deity," he even explains to her that he is not a deity at all.[29] This forms an interesting contrast to the later *Journey to the West* novel in which Sun Wukong loves to refer to himself as the Great Sage and enjoys being addressed by this title. The monkey's low standing in *Zaju* can also be illustrated by the fact that other figures at the lowest level of the deity hierarchy, such as a mountain spirit or a land spirit, can give him commands and instructions. For instance, the mountain spirit of the Flower-Fruit Mountain bade the monkey farewell with the instruction, "Xingzhe, assist your master carefully on your way."[30] This is quite different from *Journey to the West*, in which it is usually Sun Wukong who gives commands to local spirits, who are usually quite in awe of the monkey's power.

The low standing of the monkey among the celestials corresponds with his role as clown in the play. Sun Xingzhe does not act seriously, nor does he ever speak seriously. This king of demons seems to be good only at stealing and running away. Although the play records a few incidents of encounters between Sun Xingzhe and celestial warriors or demons, Sun Wukong seems to have positioned himself as a sly rascal rather than a brave fighter. In scene 9, when Devarāja Li arrives with troops to capture Xingzhe in his home, he runs away, leaving his wife behind to deal with the troops.[31] In scenes 13–16, in the episode of Tripitaka and Sun Xingzhe's encounter with Zhu Bajie the pig demon, who is converted into Tripitaka's second disciple, Xingzhe offers to help fight the pig demon, but he is more interested in the Pei girl (old man Pei's daughter) who has been abducted by Zhu. He only offers to help after old Pei tells him that his daughter is a rare beauty, and his dealings with the pig only revolve around the girl: when he visits the pig's mountain home, he sees only the Pei girl, so his first action is to take the girl back to Pei. He then waits for Zhu Bajie in the bridal chamber in the Pei girl's clothing and flirts with the pig when he arrives. Eventually Bajie is caught, though not by Xingzhe but rather by the dog of Erlang.[32] His sustained interest in women and sex is demonstrated in another encounter with a demon in the Flaming Mountain episode. In this story, he seeks to borrow the Iron Fan from Princess Iron Fan (Tieshan Gongzhu) to put out the fire, but because he introduces himself using vulgar language, the princess refuses to lend him the fan and instead attacks him. Although eventually—with the help of Guanyin and other gods—the pilgrims pass the Flaming Mountain, the battle with Princess Iron Fan, which later becomes one of the most famous battles of *Journey to the West*, seems to be caused solely by Sun Xingzhe's insolence.

The vulgarity of Sun Xingzhe's language persists throughout the drama. The *zaju* drama during the Yuan era is distinguished from most other earlier Chinese art forms by its use of informal, vernacular, and nonsensical language. The language that Xingzhe uses is the most vulgar of all, corresponding to his role as the clown. He amuses by making crude jokes and obscene references at most inappropriate occasions throughout the story. For instance, at a crucial moment of his life when Tripitaka meets him for the first time and tries to climb the mountain to have him released, the monkey starts a conversation about love and explains that Tripitaka's motivation to save him is his lust for the monkey's thin waistline, which resembles that of a desirable beauty.[33] The monkey makes a reference to Agilawood Pavilion (Chenxiang Ting), a place that is known through Li Bo's poems about the love affairs between Emperor Tang Xuanzong and his consort Yang Guifei. Agilawood Pavilion also appears a few times in Yuan playwright Bai Pu's drama *Rain on the Phoenix Tree* (Tang Minghuang qiuye wutong yu), the love story between the emperor and the consort in *zaju* form. This reference does not make sense unless we consider it as a parodic reference to the other well-known drama. The satirical cross-reference to other dramas is most obvious in the episode of Zhu Bajie, which is discussed below in more detail. Near the end of the trip when the pilgrims arrive in India, the monkey encounters an old lady who talks with him about Buddhist concepts. When asked about his heart, Xingzhe comments that he used to have a heart, but he "shit it out" because his "asshole" is too wide.[34]

In addition to his spoken parts, Sun Xingzhe also sings on four occasions in *Zaju*. According to the convention of *zaju* drama, in each act only one actor, either the male lead (*zhengmo*) or the female lead (*zhengdan*), sings. Only in exceptional situations would an actor in a supporting role sing.[35] In none of the twenty-four acts has the role of Sun Xingzhe served as the lead, but as a supporting actor he has sung four times. The first time that the monkey sings is at the end of act 9, when Guanyin puts him underneath the Flower-Fruit Mountain. Instead of singing about his failure or the consequences of his capture, he sings about how he will be missing his wife, the woman he abducted from the State of Jinding.[36] The monkey's second song explains to the old man Pei what he knows of Pei's daughter, the girl abducted by Bajie.[37] His third song occurs when he pretends to be the Pei girl and teases Bajie in her bedroom.[38] The fourth song of the monkey is a detailed description of the sexual encounters of Bajie and Sha Heshang (Friar Sand) with women in the Land of Women, while Xingzhe himself watches on the side because his sexual ability is curbed by the tightening of the headband.[39] These songs are all inserted into scenes with a female lead, either as an interruption of the woman's proper expression of their stories and emotions, or as a humorous conclusion to the act. Distinct in style and mood from the appropriate voices of the women, Sun Xingzhe's songs are apparently inserted into the scenes as amusing surprises, just like the shockingly inappropriate turns of his spoken parts. Three of these songs are used at the end of their respective acts and are blatantly about sex, conveyed in suggestive, ribald, or obscene expressions.

XIYOU JI VERSUS *XIXIANG JI*

From *Shihua* to *Zaju*, the monkey is transformed from a god who acts properly to a demon who uses foul language and makes suggestive jokes. In the hundred-chapter *Journey to the West*, Sun Wukong is turned into a multivalent figure, funny but not crude. The vulgarity of Sun Wukong seems to be peculiar to the *Zaju* version. Aside from the crude language, another special feature of *Zaju* that is not shared with the earlier *Shihua* or the novel *Journey to the West*—not even with the other extant *zaju* drama related to the Tripitaka story—is the quite apparent obsession with the theme of abduction.[40]

Glen Dudbridge has taken the frequently used "abducted maiden" theme as the dramatist's way to solve another problem: finding a singer for each scene. He believes that in "giving the stage to a heroine in distress it naturally supplies the needs of a lyrical medium."[41] However, if we count the scenes that have an abducted woman or a related character as the singer, we can see they cover a large part of the entire play: the singer for scenes 1–4 is Tripitaka's mother; for scene 9 it is Sun Xingzhe's "wife," the abducted princess; the father of a girl named Liu abducted by the demon General Yin'e sings in scene 11; the Pei girl, whom Zhu Bajie abducts to become his wife, sings in scenes 13–15. If we consider the episode of the Queen of the Land of Women forcing Tripitaka to marry her as one of reversed abduction, then scene 17 counts as one too, in which the Queen sings. In this scene Zhu Bajie and Sha Heshang are indeed abducted by women in the country, as Xingzhe's suggestive song describes. This covers most of the incidents that happen before the team arrives in India, leaving out only the episode about Guizi mu (*Hārītī*) trying to rescue her son Red Boy, who is captured by the Buddha (scene 12), and the episode about Princess Iron Fan, which can be interpreted as a story about Xingzhe's failed advances toward the princess (scenes 18–20). Indeed, the clearest themes of the play are sex and abduction, which Dudbridge's reasoning about the need for a female singer does not satisfactorily explain.

The question of why there are so many female singers, or why the focus remains on the abduction theme, is related to another curious question about *Zaju*: none of the main characters of the pilgrimage journey is designated as a singer. Singers are supposed to be the leading actors because in a *zaju* it is via the songs that the thoughts and emotions of the characters are expressed to the audience. In this play, however, the songs are all given to secondary figures, including a mountain spirit (scene 10) and a Taoist (scene 18) in addition to all the women in distress. Scene 10, for instance, is the important episode about converting Xingzhe as Tripitaka's disciple, a scene involving the major characters Sun Xingzhe, Guanyin, and Tripitaka. Instead of any of these three, the author assigned the singing position to a completely dispensable figure.

According to Dudbridge, secondary figures become singers when the major characters lack the proper character type. Sun Xingzhe, for instance, is ineligible to sing a full suite because he plays the role of the buffoon. The four single songs he sings are "distinct from the mode and sequence of the suite proper" and are ribald or obscene in content. Tripitaka and Guanyin, on the other hand, never sing in the play. Dudbridge contends that this can only be explained in terms of *zaju* conventions of casting.[42]

The narrative's obsession with abduction and the lack of singing roles for the pilgrimage characters might be pointing to something bigger than the conventions of casting. After all, if the interest of the drama is indeed in portraying the monk and the monkey as heroes, what is there to stop the author from portraying the monk, or even the monkey, as the leading *mo* role?[43] One can surmise that the drama's interest lies not so much in the pilgrimage theme as in the abduction theme. The story of Tripitaka's journey in the drama serves as a narrative theme designed to link the other separate abduction stories together. After all, there is already a tradition of anecdotal stories about lecherous monkeys who abduct women, as Qian Zhongshu points out.[44] While telling a story of *Journey to the West*, the *zaju* at the same time shows an interest in parodying a famous Yuan *zaju*, Wang Shifu's *The Story of the Western Chamber*, or *Cui Yingying daiyue Xixiang ji* (hereafter *Western Chamber*).

Even though we have no written record from the author about his intention, a commentary written by a "Yunkong Jushi," included as a foreword in a 1614 print of the drama, compares the two plays with a difference of only one character in their titles (*Xiyou ji* versus *Xixiang ji*). This stance is supported by another foreword written by a "Mijia Dizi," who apparently published this version of *zaju* in print based on a handwritten copy he possessed.[45] Both of these forewords show the connection between *Western Chamber* and *Journey to the West*. The comments of Yunkong Jushi about the links between the two dramas deserve quotation here:

> Changling was originally planning to write a *Western Chamber*.[46] Before long Wang Shifu completed the work first. Upon seeing it, Changling knew he could not possibly beat it. Therefore he wrote this drama [*Journey to the West*] instead to contend with it [*yi di zhi*]. . . . Those who live like the frogs in a well will not be able to fully appreciate it. It should be considered as a brother work with *Western Chamber*.
>
> *Western Chamber* is an account of a beautiful love story. The current story, however, provides a magnificent spectacle of the world, in which you can find the heaven, the human, the Buddha, deities, demons, and ghosts alike. . . .
>
> Dramas of the northern tunes all consist of four scenes only, except *Western Chamber*, which has twenty scenes. . . . This is the only one that has twenty-four scenes. . . . I have seen other *Journey to the West* dramas performed by vulgar entertainers, which are quite obscene and ridiculous. This version . . . can help wash away the shame.[47]

We cannot tell whether the commentator's statement about the author's intention to write a "Journey to the West" to contend with *Western Chamber* is based on sources available at the time or is merely the commentator's speculation based on his own understanding of the two dramas. Either case, however, points toward a possibly widely accepted connection between the two. Although this connection is disliked by scholars such as Yan Dunyi,[48] it does offer a viable explanation for the prominent abduction theme in *Zaju*: it works as a parody of *Western Chamber*. The scenes focusing on Zhu Bajie's subjugation serve to make the parodic intention particularly clear.

The drama devotes four scenes to Zhu Bajie's story, disproportionately long for a pilgrim of secondary importance. Besides Zhu's scenes, there are four scenes for Tripitaka's life, two scenes for Sun Xingzhe, and only part of a scene for Sha Heshang. Zhu's role in the story is limited to these four scenes. He is almost never mentioned elsewhere, except in the obscene song of Xingzhe about Zhu and Sha with the women in the scene set in the Land of Women. In other words, the lengthy description of Zhu's story unnecessarily slows the progress of the journey story, unless there is a digressive intention for it: to serve as a parody of the story. In fact, the four scenes about Zhu work nicely as a spoof of *Western Chamber*: a male protagonist that is a pig demon, and the development of the story with an opposite outcome.

Western Chamber is a popular love story between Zhang Junrui, a young scholar on his way to the civil examination, and Cui Yingying, the daughter of a late prime minister. The two meet in a Buddhist monastery and immediately fall in love. A local bandit, Sun Feihu, attacks the monastery in the hope of abducting Yingying. Yingying's mother, Lady Cui, promises the hand of Yingying to anyone who can drive the bandits away. Zhang, with the help of his friend General Du, accomplishes the task. However, at this point Lady Cui changes her mind and rejects the marriage agreement by explaining to Zhang that Yingying is already betrothed to a Zheng Heng. Yingying's maid Hongniang helps the pining young couple arrange secret meetings. When Lady Cui finds out about this, she reluctantly consents to the marriage on the condition that Zhang passes the civil examination and becomes an official. The story concludes with a happy ending: Zhang passes the exam, and the two marry.

In what is seen as a celebration of freedom of love and the happy ending of the marriage of the two lovers, little justice is given to the character of Mr. Zheng. In the story, Lady Cui essentially breaches two marriage agreements for her daughter: the one with Zheng and the one with Zhang. Near the end, Zheng appears and asks for the fulfillment of the marriage. But Zheng is followed shortly by Zhang, who with the help of his position as an official and the support of his friend General Du easily beats Zheng in the competition. Zheng then kills himself, an action the narrative ignores, turning immediately to a celebration of the happy couple's wedding.

The scenes focusing on Bajie in *Zaju* also revolve around a breach-of-betrothal theme, resembling *Western Chamber.* Pei Haitang is betrothed to a Zhu, whose family had become poor. As a result, Pei's father plans to breach the marriage agreement. Knowing her father's intention, Haitang asks her maid Meixiang to send a message to Zhu, letting him know that she will be burning incense every evening in the garden and suggesting that they could meet there in secret. So far the plot closely follows *Western Chamber.* But here the demon Zhu Bajie appears. Learning of Pei's plan, Zhu Bajie visits the garden at night, pretending to be the other Zhu, and asks Haitang to leave with him. Taking Bajie as her betrothed fiancé, Pei Haitang leaves with him in defiance of her father. At this point the story reads like a *Western Chamber* gone awry. Yingying's secret meetings with Zhang are justified by the marriage agreement of her mother and, therefore, so is Haitang's plan. However, what in *Western Chamber* is praised as the brave pursuit of love and rewarded with an eventual marriage, in *Journey to the West* can be taken as a warning: if you are thinking of following the *Western Chamber,* you will end up being abducted by a pig demon.

When Tripitaka and Sun Xingzhe arrive, the parody of *Western Chamber* opts to restore justice. The monkey plays the role of General Du of *Western Chamber,* that is to say, the outside helper who fixes things. This is actually the busiest sequence for Xingzhe in the entire drama, since he serves as an active intermediary: being the first to see Pei Haitang and the pig together, he throws a stone at the pig; after learning about the girl's story, he offers to deliver a message for her to her father; and after delivering the message, he offers to help capture the pig demon. Missing the pig at the mountain, he delivers Pei Haitang back to her home. Next, he enjoins the two families to fulfill the marriage, as they should have, and only then starts his business with the pig himself in which he first dresses as Pei Haitang and teases Zhu Bajie in the bride's room, and then seeks help from Guanyin to capture Bajie. In fact, Xingzhe shows unmatched enthusiasm in this sequence compared to any other sequences of the play and works hard to make sure things go right. The intention of the entire sequence is to correct the wrong in *Western Chamber*: it is not acceptable to breach an arranged marriage just because the groom's family becomes poor. Sun Xingzhe carries out this task with such seriousness that he almost forgets about his demonic behavior. Twice alone with a woman in the mountain, he has not made any advance toward her. Two of Xingzhe's four songs are sung in this sequence, one of which is the only song of his that delivers a message with no obscenity.[49]

In short, it can be a productive approach to consider *Zaju* as a double adaptation: an adaptation of the "Journey to the West" story combined with a parody/adaptation of *Western Chamber. Zaju* not only parodies *Western Chamber* in terms of the story and the message but also imitates the format, which both forewords of the 1614 printing are quick to point out: they are the longest dramas of the time. With *Western Chamber* already exceptionally long, *Zaju* makes sure that it has four more scenes than *Western Chamber*. The *Zaju* as a parody of *Western Chamber* thus adds an external reference to the pilgrimage story and reshapes the story through the reference.

If Hou Xingzhe is in general a god with positive qualities, Sun Xingzhe in *Zaju* shows the negative parts of his character coming into full bloom. He is much more associated with a buffoon and a demonic ape than with a celestial god. From Hou Xingzhe to Sun Xingzhe, the monkey figure is more localized, closely bound with popular culture. If we indeed can consider him as a figure on the way toward his Buddhist belief, he also remains the Taoist demon he claims to be and demonstrates his concern with keeping the order of Confucian values, as reflected in the Zhu Bajie sequence. Significantly, the monkey in *Zaju* receives the iron fillet from Guanyin, a device to control the demon in him, and which comes into use in the episode of the Land of Women. It is not until the hundred-chapter *Journey to the West* that the monkey also obtains his powerful weapon, the Golden-Hooped Rod, and hence completes the image of Sun Wukong that will become the most enduring version.

SUN WUKONG IN *JOURNEY TO THE WEST* AND THE WRITER/READER RELATIONSHIP

When Wu Cheng'en performs his creative adaptation, the sources of the journey story have been quite fully fledged. For instance, the *Pak t'ongsa onhae* (Piao tongshi yanjie), a Korean reader in colloquial Chinese first printed in the mid-fifteenth century, contains a list of references to mythic places and demons and gods, and brief accounts of episodes such as Sun Wukong's rebellion against heaven (chapters 5–7, 13 in the novel) and Tripitaka and Sun Wukong's experience in the Cart-Slow Kingdom (chapters 44–46 in the novel).[50] One of the dialogues in this record presents a picture of "ordinary people going out to buy popular stories in book form," and *Journey to the West* is one of them.[51] In the dialogue, a question arises about why people would buy popular tales instead of the Four Books or Six Classics, and the given answer is, "The *Journey to the West* is lively. It is good reading when you are feeling gloomy."[52] This conversation shows that some version of *Journey to the West* is already circulating at the time and that for an ordinary reader this kind of popular story is preferable to Confucian classics. Wu Cheng'en's task is to pull together the source materials that are available for him and transform them into a fuller text, one that is reprinted, commented upon, and continued by a large number of writers who are scholars like him. Many of these later "adaptations" take the story as serious allegories of religious teachings, instead of assuming it is just for entertainment.[53] Wu Cheng'en's adaptation of the "Journey to the West" story has accomplished its transformation from a popular-culture to an elite-culture work.

Compared to *Zaju*, *Journey to the West* has grown a great deal over time, both in terms of adding new episodes and through additions to the original narrative. It is the largest amalgamation of the pilgrimage sources, retold in a balanced style. *Journey to the West* brings the Buddhist and Taoist traditions into a new balance, despite the tensions that appear frequently in the story. Confucian principles such as the morals of loyalty and filial piety permeate the story, whether in the human world, the underworld, or the heavens. The peaceful coexistence of the three religions is pronounced repeatedly in the book and is also accepted as one of the major themes of the book by both scholars of the Ming and Qing eras and in contemporary analyses.[54] Although still full of lively local expressions, the language is more refined, without the crude references in *Zaju*.

Printed in the sixteenth century of the Ming period, a time when the printing industry grew rapidly through commercialization and many people could buy novels to read for pleasure, the concerns of this book should be different from those of earlier vernacular narratives. It is a transformational time for the writers, publishers, and readers: whereas the readership of the manuscript culture of the earliest vernacular narratives consisted of "circles of literati and admirers," for the print culture, the reading public was no longer restricted to the learned classes. There is awareness among authors and publishers that "the potential readership was a heterogeneous one of officials, literati, collectors among the new class of the nouveaux riche, members of the laity, common people, the relatively unlearned, and even the all-inclusive 'people of the empire' or 'people of the four classes.'"[55] The idea of a general reader of the novel must have contributed to the writing. Interestingly, while earlier vernacular narratives are written to be copied and circulated among the literati, the new novels are written by the literati for a wider audience. Whatever other purposes the author might have, much attention must be paid to the readability of the book: that it tells a fun story, presents interesting characters, and uses language that is accessible and lively. During *Pak t'ongsa onhae*'s time, the book *Journey to the West* had been popular because of its liveliness, which provides a rationale for the printers' interest in printing new adaptations, and both the publisher and the author must have made sure that these popular features would be included in order to ensure its continuing success in the market. The consideration of the reader and market thus supports the reading of the novel as a work for pleasure, an exemplary book of the low culture, even though it is written by a scholar.[56]

In *Journey to the West*, Sun Wukong becomes a figure of more depth, someone who does not follow any prototype. He is still the guide and protector, resourceful for the journey, and knowledgeable about Buddhist teachings, but he is not the overly serious Hou Xingzhe of *Shihua*. He is still funny and mischievous, creating trouble while pushing the narrative forward, but he is no longer the clown of *Zaju*. It seems that much of the vulgarity is redirected to the character of Zhu Bajie, which allows Sun Wukong to become a more introspective character who seeks to answer the question "Who am I?" or, more accurately, engages the reader to ask the question.

Compared to the earlier versions, the most significant change of *Journey to the West* is the change of protagonist. In *Zaju*, Tripitaka is still the main pilgrim on the journey and the main character in the entire play. Besides the incidents during the journey, the drama starts with Tripitaka's legend and ends with Tripitaka's accomplishment of the pilgrimage. In *Journey to the West* this structure is changed. The novel begins instead with a seven-chapter-long account of the monkey's story, which is elaborated more than in any earlier account. It is here that Sun Wukong obtains his weapon, the Golden-Hooped Rod, which does not appear in the previous monkey stories.[57] This addition completes the other side of the multivalent figure of the Monkey King. In *Zaju*, Sun Xingzhe is associated only with the fillet over his head. His actions, from stealing peaches from heaven, to making advances toward Princess Iron Fan, are all actions of a mischievous demon that needs to be controlled by the fillet. In *Journey to the West*, Sun Wukong finds his rod, and his experience—from the learning of skills, the testing of territory, the freedom of doing what he wants, to the kind of fun he enjoys no matter what he does and where he is—seems to be associated with, or represented by, the rod. Indeed, the narrative particularly makes the point that the monkey is meant to be the owner of the rod.[58] The narrative also notes in one episode that without the rod he is no longer the monkey.[59] The pleasure and freedom that Sun Wukong enjoys with the rod, or the Compliant Golden-Hooped Rod (Ruyi Jingu Bang), is only to be met by the fillet from the Buddha, given to him by Guanyin via the hands of Tripitaka. The fillet is not compliant to his will; instead, it controls him against his will. From the moment that Sun Wukong puts on the fillet, he is transformed from a free monkey—or a demon from the viewpoint of the Taoist and Buddhist deities—to a disciple of Tripitaka, a "compliant" good pilgrim for the journey. In a sense, he becomes the "compliant rod" for his master and Guanyin, since they can use the Tightening Fillet to force him to do what they want. However, the story is told mainly from the monkey's point of view, as is established in the beginning chapters. Thus, the conflict between the rod of free will and the fillet that constrains the will becomes fundamental for the character Sun Wukong, providing the exigencies for his behavior. The narrative makes sure that the power of the fillet is exercised later, too, for instance in the episode where Sun Wukong fights against the White Bone Demon.[60]

The conflict between the rod and fillet is also the conflict between a god and a demon. Sun Wukong represents both god and demon in one body. Unlike previous vernacular narratives where the monkey may have different titles, which are self-made titles that qualify him as a demon in the mythical hierarchy, in *Journey to the West*, Monkey is twice given official titles by Jade Emperor: the Supervisor of the Imperial Stables (Bimawen) and Great Sage, Equal to Heaven (Qitian Dasheng). The reason that he creates the trouble in heaven is because he sees the contradiction between his two identities: the god and the monkey, in contrast to Sun Xingzhe in *Zaju*, who steals because he wants to enjoy the treasures at his demon home with his wife. Sun Wukong of *Journey to the West* wants to be treated as a Great Sage, but unfortunately when he is seen as a monkey, he cannot possibly be treated like the other gods. When his rod is reaching so far that he creates turmoil in the Jade Emperor's palace and even wants to create a new order, it is time for the fillet to let him know the boundary of his power.

The conflict of the rod and fillet provides a kind of interior conflict that resonates with readers who must balance freedom and responsibility in their own lives. This conflict earns readers' sympathy for the monkey figure and possibly contributes to their identification with him. It points to a new kind of relationship between the writer and the reader. Examining the writing of the various versions of the "Journey to the West" story, including *Shihua, Zaju, Xiyou ji*, and later adaptations, there are two interrelated tracks during the adaptation process: one, the writing is for the purpose of entertainment (including religious entertainment) within popular culture; and two, the making of a version is a writing game for the literati himself. Although all these adaptations follow the two tracks at the same time, they probably lean more heavily on one of them. While *Shihua* and *Zaju*'s readers can be easily outlined—those who are interested in Buddhist teachings and the *zaju* drama—the writers' attention lies more in satisfying these outward needs (religious references and intertextual references to other drama, for instance). However, *Journey to the West*'s readers, the general readers of late sixteenth century and after, have wider interests owing to the heterogeneity of the reading population. To satisfy their needs, *Journey to the West* provides "liveliness" of writing, encyclopedic content, and most importantly, it focuses on the monkey's identity quest. Therefore, besides the lively incidents between the pilgrims and demons, it provides above all a story of a monkey who seeks to understand who he is and his position in the world, a monkey who refuses to accept his limits but in the end has to accept the tragic solution of his life—all of which can be wrapped in the contradictory bundle of the rod and the fillet. In other words, Wu Cheng'en's work establishes the protagonist as a "self" that can be identified by the reader. This concern with the self and the communication between the writer and the reader begins with the addition of the monkey's story at the outset of the novel.

My discussion of the inward interest of the Monkey King image corresponds with the trend of the "inward turn" in the Ming cultural milieu. This trend is manifested by the interest in the mind/heart (*xin*) by the three religions in the Ming and culminates in the *xinxue* (learning of the mind/heart). Plaks's study of the four masterworks of the Ming novel posits the study of the works, including *Journey to the West*, in the context of *xinxue*.[61] Yu's reading of Monkey as the heart/mind of the pilgrim team also relies heavily on the Neo-Confucian understandings of the mind.[62] In fact, the term *xinyuan* (mind monkey) is generally accepted by analysis today as representing Sun Wukong's crucial role for the journey. I argue that the inward emphasis exists not just in the wordplay of the author: the philosophical terms that mostly appear in the poems embedded in the text and in chapter titles. It is obvious also for readers who are not familiar with these terms, in the structure of the book, in the fundamental features of the monkey Wukong. It is more in the sense of identity than in the play of the word "mind monkey" that many adaptations of *Journey to the West* in later popular culture place their focus. It is also around the Monkey King's sense of identity that the later chapters develop.

Journey to the West becomes an example of how popular culture and elite culture merge in a literary vehicle. Having been rewritten within "low" culture, the story is taken over by an elite scholar and made into a classic, a work that is recognized by elite literati as exceptionally well written. The novel has established itself as the "original" for future adaptation, both by elite scholars and by popular culture. In late Ming and Qing periods, there appeared sequels (*xushu*) to *Journey to the West*, in which the journey either continues or episodes are added in the middle. According to literary scholar Qiancheng Li, these sequels demonstrate an increasingly "inward turn," in which the journey is internalized.[63]

This "inward turn" has been examined in studies of seventeenth-century Chinese literature, such as Robert Hegel's discussion of the interest in exploration of mind in literary novels, and Andrew Plaks's observation about "private sensibility":

> Whereas the sixteenth-century novels were all based on pre-existing sources from the popular tradition, the seventeenth-century works come more and more to be based on personal experience, so that the public focus of the earlier work becomes increasingly one of private sensibility. This tendency is most marked in the exploration of dream psychology in the *Xiyou bu*, although the interest in subjective experience dominates a number of other works of the period.[64]

Sequel to the Journey to the West (Xiyou bu) is one of the three sequels of the late Ming and Qing periods, and the one with the strongest emphasis on the mind among the three.[65] Written by Dong Yue in 1641, the story focuses on the character Sun Wukong and takes place between chapters 61 and 62 of *Journey to the West* in a series of dreams of the monkey, whose mind is controlled by a mackerel demon (*qing yu*).[66] Dong, a scholar who became a Buddhist monk later in his life, is eager to teach the reader through his reinterpretation of *Journey to the West* that the root of evil is inside oneself and that the way to enlightenment is to use emptiness to destroy desire. This eagerness, as well as the intended message of his novel, is clearly stated in the question-and-answer session appended to the novel. Qiancheng Li states that all three sequels probe the human mind, and that *Xiyou bu* is the one that explores the deepest, at "the workings of human psychology and experiments with fictional representations of the human mind."[67]

Each sequel, however, uses its own adaptations to prove its points about the allegorical meaning of *Journey to the West*. The authors are interested in making obvious what they think is not articulated clearly enough in the novel, or correcting what is presented incorrectly.[68] In other words, they use Sun Wukong to teach the reader a lesson, to explain an idea, rather than to ask the reader to relate to their own life and to engage in questions of identity. Such rewritings require less identification on the reader's part with Sun Wukong than do later adaptations from popular culture.

CHAPTER 3

From Trickster to Hero

National Mythmaking in Wartime and Maoist China

Growing up in the People's Republic of China shortly after the Cultural Revolution, I first encountered the "Journey to the West" story in children's picture books (*xiaoren shu*), television series, and stage performances. Only years later did I realize that the hero of my youth was a contemporary adaptation, and not identical to the figure in the original novel or other forms of the "Journey to the West" narrative from earlier times. The contemporary images of Sun Wukong have been so overwhelmingly positive that to me—and to millions of other Chinese readers—the Monkey King is a hero, a role model, and one who is not only fearless and willing to challenge authorities but also loyal to his master Tripitaka and devoted to the goal of the band of pilgrims. Although he had been a trickster figure who embodied contradictory values as portrayed in *Journey to the West*, or a monkey who made funny moves and demonstrated opera skills in the late Qing dynasty, the Monkey King in the new China epitomizes positive and progressive values for the proletarian revolution and socialist construction.

The early twentieth century was a time of turmoil in Chinese history, particularly the years between the 1930s and 1950s. This period was marked by the Japanese invasion, an occupation of China (1931–45), the Second Sino-Japanese War (1937–45), and the Chinese Civil War (1945–48). During the transformational Communist Revolution, with 1949 as the watershed year, the connection of the Monkey King image with the idea of revolution was established. Unlike many other artistic works affected by the Cultural Revolution, *Journey to the*

West was not discarded as literary nonsense from the past; to the contrary, its protagonist was taken up and reshaped to represent the revolutionaries. The reshaping of the Monkey King image is so powerful that it changed the position of Sun Wukong in literary tradition and made him one of the most popular literary and cultural figures for both old and young readers. Sun Wukong was transformed from a trickster, a figure whose role in the play is more for humor and stunts than serious conversation, to a sublime and honorable protagonist. This trajectory sheds light on the power of the political discourse of the state, which remodels images not only of historical figures but also of popular folkloric and mythical figures such as Sun Wukong.

PRINCESS IRON FAN

The effort to positively transform the trickster Monkey King into a heroic figure and role model for a modern Chinese audience can be clearly traced to the first animated feature film in China, the 1941 *Princess Iron Fan* (Tieshan Gongzhu). The film, produced by the Wan brothers, was influenced by the success of the American animated feature film *Snow White and the Seven Dwarfs* but was made as a response to the Japanese invasion of China.[1] Significantly, from the very beginning of Chinese animated films, there was clearly a twofold task for the animators: to experiment and build a Chinese style of animation, and to make the films educational in response to the political situation of the time. In a 1936 article, the Wan brothers wrote that "one ought to have a story based purely on real Chinese traditions and stories, consistent with our sensibility and sense of humor. . . . Also, our films must not only bring pleasure, but also be educational."[2] As the leading figures in the Chinese animation industry, the Wan brothers placed an emphasis on social and political functions throughout their filmmaking in the 1930s and 1940s. Wan Laiming has explicitly stated that his experience living in Shanghai under imperialist control from the 1920s to the 1940s, as well as the influence of progressive people in literary and art circles, convinced him and his brothers to use the weapon of fine arts to fight against imperialism, thus enabling them to contribute their animated films to the joint anti-Japanese enterprise.[3]

In *Princess Iron Fan* in particular, by choosing an episode of *Journey to the West* as the topic, the Wan brothers not only tried to make an animated film with a Chinese theme in a Chinese style—a Chinese princess in response to the American princess Snow White—but also intended the story as a metaphor, referring to the current war between China and Japan. The two conflicting factions of the story, Sun Wukong versus the Bull Demon King and Princess Iron Fan, represent the two sides of the war. The film made it quite obvious that the Monkey King's victory over the Bull Demon King, a collective victory in collaboration with Zhu Bajie (Pigsy) and Sha Seng (Sandy) as well as the villagers, is the victory of the Chinese people against the Japanese invasion, thus making the theme of the film "all Chinese people must unite for victory against the Japanese invasion."[4] These exact words were supposed to be embedded in the film, but because the end of the shooting occurred just at the time of the Japanese invasion of the foreign concessions in Shanghai, they were censored from the final cut. However, even without these words spelled out in the film, the trope is easily recognizable.

In a textual prologue of the film, the audience is informed that "*Journey to the West* was at the outset an excellent fairy tale for children, but it has been taken as a novel of gods and spirits [*shenguai xiaoshuo*] by mistake." Not intending to repeat that mistake, the prologue states that the film instead aims at "encouraging a healthy mentality for children." The prologue also spells out the moral of the story for the audience: "The pilgrims' story at the Flaming Mountains represents the difficulties in life, and in order to overcome these difficulties, we have to keep our faith and work together."

As a vehicle for this message, the film offers a revised plot, so the new story resembles a bildungsroman. Sun Wukong, Pigsy, and Sandy are presented as children-friendly figures learning an important lesson in life: the value of collaboration. When they arrive at the Flaming Mountains, they find it impossible to cross because of the roaring blaze. Learning that the only way to extinguish the flames is to borrow the magic fan from Princess Iron Fan, who is unwilling to lend it, they each decide to do it individually to prove their ability. After their individual efforts all fail, they realize that their mistake lies in being divided among themselves. As Tripitaka tells them in his teaching: "Your failure is owing to poor coordination. If the three of you can make a concerted effort, you will definitely be able to beat the Bull Demon King." Tripitaka also mobilizes the villagers to join the battle, who fight in solidarity against the demon. A victory that appears in *Journey to the West* as mostly the accomplishment of Sun Wukong himself is ascribed in *Princess Iron Fan* to the collective effort of all the pilgrims and villagers.

The new plot contains two major points of revision to the *Journey to the West:* first, the monkey's earlier failed efforts to trick the fan away from the princess are changed into failures caused by the division among the three; second, the celestial help that Sun Wukong receives in his duel with the Bull Demon King is replaced with help from the villagers. These alterations help to formulate the moral of a story that points to the political situation of China: uniting the efforts of all Chinese against the common enemy. The encouraging ending adds glory to the image of the monkey, associating it with the heroic Chinese people fighting against the enemy of the nation.

This revised story plants a seed for the future exaltation of the image of Sun Wukong, although in the current film the image of the monkey still shows the influence of the traditional representation of him as a trickster. With his beak-like mouth, skinny limbs, and white gloves, Sun Wukong appears as a funny and small figure, resembling Mickey Mouse or Donald Duck more than a charismatic hero. He is better at running about and fleeing from danger than at fighting the enemy head-on. He uses transformation in order to try to cheat the princess into giving him the fan, but all his tricks fail. In the end, during the battle with the Bull Demon King, it is the small Sun Wukong who, without using transformation or grandiose size as he did in the novel, leads the gigantic bull into the trap prepared by the villagers. The contrast in size points to the reason for the eventual victory: individuals with little power can together form into strong bands. In such a case, the individual value of the Monkey King is represented by his size, which is just the same as that of every villager. The Monkey King remains tiny so that collective heroism can be presented as superior to individual heroism.

HAVOC IN HEAVEN

The trend of portraying the Monkey King positively as a hero continues in Mao's era. One episode that receives special attention and is crucial in the Monkey King's transformation into a hero is *Havoc in Heaven* (Da'nao tiangong; *or* Nao tiangong), which first stands out as an important title in Peking Opera and is later adapted as a milestone animated feature film in China. All of the adaptations that take place after Mao's rise to power are under the direct influence of his 1942 speech at the Yan'an Forum of Literature and Art. A major guideline and dominant principle for literary and artistic works during the Mao era, the speech was published in *Liberation Daily* (Jiefang ribao) in 1943, was included in *Selected Works of Mao Zedong* (Mao Zedong xuanji) in 1952, and was widely studied and promoted in China through the 1980s. Mao emphasizes that literature and art should serve both the people (including the worker, the farmer, the soldier, the working class, and the intellectual) and the purposes of the Revolution. The legacy of literature and art from the past should be inherited but only when it serves the revolutionary end of the people after necessary reform in both form and content.[5]

To meet the end of "serving the people," the dominant form of literature and art in post-Revolution China is socialist realism, a form and genre that does not leave room for most classical works. Even before the founding of the People's Republic of China, there were heated discussions about the proper attitude toward classical works: which ones to discard as the "dross" from older times and which ones to take over, reform, and reuse. Such discussions and efforts to reform and reuse works from the past continued well after 1949. Surprisingly, *Journey to the West*, with its religious and fantastic stories, deities, and demonic characters—seemingly the furthest from being acceptable for the socialist realistic discourse—became one of the few that was still considered appropriate and usable after the socialist revolution, although this acceptance came only after confusion and disagreement. *People's Daily* (Renmin ribao), the official newspaper of the Communist Party, bore witness to such discussions, especially of the episode *Havoc in Heaven* (Da'nao tiangong). On November 13, 1948, an editorial titled "Undertaking the Reformation of Traditional Theater Step by Step" appeared in *People's Daily,* stating that those theatrical works that advocate for ignorance and superstition should be banned. But it continued to argue that even though most plays about gods and ghosts belong to this category, "normal mythic stories" such as *Havoc in Heaven* should be kept. Why the story about the Monkey King creating turmoil in the Jade Emperor's heaven should be considered "normal" rather than "superstition" is left undiscussed. On December 24, three more articles about theater reformation appeared in *People's Daily*, two of which focused particularly on *Havoc in Heaven*: "On *Sun Wukong Creating Havoc in Heaven*" and "Some Questions on Reforming Traditional Theater." Both articles recognized that creating uproar in the celestial palace is a revolution and that Sun Wukong represents the class of the farmer rising up against the ruling class. Both also admitted that the appearance of gods and demons onstage can be misleading to the audience. Despite these reservations, it is clear that the traditional play *Havoc in Heaven*, with revisions, stayed onstage owing to the revolutionary reading of its content. In 1951, articles in *People's Daily* all cited *Havoc in Heaven* as representative of approved traditional plays. For instance, Ma Shaobo's article "Eliminate the Ugly and Unhealthy Images on the Opera Stage," published on September 27, cited *Havoc in Heaven* as a "healthy and good" play, whereas *Uproar in Hell* (Nao difu, another episode of *Journey to the West*) is unhealthy and ugly because the latter is only related to horror and superstition. The argument itself can hardly hold its ground, since it is based on ignoring the fact that in *Uproar in Hell* Sun Wukong is also fighting rebelliously against the ruling class, and in *Havoc in Heaven* there are also superstitious figures. On the other hand, confirmation bias indicates clearly that *Havoc in Heaven* had soundly established its status as a "good" traditional play by this time.

The discussions about the nature of the opera accompany the transformation of the Monkey King onstage from a naughty troublemaker into a brave, rebellious, and heroic figure representing the revolutionary classes of the new China. The 1950s see a major revision of the ending of the "Havoc in Heaven" story. The subjugation of Sun Wukong is replaced by his victory, and his reasons for creating the uproar (*nao*) in heaven are also rendered more justifiable.

OLD PLAY, NEW ENDING

The traditional Peking Opera play based on the episode "Havoc in Heaven" focuses on the taming of the monkey. The two extant versions of the transcript, titled *Antian hui* (Pacifying heaven) and *Nao tiangong* (Havoc in heaven), closely resemble each other except the ending, but this small difference does not affect the image of the Monkey King. The play begins when Sun Wukong, officially the "Great Sage, Equal to Heaven" who has the responsibility of guarding the Peach Garden, eats up the peaches and then vandalizes the celestial banquet. Leaving the "scene of the crime," he accidentally arrives at Laozi's residence and devours all the Elixir of Life that Laozi made before returning home (as described in chapter 5 of *Journey to the West*). When he learns about the monkey's offenses, the Jade Emperor sends Devarāja Li (Li Tianwang) and a battalion of heavenly troops to subdue him. After some combat, Immortal Master Erlang (Erlang

Shen), the well-known foe of the Monkey King, has him captured with the help of his dog (chapter 6 of *Journey to the West*). But whereas *Antian hui* ends with his capture, *Nao tiangong* continues on with the story, revealing that Sun Wukong cannot be decapitated because of the Elixir he consumed. As a result, Laozi decides to burn him in the Eight-Trigrams Furnace until only the Elixir remains (from chapter 7 of *Journey to the West*). Despite the difference, both endings emphasize the peace that is restored after the subjugation of the monkey, and both end with Devarāja Li singing about the promised demise of the monkey. In *Antian hui*, Li summarizes: "You have boasted about your magical power, but it has only prepared you for the magical guillotine!"[6] In *Nao tiangong*, the promised ending place of the monkey is the furnace, so Li sings: "The monkey is wild in nature and erroneous in behavior. Appointed the official position of 'Great Sage, Equal to Heaven,' you acted foolishly, and broke the celestial laws. The Great Banquet at Yaochi was destroyed by you. Now you will be burnt to ashes, leaving only the Elixir that you consumed which will then be sent back into Laozi's care."[7]

Out of the larger "Journey to the West" story, various versions of the "Havoc in Heaven" episode can end at different points, resulting in varied images of character and different messages. The two Peking Opera versions under discussion, although ending at different points, follow the tradition of the Yuan *zaju* theater, both presenting the Monkey King as wicked and mischievous, someone to blame for the turmoil and who is rightfully subjugated in the end. *Dagu* performance—a form of storytelling performance accompanied by drum (*gu*) that originated from storytelling about the Monkey King and was popular during late Qing and the Republic era—also follows this tradition. The song about the "Havoc in Heaven" episode is similarly titled *Antian hui* (Pacifying heaven) or *Da'nao tiangong* (Havoc in heaven), two versions that are almost identical. It allows the story to go a bit further and ends after the Monkey King is sent to the Eight-Trigrams Furnace to be burned. The monkey, however, knocks down the furnace, has a fight with the celestial forces, and is eventually confronted and defeated by Buddha, whom he begs for mercy. The song concludes with Buddha's words: "You should stay suppressed under Five Phases Mountain, and will not get out until Tripitaka releases you!"[8] This ending allows the monkey to make even more trouble and to show his power before his eventual subjugation, but the message about taming is unmistakable.

In 1951, playwright Weng Ouhong and Peking Opera performance artist Li Shaochun joined the China Traditional Opera Institute, and Weng revised *Nao tiangong* (Havoc in heaven) together with Li, who played the monkey.[9] The most important revision in the plot was the omission of the Monkey King's subjugation and his begging for mercy, ending with Sun Wukong celebrating his victory. Meanwhile, the discussion of the reformation of traditional art continued, and the new ending of *Havoc in Heaven* was positively received. On November 15, 1951, the *People's Daily* published a few readers' letters about art reformation. A letter from Jiang Ping, titled "Against the Trend of Anti-Historicism in the Reformation of Traditional Opera," discussed some traditional plays that had been successfully reformed, such as *Sun Wukong Creating Havoc in Heaven,* which "represents the people's rebellion against the feudal rulers, and demonstrates the infinite power of the people." According to Jiang, the most impressive scene in this play is at the end, when Sun Wukong, "having defeated the celestial troops, fights his way to the Hall of Lingxiao and chases away the Jade Emperor. This act breaks to pieces the glorious icon of the feudal rulers, and is both cathartic and educational for the audience." The scene being praised was newly added and did not exist in previous versions.

The success of *Nao tiangong* prompted a more extended version of the opera. In 1955, Premier Zhou Enlai asked for the play to be extended to a fuller version, as *Da'nao tiangong.* Zhou particularly noted three positive aspects that could be emphasized: first, Sun Wukong's resistance to oppression; second, the scheme that the celestial court set up against the Monkey King; and third, Sun Wukong's working-class wisdom with which he defeats Tianxi xingjun, the literati in the celestial court.[10] None of these three aspects existed in the traditional versions. Accordingly, Weng modified the plot to better sculpt Sun Wukong as representing the revolutionary people.

Whereas in previous versions, the monkey's mischief in the heavenly court is what causes the conflict between him and the Taoist gods, in the new play the problem arises from the celestial court's scheme against him. The relationship between the monkey and heaven is described oppositionally: heaven treats the monkey deceptively, and Sun Wukong responds with anger and rebellion. For instance, when Sun Wukong is invited to heaven for the second time, he is told that the Jade Emperor has planned a Peach Banquet for him as an apology, and as a celebration of his new title "the Great Sage, Equal to

Heaven." But in reality, the intention of the celestial court is to lure the monkey into heaven so that the troops could apprehend him. Sun Wukong, for his part, is on the alert for any tricks. He makes sure to arrive in heaven early so he has some time to investigate the Peach Banquet. Finding out about the set-up, Sun Wukong is filled with anger and decides that he has to "turn the banquet at Yaochi upside down and engulf everything, to alleviate [his] anger."[11]

In the setting of an unjust and oppressive heavenly court, Sun Wukong is transformed into a soldier who is full of hatred for oppression. Even the little monkeys in his kingdom are also presented as highly aware of the political importance of their battle. When Sun Wukong leaves the turmoil at the Peach Banquet and makes his way back to the Flower-Fruit Mountain, he is met by a monkey soldier who reports that the celestial troops had slaughtered his subjects while he was away, singing, "I am risking my life to report to you, oh Great Sage; fight against the celestial court and take revenge, revenge!" In response, the Monkey King addresses the monkey as "my good brother" and arranges a plan to fight back up to heaven with the surviving monkeys as his backup. In this light, Sun Wukong's battle with heaven becomes the battle between the monkey class and the celestial lords, thereby allowing the Monkey King's victory in the end to belong to all monkeys. After battling with the generals and then breaking free from Laozi's furnace, the Monkey King reunites at the Flower-Fruit Mountain with the little monkeys. The story here ends with the monkeys' celebration of their victory over the heavenly troops, singing in ensemble: "Paean all over the Flower-Fruit Mountain! Paean all over the Flower-Fruit Mountain!" Aside from creating a victorious Monkey King image instead of a monkey loser as portrayed in earlier versions in popular culture, this note also offers a finishing touch for the new image of the Monkey King as a revolutionary: the hero does not fight alone and for himself. He is the leader and a representative of the entire monkey class, representing the oppressed, and his battle is the battle between the mountain and heaven. Flower-Fruit Mountain, in such light, can be seen as a base for revolution (*geming genjudi*), such as those bases for revolution built by the Communist Party in mountain areas during the civil war. In fact, the first line of the opera, sung by monkeys in the mountain, makes explicit this resemblance: "Defending the Flower-Fruit Mountain, crossing the sea to enter the dragon's pool." The first word, "defend" (*baowei*), is often used in the context of battles against the Nationalist attack. This opening is notably echoed by the ending, "Paean all over the Flower-Fruit Mountain," which is again sung by the monkeys, not by the deities from heaven. In contrast to the previous plays, which are about the subjugation of the Monkey King, this new play is a very loud celebration of the voice of the monkeys.

In transforming the mischievous into the righteous, Sun Wukong's drunken misconduct is repackaged as conscious rebellion. After eating and packing up the food and drink from the banquet as an expression of anger, Sun Wukong steals the pills of life from Laozi's residence as he leaves the Peach Banquet. In *Zaju Xiyou ji* he openly admits that he stole from the Taoist heaven for his own pleasure. In both *Antian hui* and *Nao tiangong,* the monkey enjoyed the pills of life "like eating fried beans" and then immediately realizes that he has made a mistake and should leave quickly. In contrast, in the new Peking opera, stealing the pills becomes a righteous action against the oppressive privilege that the Jade Emperor enjoys. Seeing the words "For His Majesty the Jade Emperor Only" on the container of the pills reignites the Monkey King's anger: "My wrath is enkindled by the name Jade Emperor. Let me devour it all! Jade Emperor, pigs!"[12] This version of the Monkey King is not indulging in the hedonism of mischief—rather, he is portrayed as a fearless and angry fighter, a strong-willed crusader against evil.

The new opera *Havoc in Heaven* was considered a success. The victory story of the Monkey King was well suited to the task of representing the new victory of the Chinese people to foreign audiences. As a member of the Chinese art representative team, Li toured many countries in the world with the opera, which became a part of the regular repertoire and one of the most popular performance pieces. As a result, Sun Wukong became an ambassador of Chinese art, touring countries including France, Belgium, Holland, Czechoslovakia, Switzerland, Italy, and England. In *Cartoon Monthly* (Manhua yuekan) in 1955, a cartoon image of the Monkey King standing on top of the plane of the Chinese Art Troupe (Zhongguo yishu tuan) appears, celebrating the successful tour and the new heroic image of the Monkey King (figure 3.1). The names of the countries visited are listed on the body of the white plane, underneath of the feet of Monkey. The cartoon indicates that it is now the plane, instead of the Somersault Cloud, that flies Monkey around. Both a welcomed witness and a most prominent passenger, the Monkey King travels like an emissary, representing Chinese art and Chinese culture.[13]

Figure 3.1. Sun Wukong standing on top of a plane. The words on the plane read "Chinese Art Troupe" and list the countries visited, including France, Belgium, Holland, Czechoslovakia, Switzerland, Italy, and England (Mi Gu and Jiang Fan, *Cartoon Monthly* [Manhua Yuekan], November 18, 1955).

"HAVOC IN HEAVEN" IN NEW GRAPHIC FORMS

Around the time of the new opera, the "Havoc in Heaven" story that portrayed the Monkey King in a heroic light was also widely circulating via books and graphic prints. Newly founded publishing firms all worked to print the traditional works that were already accepted by the authorities as healthy, including the Ming novel *Journey to the West*. In 1954, China Writers Press (Zuojia chubanshe, founded 1953) published the one-hundred-chapter Shidetang edition of *Journey to the West*, with 130,000 copies in the first printing. It was followed by a 1955 edition published by the People's Literature Press (Renmin wenxue chubanshe, founded 1951) that featured more annotations and that enjoyed many later reprints, also with 130,000 copies at first printing. Even before these full versions of *Journey to the West*, 1953 had already seen the People's Literature Press bring out a series of "literature starters," including both modern and contemporary works and selected portions from three classical works: *Yellow Mud Hills* (Huang ni gang), *Chang ban po*, and *Havoc in Heaven*. Like *Havoc in Heaven*, the two other episodes, taken from *Outlaws of the Marsh* (Shuihu zhuan) and *Romance of the Three Kingdoms* (Sanguo yanyi) respectively, are about rebels fighting with valor and strategy. These starter readers represent an act of selection but not of adaptation. The story of Sun Wukong's troublemaking with heaven is based closely on the book *Xiyou ji* and ends at the end of chapter 7, where he is trapped by Buddha under the mountain.

Adaptations of *Havoc in Heaven* in graphic forms shortly after, however, all eliminated parts of the seventh chapter to give the story a triumphant ending. A version of *Havoc in Heaven* in the form of *lianhuan hua*, a palm-sized picture book with one drawing and a brief text on each page, coauthored by Liang Shi and Chen Guangyi, was published in 1954 by New Fine Arts Press (Xinmeishu chubanshe, founded 1952). By the third printing in September 1954, 135,000 copies had been printed. This story followed the Ming *Journey to the West* quite closely except in the ending, where Sun Wukong jumps out of Laozi's furnace, chases the Jade Emperor from Lingxiao Hall, and defeats the celestial warriors. He then returns to his mountain and celebrates his victory. The scene of Sun Wukong fighting his way into Lingxiao Hall and chasing away the Jade Emperor is highlighted in the book and used as the cover page (figure 3.2). The Monkey King occupies the dominant top-right section of the cover image, leaping high in the air, taking a mighty swing with his magic rod, ready to hit the celestials. Everyone else is falling to the ground, including the Jade Emperor, who is on all fours trying to crawl away. The scene no doubt served as a good portrayal of the victory of "the people" over "the ruler," echoing the Peking Opera version. This scene is a bold revision of the original. In chapter 7 of the novel *Journey to the West*,

Figure 3.2. Sun Wukong breaking into Lingxiao Hall and chasing away the Jade Emperor. From Liang Shi and Chen Guangyi, *Da'nao tiangong*, front cover.

Sun Wukong does not even get into Lingxiao Hall: he was still outside of the hall fighting with the celestial generals when the Buddha, the pacifier invited by the Jade Emperor, approaches the monkey and subsequently subjugates him.

The last page of the book pictures the moment of rejoicing when the Monkey King drinks the victorious wine with other monkeys (figure 3.3). Note the red-tasseled spear (*hongying qiang*) the celebrating monkeys hold in their hands. This weapon, utilized by the Communist militia before and during the anti-Japanese war, is often associated with the emergent Communist militias of the time. The 1954 film *The Letter with Feathers* (Jimao xin), as well as Liu Jiyou's 1950 picture book of the same title, for instance, centers around a boy who is the commander of the children's corps always carrying a red-tasseled spear with him. The image of the celebration of the monkeys thus is linked to the recent victory of the Chinese people led by the Communist Party. As with the Peking Opera, this new ending of the rebel story was well-promoted and well-received. When New Fine Arts

（84）悟空回到花果山，小猴们都喜出望外，拿出椰酒、瓜果，大摆筵席，庆贺大王归来。

Figure 3.3. Monkeys drinking the victorious wine. From Liang Shi and Chen Guangyi, *Da'nao tiangong*, 84.

Press merged into Shanghai People's Fine Arts Press (Shanghai renmin meishu chubanshe) in 1956, the latter reprinted the book again in February of the same year, and by the third printing in October, 260,000 copies were in circulation.

The idea of *Havoc in Heaven* as depicting a revolution was further promoted by the publication of Liu Jiyou's painting series *Nao tiangong* by the Shanghai People's Fine Arts Press in the same year. This group of "New-Year paintings" consists of eight paintings in *gongbi* style, a technique in traditional Chinese painting that uses meticulously detailed brushstrokes for realistic effect. Seven of the eight paintings contain the Monkey King, all in a dominant or central location of the painting (figure 3.4). These paintings became widely popular, and the original copies were sent to international exhibits as representing the achievements of Chinese art in the new era.

In the three fight scenes, Sun Wukong is always in the commanding position of the upper corner, coming down from above with unstoppable force upon the celestial generals. The eighth painting ends the

Figure 3.4. Sun Wukong knocking down the furnace of Laozi. From Liu Jiyou, *Nao tiangong*.

story with Sun Wukong defeating the celestial fighters, with the Jade Emperor's Lingxiao Hall in the background (figure 3.5). The celestial generals, collapsing on the ground, are all looking up at the Monkey King, whose golden rod is raised high, ready to fling forward, feet ready to stamp.

Even the more peaceful paintings position the monkey in a commanding position. In the tableau of Sun Wukong interrogating the seven fairy maidens (figure 3.6), the monkey sits high upon the base of a tree, looking angrily down at the seven maidens, who are all on their knees and looking up at the Great Sage apologetically. The monkey, on the other hand, is not being apologetic for the tree branches deprived of peaches, or for the disorder he creates at the banquet as depicted in another tableau. Instead, he is in the position of making judgment, correcting what he perceives as an injustice. Overall, the tableaux represent a glorified Monkey King with a commanding presence, echoing Liang and Chen's 1954 book and the revised Peking Opera. Liu's choice of *gongbi* style, furthermore, gives a realistic visual tone to the mythical story.

In the same year, *Picture Stories* (Lianhuan huabao) carried Xu Hongda's "picture story" *Nao tiangong.* The total of thirty-six images plus the brief text along with each image relates the story of the Monkey King corresponding to the first seven chapters of the novel *Journey to the West.* Although the book is unfinished, and the thirty-six pictures follow the *Journey to the West* major plot quite closely, it unmistakably shows the Monkey King as a hero. From the detailed portrayal of Sun Wukong's battle with the celestials, one can safely conclude that were the book to have been completed, it would most likely end with the victory of the Monkey King, in line with contemporary adaptations. All the battle scenes treat the Monkey King as a valiant warrior, while the celestial generals are shown as good-for-nothings. Although outnumbered, with one swing of his rod Monkey breezily knocks down the Nine Stars (figure 3.7). The last image of the unfinished series portrays Sun Wukong standing in the middle of all of his rivals in a gigantic form taller than the mountains, towering over the celestials swarming around him like ants. The greatness of the Monkey King controls the entire scene with irresistible force (figure 3.8).

Otherwise following the *Journey to the West* plot quite closely, this comic version readily upsets the power relation between Sun Wukong and Erlang Shen, with Erlang capturing Sun Wukong at the

Figure 3.5. Sun Wukong battling with celestial generals. From Liu Jiyou, *Nao tiangong.*

Figure 3.6. Sun Wukong interrogating the seven fairy maidens. From Liu Jiyou, *Nao tiangong*.

end of their battle. In *Journey to the West*, as well as the other Ming and Qing versions discussed earlier, Erlang holds the advantage in the transformation competition between the two, an advantage that enables him to see through Sun Wukong's camouflage and then to take a form that can beat that of the monkey. Xu's version changes Sun Wukong's passive transformations into active ones, creating moments when Sun Wukong takes stronger forms than Erlang and

31 一轉眼对面跳出九員將，
原是有名的凶神九曜星。
美猴王輕輕一点金箍棒，
九曜星丢盔落甲敗陣中。

Figure 3.7. Monkey knocks down Nine Stars with his rod. From Xu Hongda, *Nao tiangong*, 31.

furthermore takes advantage of those moments to chase Erlang. Page 34 illustrates the moment when the Monkey King transforms himself into a crane to peck at the hawk into which Erlang transformed himself (figure 3.9). In the following moment, portrayed on page 35, Erlang changes into a little fish to escape from the crane, after which Sun Wukong is immediately transformed into a big fish to chase after the little one (figure 3.10). By comparison, the sixth chapter of *Journey to the West* actually recounts the Monkey King's transforming himself into a little fish in order to escape from the Erlang transformed into a sea eagle.

Although the rhymed poems in the comic series read like those from the oral performance of an earlier time, and although the first page starts the story like that of the *dagu* performance, the image of the Monkey King in this version differs distinctly from that of the singing performance mentioned earlier. This again is owing to the

Figure 3.8. Monkey in giant form. From Xu Hongda, *Nao tiangong*, 36.

contortion of the plot. Like the Sun Wukong of the operatic version as well as other graphic retellings, this Monkey King is undoubtedly a champion, representing the recent victory of the people who had built the new China.

THE ANIMATED FILM *HAVOC IN HEAVEN*

The 1961–64 animated film *Havoc in Heaven* (Da'nao tiangong) epitomizes the transformation of the Monkey King image and brings it to its peak. The director Wan Laiming and his brothers had the chance to make an animated version of *Havoc in Heaven* in 1939, but halfway through the project, the investors decided to sell the film stock and photographic chemicals instead, as it was more profitable due to a price hike during the war.[14] In 1961, after more than twenty years, Wan Laiming once again had the opportunity to make his favorite story into an animated film. The twenty years between

Figure 3.9. Monkey and Erlang fighting in transformation: the crane (Monkey) pecks at the hawk (Erlang). From Xu Hongda, *Nao tiangong*, 34.

Princess Iron Fan and *Havoc in Heaven*, however, witnessed massive social transformation along with a corresponding change to the image of the Monkey King. Wan Laiming's understanding of art under the influence of Hollywood animation was changed, or "reformed," after his study of Mao's *Speech at the Yan'an Symposium of Literature and Art*. He wrote that although he had always loved the Monkey King character and had been thinking about re-creating the image again since his last Sun Wukong movie, in the past he never really understood this character and had treated him almost like a comic figure. With the new and corrected understanding, Wan decided "to look at Sun Wukong from a brand-new approach, to remold the character thoroughly, producing a new image of a rebel."[15]

35 楊二郎回头一看海鶴到，
急忙忙变只小魚入水中。
孙悟空变成大魚鑽下水，
他窮追直赶一步不放松。

Figure 3.10. Monkey and Erlang continue their fight in transformation: the big fish (Monkey) chases the small fish (Erlang). From Xu Hongda, *Nao tiangong*, 35.

Accordingly, in contrast to *Princess Iron Fan*, in which Sun Wukong represents a heroic human who learns from his mistakes, *Havoc in Heaven* celebrates the established glory of the Monkey King as an indomitable rebel and invincible warrior. In the latter film the Monkey King does not seem to have any human faults. Reminding us of Weng's Peking Opera version, even the actions of stealing celestial wine and elixir here are presented as acts of rebellion, not as mischief or mistake.

The most conspicuous revision aimed at the glorification of the Monkey King image appears again at the ending of the film. As with the Peking Opera script and Liang and Chen's picture book, the animated film ends with Sun Wukong's victory over the celestial court. But in this version, animation as the medium enables a more striking visual depiction of the Monkey King breaking Lingxiao Hall into pieces. In the portrayal of Sun Wukong's dash into Lingxiao Hall, the

Figure 3.11. Monkey laughing after breaking down the Lingxiao Hall. From Wan Laiming and Cheng Tang, *Da'nao tiangong*, 1961–64.

shot of his back is enlarged in the foreground, with the tiny profile of the Jade Emperor and two celestial generals at the far back visible from beneath the monkey's legs. This change reverses the haughty blown-up image of the Jade Emperor at the beginning and indicates a shift of power that now favors the Monkey King.

The dominant weight of Sun Wukong in these scenes makes the Jade Emperor's escape a predictable next step of the story, although the Emperor is only able to accomplish it with the help of Li Tianwang's magic weapon, the golden tower. The subsequent scenes of Sun Wukong breaking up the golden tower and the sign that reads "Lingxiao Hall" provide a strong message of the strength of the people (encapsulated in the heroic figure of the Monkey King), visually articulating the breaking up of the control of the oppressors. This victory of the Monkey King leads naturally to the final scenes of the film celebrating the power of the people: after clearing up the tyranny of the feudal emperor, the Monkey King laughs as heartily as he can, his image striding over the entire screen (figure 3.11). In the subsequent and ending scene, resonating with the Peking Opera and the picture book versions, the masses of monkeys jump and cheer for their victory at the Flower-Fruit Mountain.

As Wan wrote in his memoir about the ending of the animated film:

> After repeated discussion, we decided to boldly remove the section about Sun Wukong being imprisoned by the Buddha, and replace it with an ending that results in an image of Sun Wukong that was more lively and more thorough, one that jumped out of the furnace, picked up his rod, fought his way to Lingxiao Hall, forcing even the Jade Emperor to leave his throne. I was quite anxious with the revised ending, not sure whether it would be accepted by the audience. But it was later clear that the audience shared my vision.[16]

Wan was apparently aware of how much the revised ending digresses from the traditional story, but he seemed to have forgotten about the immediate antecedents of *Havoc in Heaven* in popular art forms and in print, which had all made the same change to the ending. With the successes of those precedents, Wan's audience should already have been well prepared for the victory of Sun Wukong in the final scene. The revised ending followed the guidance of the dominant thought being propagated from the center of the Communist Party. Repeating words that have been reiterated in discussions in the late 1940s and 1950s, Wan wrote that the central theme of the animated work was to represent "the conflict and battle between the oppressor and the oppressed, between the feudal rulers and the people," and that "Sun Wukong as a rebel demonstrated an uncompromising rebellious spirit and a strong will to fight in his unrelenting war against feudal forces," until he grew "stronger and stronger, and earned his final victory."[17] What seems to Wan as a new revision and new meaning for the Monkey King story is actually following a path that had already been clearly marked.

The valorization of the Monkey King image in *Havoc in Heaven* is tightly interwoven with the task of building a distinctive style for Chinese animation. Wan, conscious of this task, also noted the importance of considering a much wider audience: "Constantly seeking the Chinese style is an important issue, which has much effect on whether Chinese animation film can assure its space in the world."[18] Reflecting on his experience making *Havoc in Heaven*, Wan Laiming summarizes three lessons for animated film: one, walking firmly on the road of Chinese style; two, adapting classical works for topics; and three, the form has to serve the content.[19] In other words, the task of finding a Chinese style should serve to help the portrayal of the hero of the Monkey King.

Many components of *Havoc in Heaven*'s design were based on traditional art. Not only was much of the movement design based

Figure 3.12. Fairies that resemble the *feitian* figures in Dunhuang frescoes. From Wan Laiming and Tang Cheng, *Da'nao tiangong*, 1961–64.

on Chinese opera tradition, including dancing and martial art movements, but also the intonation of lines and the musical accompaniment. The design of characters, use of color, creation of scenes, and decorations originated from fresco paintings and Chinese New Year paintings (figure 3.12). The image of the Monkey King itself incorporated the idea of "monkey, god, and human in unity" (which closely aligns with the traditional "Monkey Opera") and utilized facial makeup patterns in traditional theater and popular prints as sources of reference. The artists thus revealed their search for a distinctly Chinese style of animation by rooting the images deeply in Chinese artistic traditions.

While using details from the Ming novel, the visual glamour and the humorous scenes in the film do not work against the effort of glorifying the Monkey King image. The heroic side of the monkey character is never forgotten, even when the movie explores his humorous features. On the one hand, the representation of the heavenly court in the animation is highly embellished, including many beautiful scenes such as Sun Wukong rejoicing with the celestial horses under his care; the Peach Garden in which Sun Wukong enjoys eating the celestial peaches he is supposed to guard; and the seven singing and flying fairies fetching peaches for the Banquet. On the other hand, the film then gives a justifiable motivation for the turmoil that the Monkey King creates, just as with the opera version: he is enraged upon learning from the seven fairies that he had not been invited to the Peach Banquet. Overhearing the fairies mocking his low rank as a garden-keeper and his dream of being invited to the banquet, the monkey jumps up with anger: "Jade Emperor you old man, you have pushed me around again and again, it is not possible for us to exist together!" However, this sudden rage of Sun Wukong seems to be a bit ill-founded, since the film had stated earlier that his interest was not in the position, and he had no complaints about his experience in the Peach Garden where he enjoyed the best peaches. This inconsistency comes from portraying Sun Wukong as a heroic fighter, modeled after the angry Monkey King in the Peking Opera, while at the same time allowing much of the idyllic illustration of heaven as a way to feature the beauty of Chinese culture in Chinese style.

Following the example of the graphic books that portray the Monkey King as a hero, the animation's depiction of the fighting scenes between Sun Wukong and Erlang Shen gives prominence to the monkey's strength and capacity. Not only does he manage quite well in fighting with Erlang and his dog, he can at the same time use the body-dividing method to defeat the six brother generals of Erlang. Wukong also wins in the transformation competition with Erlang, changing into a huge mythical animal and defeating the tiger into which Erlang had transformed (figure 3.13). He is caught only because of Laozi's sneak-attack, and the heroic monkey indignantly states: "You use a despicable method to win against me, this is not what a true man would do!" By criticizing his opponent, he claims himself as a true man, or a real hero. The vigor that the Monkey King demonstrates here against his enemy, and later the bravery and pride he shows while enduring the "torture" of the celestial court, remind one of the revolutionary heroes that many communist films of the time offered.

Havoc in Heaven has travelled to many other countries and has been well-received ever since the release of the first part in 1961. In Wan's own words, it served as an unofficial diplomatic envoy through its screenings.[20] The establishment of a Chinese style was so closely tied to the political task—representing the Chinese people for both the Chinese and the international audience—and had such long-reaching

Figure 3.13. The Monkey King's transformation beats out Erlang's. From Wan Laiming and Tang Cheng, *Da'nao tiangong*, 1961–64.

influence that years later, after the time of the Peking Opera and the animated film, the heroic image of the Monkey King continues and has itself become a tradition.

SUN WUKONG SUBDUES WHITE BONE DEMON

The image of Sun Wukong as a rebellious hero in *Havoc in Heaven* merged with the image of the Monkey King as a heroic communist in *Sun Wukong Subdues the White Bone Demon* (Sun Wukong sanda Baigu Jing) in the *shao* opera of 1960–62, which was also made into a *shao* opera film and a picture book (1962).

The White Bone Demon (Baigu Jing) is one of the many enemy-spirits of the Monkey King and his fellow pilgrims on their way to India. In the original *Journey to the West*, this episode occurs shortly after the pilgrim team of five is formed: after setting off on his journey, Tripitaka first meets Sun Wukong, who becomes his first disciple and in turn helps him subdue three other demons who also become his disciples. When the team meets the White Bone Demon, each member has yet to negotiate their role and position in the group. The leadership role of Sun Wukong is established after the White Bone

Demon episode: the Monkey King is the only one who recognizes the White Bone Demon's disguises when she successively transforms into a pretty village girl, an old lady, and an old man, approaching the pilgrims repeatedly with her lure in order to snatch Tripitaka from his protectors and eat him to prolong her own life. Sun Wukong's actions to protect Tripitaka are mistaken for undue aggression by his compatriots, and he is ousted from the group. The remaining pilgrims promptly fall prey to another demon and must ultimately be rescued by the Monkey King. Tripitaka, recognizing his own mistakes, thanks Sun Wukong and praises his contribution to the pilgrimage as "number one."[21] With the central role of the Monkey King in the group thus acknowledged, Tripitaka then gives Sun Wukong permission to deploy the other disciples as his subordinates at the beginning of the following episode.[22]

While the 1960s White Bone Demon stories preserve many details of the original, the changes made emphasize that the Monkey King is the only one who is correct, and yet repeatedly wronged by the other characters. The correctness of Sun Wukong echoes his canonization as a revolutionary hero by the *Havoc in Heaven* adaptations. The most apparent changes in the new versions are the ways in which Sun Wukong is exonerated and the other team members learn they are the ones who are wrong. The new versions merge nine chapters of the original *Journey to the West* into one episode, and any parts that work against Monkey's heroic image are deleted from all adaptations of this period, such as the quite detailed description of how Sun Wukong himself used to capture humans when he was a demon in the Flower-Fruit Mountain.[23]

Rudolf Wagner's *Contemporary Chinese Historical Drama* devotes one of its four chapters to the case of "Sun Wukong Subdues the White Bone Demon," providing historical background and elaborating on the revisions the story went through at the time. As Wagner argues in his study, the meaning of the new White Bone Demon episode goes hand in hand with the political situation of the time, when China had just been through the disastrous Great Leap Forward (1958–61) and was simultaneously experiencing a worsening of relations with the Soviet Union. While "the journey to the west" represents the socialist road that the new China was taking, that is, the transition period from capitalism to communism, the White Bone Demon represents the "revisionist" currents led by Khrushchev—or, in Mao's words, the "opportunists who capitulate to imperialism"—and the disagreement between the four pilgrims represents the inner battles within the Communist Party.[24] The play received close attention from top political leaders and intellectuals and was interpreted and revised multiple times.

Indeed, after seeing the *shao* opera, Guo Moruo, the then-president of the Chinese Academy of Sciences, published a poem on the play in *People's Daily* on October 25, 1961. The poem targets Tripitaka's lack of insight in discerning friend from enemy, and on the other hand praises the Monkey King's vitality, making up the phrase "Great Sage Mao" (*Dasheng Mao*, or hair of the Great Sage), a deliberate pun referring to "Hair of the Monkey King" or "Mao Zedong the Great Sage."[25] In response to this poem, Mao wrote a poem on November 7, 1961, correcting Guo's misunderstanding of the play regarding what the demon and the monk each represents in the sociopolitical world. This poem turns from criticizing Tripitaka to extolling the "Golden Monkey," with the famous line, "The Golden Monkey wrathfully swung his massive cudgel, and the jade-like firmament was cleared of dust."[26] Guo saw Mao's poem on January 6, 1962, and immediately published yet another poem in response to Mao's in *People's Daily*. On May 30, 1964, Guo further published a long article in *People's Daily*, analyzing Mao's words and his own improved understanding of *Journey to the West* as well as of the political situation of the day. Here, Guo identifies the demon that the monkey killed as "the opportunists that have yielded to Capitalism," and Sun Wukong as the revolutionary "dragon's seeds," or "the developed revolutionary of Marx-Leninism." Throughout the discussion, Mao showed no doubt or objection to Guo's suggested identification between himself and Sun Wukong, and their later commentary only strengthened this connection.

In this interpretation of the White Bone Demon story, the image of the Monkey King stands as the central figure among the pilgrims, the only one who is both insightful and loyal to the communist goals of China. This image of Sun Wukong merged with the revolutionary Sun Wukong of *Havoc in Heaven*, becoming the standard image of the Monkey King in the years to follow. It is important to note that these two episodes reveal the two aspects of the multivalent nature of the Monkey King. While the episode "Havoc in Heaven" emphasizes Sun Wukong as a rebel, the episode about subduing the White Bone Demon underlines the quality of Sun Wukong as a worthy socialist, conforming to the true values of the socialist construction of China.

The first story is about the rod, and the second story about the fillet.[27] It is profoundly interesting to see that during the time when China is rethinking its revolutionary victory and evaluating its current political route, it is these two episodes of *Journey to the West* that have been popularized. The combination of the Havoc episode and the White Bone episode forms a polyphonic narrative for the ideological stability of the time.

In an interview in Carma Hinton's documentary *Morning Sun*, Luo Xiaohai, a leader of the group of high school students who founded the Red Guards in 1966, states that the beginning of the Cultural Revolution, or more particularly the feeling that young students like Luo himself share at the time about their right to rebel (*zaofan*), is encouraged by the animation *Havoc in Heaven*. The influence of the animated film should not be underestimated. Quite coincidentally, Hinton's other example of the popular culture of the 1960s is Lei Feng, the exemplary soldier whose image counteracts the rebellious Monkey King image.[28] The ideal of Lei Feng—to function as a bolt for the machinery of socialist construction in China—corresponds perfectly with the image of the Monkey King constrained by his tightening head fillet, strengthening the opposing end of the image of the rebel.

Wagner rightly states in his analysis of the case of the White Bone Demon that "as long as opera, film, and text with their strong political load were reshown and reprinted, they were read and reread against the changing political realities."[29] And indeed, both the "Havoc in Heaven" and the "White Bone Demon" episodes were continuously revised in the later adaptations of the "Journey to the West" stories, becoming the most popular episodes of *Journey to the West.* But despite the constant changes, the image of Sun Wukong as the most capable, undeceivable, and faithful hero persists.

From the CCTV series *Journey to the West* (1982, 1998) directed by Yang Jie and starring Zhang Jinlai (known as Liu Xiao Ling Tong), to the more recent TV series of the same title (2010) directed by Zhang Jizhong, from the 2001 cyber novel *Biography of Wukong* (Wukong zhuan) by Jin Hezai, under the direct influence of the 1995 Hong Kong film *A Chinese Odyssey* (Xiyou ji di 101 hui) by Jeffrey Lau, to the 2015 animated film *Monkey King: Hero Is Back* (Xiyou ji zhi dasheng guilai), which was highly successful as a Chinese animation, the Monkey King as a hero is presented again and again for the Chinese audience, even though the heroic theme is addressed from different approaches each time.

An episode in the 2001 film *The Guasha Treatment* describes the resistance one should expect to meet when presenting the Monkey King as a nonhero. A first-generation Chinese American, Xu Datong is a successful video game designer who has just invented an award-winning game based on the hero of his heart, the Monkey King, but has been charged by the Child Welfare Agency with abuse of his son. As evidence of Datong's violent personality, the prosecutor resorts to a reading of the "Havoc in Heaven" story of the Monkey King. He cites examples of stealing the peaches and the elixir pills to present the Monkey King as a "murderous, vulgar, and devious" figure, and the culture Sun Wukong represents as a violent culture. Xu Datong defends Sun Wukong as a "good-hearted, compassionate, and righteous hero" and maintains that he represents the traditional values and ethics of the Chinese. Although Xu knows well that he needs to behave well at the court to present the image of a good father, he cannot help but lose his temper when the prosecutor purposefully smears the image of the Monkey King. The prosecutor holds a copy of *Journey to the West* in his hand while he gives his speech about the Monkey King, which is not totally ungrounded, according to the book. The contradictory reading of the Monkey King figure in this case stems not just from a different understanding of traditional Chinese culture. There was a consistent reshaping of the monkey figure during the Maoist time in China. The reshaping of the image is so powerful that it becomes difficult for people accustomed to this culture to see the image otherwise. It will take another "revolution" to change that image again.

CHAPTER 4

From Fighter to Lover

The Postsocialist Hero in the PRC and Hong Kong

Since Socialist China has reconstructed Sun Wukong as a revolutionary hero, the image of the Monkey King as a more heroic figure followed suit. This tradition persisted until the end of the twentieth century, when a film coproduced by Hong Kong and mainland China, *A Chinese Odyssey* (Xiyou ji di yibai ling yi hui, known in China as *Dahua Xiyou*; 1995), starring Stephen Chow as the Monkey King, once again redefined the character. Although considerations of the body and sexuality are largely unaddressed in *Journey to the West*, the film subverted the heroic image of Sun Wukong and replaced it with a comedic character who is also a romantic interest. Many subsequent adaptations of *Journey to the West* followed this example, such as the novella *Another Voice* (Ling yizhong shengyin) by Li Feng, and the Internet novel *Story of Wukong* (Wukong zhuan) by Jin Hezai, which also became phenomenally popular.

The transformation of the Monkey King from a fighter to a lover at the turn of the twenty-first century foregrounds body and sexuality as a central issue in *Journey to the West*. These adaptations, produced during a period of social transformation and widespread anxiety about changing sexual mores, made the Monkey King's body and even gender a significant concern. When this new image of Sun Wukong travels and adapts from Hong Kong to mainland China, the message that it carries changes dramatically. While the Monkey King in *A Chinese Odyssey* may be indicative of apprehension about the transfer of sovereignty over Hong Kong when it was made in Hong Kong, the same movie reflects a different set of social concerns when it circulates in the mainland. In a sense it is precisely the creative misreading of the original film that has led to its success. Together with later adaptations under its influence, this misreading created a postsocialist hero for the large population of young people who became its fans. Starting with the creative adaptation of *A Chinese Odyssey*, a new type of Monkey King began to replace the revolutionary hero.

THE *DAHUA* PHENOMENON

A Chinese Odyssey is a two-part comedy that is built on the basic structure and includes the major characters of *Journey to the West*, but the plot and style deviate from the original. It takes the form of an additional chapter—inserted into the middle of the one hundred chapters of the book—when the pilgrims are halfway to Western Heaven. The film marks a temporary departure from the original journey, with major deviations at the beginning, and a realignment with the original narrative at the end. While making fun of many characters in *Journey to the West*, the two-part comedy now also serves as a tragic love story.

The beginning of *A Chinese Odyssey: Part One, Pandora's Box* (Dahua Xiyou zhi Yueguang baohe) finds Sun Wukong in rebellion against Tripitaka and Guanyin. In an attempt to force Sun Wukong to learn from his mistakes, Guanyin causes Sun to be reincarnated five hundred years in the future as "Joker," the leader of a bandit gang. The movie recounts how Joker finds his way back to his real self—Sun Wukong—and eventually returns to the journey to the West. Having forgotten everything about his previous life, however, Joker falls in love with Jingjing, the White Bone Demon, who had been working with the Spider Demon in searching for reincarnations of the Monkey King and Tripitaka. In order to save Jingjing from suicide and clarify the misunderstanding between them, Joker travels back in time five hundred years, using a time machine called the Moonlight Box. When he arrives in his own past, everyone from that time treats him as the Monkey King. The story continues in *Part Two, Cinderella* (Dahua Xiyou zhi Xianlü qiyuan), where Joker devotes himself to finding the Moonlight Box (which had been lost after its first use) and returning to the future. He meets Zixia, a fairy who sacrificed everything for love and who sees him as her true love, but he denies his feeling for her until the moment he dies and his spirit becomes the Monkey King.

Devoted to his duty for the journey, the Monkey King fights with and defeats the demons, but he loses Zixia, who dies in his arms.

When first released in Hong Kong and mainland China in 1995, *A Chinese Odyssey* was a box-office failure. The film's slapstick humor that later was admired by its followers was initially unappreciated. But two years later, when the film was shown on TV film channels, it caught the attention of college students and grew a large fan base on college campuses in the mainland. The growing popularity of the film occurred at a time when bootleg disc markets mushroomed in China, and the Internet and BBS (Bulletin Board Systems) became important social networking platforms for university students. For a while, *A Chinese Odyssey* was vigorously traded in the bootleg disc market. According to a bootleg disc seller quoted in a *Beijing Evening News* article, no matter how many copies of *A Chinese Odyssey* he took to the market, they would be sold immediately, and in this way he alone sold several thousand copies of the film.[1] Fans of *A Chinese Odyssey*, known as *Dahua* fans, exchanged their interpretations and readings of the film on the Internet, on popular sites such as SMTH BBS and YTHT BBS, based in Tsinghua University and Peking University respectively.[2] Many forums on such sites were devoted to or named after *A Chinese Odyssey*.[3] Between 1998 and 2002, more than one hundred *Dahua* fan websites were established, and the fans' passion for the film served to change its reception.[4] Instead of criticizing the movie for deviating from the original, or changing and subverting the images of the characters, *Dahua* fans found a new aspect of the Monkey King story that spoke to them. Their discussions did not treat the story as a myth; rather, they took the Monkey King as representing themselves and the story as reflecting the problems they faced in their lives.

The *Dahua* craze spread quickly, with the help of the rapidly growing Internet culture in China. While in many physical locations, one could overhear *Dahua* fans using various lines from the movie, on the Internet they also shared their personal interpretations of the movie or creative rewritings of the story. Rewritings of *A Chinese Odyssey* locate the story in realistic settings, using the legendary figures to speak about the hardship of life through black humor. A book titled *Bible of "A Chinese Odyssey"* (Dahua Xiyou baodian), edited by Zhang Lixian and others, brought together a collection of fans' writings that had been circulating online, some of which had been reposted so many times that the original author was unknown. One section of the book starts with a statement in *Dahua* style: "Last night I searched for websites related to *A Chinese Odyssey* on sina.com, and got 38 results. Then I searched again using the search engine on sohu.com, and hit 55 results—This *A Chinese Odyssey* must have owed everyone a lot of money."[5] This statement parodied lines from the film, a practice widely adopted by *Dahua* fans. Shortly after, according to Hou Zhenwei's article in the *Beijing Evening News*, a search of "Dahua Xiyou" on sina.com on August 23, 2000, returned a list of 108 websites.[6]

As an adaptation of a classic, *A Chinese Odyssey* has itself become a classic. It has not only developed a cult following in China, but it has also drawn the attention of academics and become the subject of research for multiple disciplines. Academics paid attention not only to the popularity of the film itself but also to the special phenomenon created by its influence over popular culture, which is called "*Dahua* Culture." A January 2015 search of the CNKI (China National Knowledge Infrastructure) database finds 1,166 articles published between 2000 and 2014 with "Dahua Xiyou" as key words. These articles focus on a wide range of aspects, including postmodern culture, adaptation, intertextuality, cultural studies, Internet culture, performance, language, time and space, and also include creative writing—*A Chinese Odyssey*'s appeal to both fans and academics is steady. In October 2014, twenty years after its first release, *A Chinese Odyssey* was shown again in movie theaters in China, this time as a "classic," as part of "The Good Movie We've Missed in Those Years" event organized by Huaxia Film Distribution Company. The event was reported on widely by many Internet sites, predicting, reporting, and analyzing box-office returns, audience response, and fans' wish to "finally pay Stephen [Chow] his due." According to a Xinhuanet report, showings were arranged on a volunteer basis, and 1,166 movie theaters out of 3,831 total in China had volunteered to show the film. Chinanews.com reported on the second day of the rerelease that the box-office sales were "surprisingly high," given that the movie was screened side by side with new blockbusters, and on a weekday during business hours. The social network service douban.com, known for its focus on books, movies, and music, carries 66,480 entries of short reviews of the first part of *A Chinese Odyssey* (*A Chinese Odyssey: Part One, Pandora's Box*) alone, and 1,787 full-length reviews (as of March 7, 2016). Writers of these posts often relate the challenges that Sun Wukong faces in the film to the challenges they face in their own lives.[7]

A central question to be asked of "*Dahua* Culture" is one of identification: Why does this particular generation in China so readily identify with the Monkey King in *A Chinese Odyssey*? What does the Monkey King in this movie represent that speaks to the young people in mainland China around the turn of the twenty-first century but not to people in Hong Kong? Many comments about the movie have pointed to the "postmodern" factors in Stephen Chow's "nonsensical" (*mou-lei-tou*) style, and the subversive pleasure that the young audience derives from the film's excessive play with the grotesque and the violation of social norms. Indeed, Stephen Chow has transformed the story of pilgrimage into a slapstick comedy. The audience's laughter at the gods, pilgrims, and demons dissolves the awe they used to reserve for these characters, and such laughter serves as an outlet in a political environment where authorities are supposed to always be respected, effectively functioning as a form of the Bakhtinian carnivalesque. But the carnival effect is only partially responsible for the success of the film, as many fans take the story seriously, discussing the allegorical levels of meaning in the film. The following example demonstrates the kind of analysis that circulates among fans:

> If you double over with laughter when watching this movie, it means you have a sense of humor. But if you're still laughing when the movie is over, you actually understand nothing of the film. When the film is over, if you find your face is covered with tears, you have come to understand the first layer of its meaning. If after all your laughter and tears you are stunned, not knowing whether to cry or to laugh, you understand the second layer of its meaning. If you sit there speechless, dejected and despondent, not knowing where you should go, you understand the third layer of its meaning.
>
> *A Chinese Odyssey* is an allegory. Hidden within the shell of an ancient myth, it appears to be a very funny and sad, bawdy but pure love story, but actually it is about the problems caused by the uncertainty of time and the hesitation of the individual.[8]

Besides listing four different levels of understanding, the post also provides its own allegorical reading: Joker's transformation into Sun Wukong represents the spiritual journey that a man experiences growing up, and Tripitaka and the Bull Demon King each represent different social powers around him. Many fans speak about their experience watching the film repeatedly, and how their understanding deepens after each viewing. Another fan, in a review titled "What We Cannot Resist Is Only Love and Death," writes about her understanding of love, which changes through the years in which she watched the film repeatedly: from the 1990s, when she was in elementary school, until 2008 when she graduated from college, the film in her eyes has evolved from a horror film to a love story, from an avant-garde film to a love story that is all based on a lie.[9] A review that was reposted on douban.com as well as many other websites, titled "*A Chinese Odyssey* in My Eyes Two Years after Graduation," speaks about the author's deepened understanding of the film after college:

> I suddenly understood the beginning of the movie: A young guy who is talented but does not respect rules (Sun Wukong) loathes the big and important cause that he is assigned (the pilgrimage to India). He especially cannot bear the nagging preaching of his teacher (Tripitaka), but the rules and regulations in the world (Guanyin) won't let him go. In order to transform him into a devoted pilgrim, Tripitaka and Guanyin have reached an agreement: let him get reborn and start anew five hundred years later. Such a foreordained beginning.[10]

The review goes on to state that Sun Wukong's "Havoc in Heaven" takes place during the golden era of four years in college. After he leaves the campus and finds a job he realizes that all his talents and personality do not matter underneath the mountain of Buddha's palm.

In short, while *A Chinese Odyssey* subverted *Journey to the West*'s status as a revered classic, it managed to establish itself as a classic. The parody did not just ridicule the gods and teachers in the original story, but it also drew new images for the main characters, establishing new meanings related to the social milieu in which it was produced. It influenced later adaptations of *Journey to the West* and deeply changed the normal depiction of characters such as Sun Wukong and Tripitaka.

ABSTINENCE FROM SEXUALITY IN *JOURNEY TO THE WEST*

In the novel *Journey to the West*, themes of the body and sexuality are sublimated due to the nature of the story as a religious allegory. Sex is a formidable sin from which all of the pilgrims except Zhu Bajie abstain. The only one who shows weakness toward the temptation of sex, Bajie is repeatedly tested, warned, and punished.[11] In contrast, Tripitaka has sustained his pure virgin body for ten reincarnations, and it is believed that because of this his flesh has magic power: eating one piece of it is sufficient to grant the consumer longevity. For this reason, throughout the journey Tripitaka encounters many demons who want to eat him, and sometimes female demons who want to have sex with him.

If Tripitaka has to constantly work against the idea of sexuality and make an effort to abstain from it, for the Monkey King sex has never been an issue. In his own words, he was born without *xing*. When Patriarch Subhūti asked him about his *xing* (surname), he took it as a question about his *xing* (temperament/nature) and responded that he did not have any temper (*xing*), and had never lost his temper (*yisheng wu xing*). This statement also holds true if we take the liberty of relating the pun of *xing* to sexuality.[12] When it was clarified that the question was about the surname that he would have received from his parents, Monkey responded that he did not have any parents, since he was born from a piece of stone on top of the Flower-Fruit Mountain. Subhūti was much delighted upon hearing this, saying that the monkey was born of heaven and earth. Although the narrative of *Journey to the West* never explains the ways in which Monkey's birth from stone function as an asset, it is clear that his parentless birth (a birth that is not as a result of sexual activity) distinguishes him as a model for religious practice. Quite relatively, throughout the journey sex simply never constitutes a temptation for him, as if his mind cannot fathom the idea of sexuality.

The correspondence of the five members of the pilgrimage group with the Five Phases of Chinese philosophy is widely accepted, with Monkey related to Metal (Jin) and Heart/Mind (Xin). Metaphorically Monkey functions as the mind/heart of the group, who is focused on defeating demons and directing the group toward the religious holy land. This is perhaps why the narrative of *Journey to the West* constantly refers to Sun Wukong as the "heart monkey" (*xinyuan*).[13] If the heart/mind of the pilgrims should be directed toward attaining Buddhist sutras for the world or attaining Buddhahood for themselves, the body that is attached to the worldly pleasures constitutes obstacles for the heart. For Zhu Bajie, the obstacle of body is significantly greater than it is for Tripitaka. But for Sun Wukong, his body does not stand in the way—born from stone and smelt in Laozi's elixir furnace, his body is built for battles and transformational magic, not for the sin of desire. The text of *Journey to the West* actually contains many detailed descriptions of Monkey's body—from his birth from the stone, to his transformation training, to the numerous bodily tricks he plays when encountering demons during the journey—but the writing about the body is paradoxically for the purpose of eventually transcending it, and his physical capacity greatly facilitates that process. It is precisely this feature of his body that facilitates his image being transformed into the revolutionary hero during Mao's era, through a series of revisions of both the episodes the havoc in heaven and the White Bone Demon, as discussed in chapter 3. These adaptations emphasized the heroic aspects of Sun Wukong and reconstructed him as a brave warrior who fights against the oppression of the feudalist heaven controlled by the Jade Emperor, and a true pilgrim who can see through the disguises of forms and catch the White Bone Demon despite her transformations. What is unchanged from the religious "heart monkey" to the communist revolutionary monkey is the agreement in his "heart" and his body, originating from his miraculous birth and well suited to the purposes of pilgrimage and revolutionary cause alike.

BODY VERSUS HEART: HUMANIZATION OF THE MONKEY KING

In contrast, in *A Chinese Odyssey* the Monkey King's story becomes one of body working *against* heart. With the entire story focusing on Joker's romantic adventures, love and sexuality become central themes of the film, and the meaning of "heart" in "heart monkey" changes to refer to love. Correspondingly, his body quite frequently becomes the focal point of the camera. *A Chinese Odyssey* gives the Monkey King (reborn as Joker) a mortal human body, and Joker's adventure involves various sorts of mistreatment of this body. Joker appears near the beginning suffering from a severe injury. He cannot see or speak properly, and it is predicted that if the wound spreads, his entire body will explode. His legs soon give out, and he can only walk upside down with his arms. His body continues to be treated cruelly when the gang proceeds to fight against the spider demon, "Ma'am Thirty": Joker is seen falling into a pit of feces; trapped by a spider net; breaking his own teeth; being beaten, burnt, and repeatedly trampled on by his gang members. His private parts particularly become the target of trampling quite a few times. When Joker and Jingjing fall in love, in the short moment when they were together, sex was never consummated. Paradoxically, the narrative of this film about love seems to focus unmistakably on castration.

Whereas part 1, *Pandora's Box*, tells the adventures of Joker's body, part 2, *Cinderella*, becomes the story of his heart. But just like the mistreatment of body in the earlier part, something always goes wrong with his heart in part 2. Joker spends this part of the journey in denial: of both his love for Zixia and his identity as the Monkey King. It is only by means of the literal separation of his heart from his body that he is eventually able to find and recognize his heart—he is killed by Ma'am Thirty, who cuts open his chest and takes his heart out, so he sees it with his "eyes of the heart/soul" (*xinyan*). At this moment, after his heart leaves his body, he becomes the Monkey King, who has to put the golden ring on his head to control his worldly desire. Later, when the new Sun Wukong is faced with a hard choice between saving his true love Zixia and saving his master Tripitaka, the golden ring tightens to make sure he makes the right choice.

With its depictions of the body and the search for love, *A Chinese Odyssey* seemingly delivers a message that is diametrically opposed to that of *Journey to the West* until the ending, when it hits on a conclusion that is much in agreement with *Journey to the West*: abstaining from worldly pleasure. The last scene of the movie sees the group of pilgrims set off once again on their journey to the West, when they come across a couple, the exact replica of Joker and Zixia, repeating the scene that Joker once experienced when he refused to kiss "Zixia" and profess his love for her. Possessing the body of the replica Joker, Sun Wukong embraces "Zixia," gives her the requested kiss, and tells her that he will never leave her. Having done this, Sun Wukong leaves the body of "Joker" and sets off on his journey, leaving the embracing couple behind. Although this ending provides Sun Wukong the chance to make up for his regret by means of the body of the substitute, it also concludes the separation of the body and the heart, permanently.

By the same token, although the film is replete with sexually charged language and images, sex is never directly represented. Sexual expectations are subverted and rebuffed. For instance, while Joker and Jingjing are well on their way toward a physical encounter, they give up their attempt abruptly for a seemingly arbitrary excuse: waiting until it becomes dark. While Ma'am Thirty is immediately seen as the object of sexual abuse for the bandits when she appears at the very beginning of the film, in reality, she takes sexual advantage of the bandits. In general, sex in the film is often referenced but not demonstrated (and usually not consummated).

The story of the conflicting body and heart of Joker ends with a symbolical self-castrating action, when we see Sun Wukong eating a banana, during two occasions near the end of the movie, with peels dangling at his mouth and the banana bitten off (figure 4.1). These scenes, echoing the trampling scene described earlier, epitomize the conflicting relationship between body and heart. Although they no doubt create a humorous effect, part of the "nonsensical" style for which Stephen Chow is known, the Monkey King image created by such effect forms a stark contrast to that of the successful and capable fighter in earlier adaptations. Now that he knows love, his body is working against his heart. Thus, the new Sun Wukong must bear the vexing challenges of life, just like a normal human being. It is this contradiction between body and heart that has become the source of inspiration for many *Dahua* fans who see the story as reflecting their own: the dreams of the young heart and its obstructions in reality.

BETWEEN DEMON AND DEITY

A Chinese Odyssey presents us a Monkey King who has lost the godly control and coordination of body and heart that he enjoyed in *Journey to the West.* Nevertheless, the film still resists a simple dichotomy between deity and demon. In fact, blurring the line between the demon and the god is a major endeavor of the narrative. Not only does the film question the categorical nature of the Monkey King, but it also ridicules the differentiation between deity and demon. As for Sun Wukong, after he is reincarnated as Joker as a punishment for his demonic behavior, he repeatedly refuses opportunities to be transformed back into the deity Monkey King. When he realizes that he has finally become the Monkey King reincarnate, seeing the image of a monkey in the "Mirror of Demon Revelation," he immediately throws the mirror to the ground, tramples on the mirror (and his predestined identity), and runs away. Thus the final transformation into Sun Wukong at the end concludes the human Joker's resistance with his eventual submission to his predestination (or the pressure of the social environment, in one *Dahua* fan's interpretation).

The question of "deity or demon?" as a major theme is represented by what Zixia asks Joker when she first meets him: "Deity? Demon? Thanks." Indicating her immediate need to categorize Joker as a deity or a demon, the question reflects her interest in

Figure 4.1. Sun Wukong eating a banana when the pilgrimage team sets off on their journey. From Jeffrey Lau, *A Chinese Odyssey*, 1995.

detecting disguises, as deities and demons frequently transform themselves into human form. In her short earlier encounter with Erlang Shen and the Four Heavenly Kings, the gods transformed into humans to deceive her. While the "Mirror of Demon Revelation" can tell demons from humans by revealing one's spiritual identity, depictions of demon and deity in the film blur and confuse the good-versus-evil stereotype. Gods such as Erlang Shen and his team are represented as quite ungodly, their conversations indicating that they all have ordinary humanlike faults and concerns. Joker relies on the magic mirror to try to tell demons from humans, but the demons identified by the mirror turn out to be as lovable as their human disguises: Jingjing is devoted to love, and Ma'am Thirty sacrifices herself to save her partner and baby. The triangle formed between Joker, Jingjing, and Zixia involves a human, a deity, and a demon, and the fact that they fall into different categories never constitutes a problem for them. In general, the narrative presents the human side of all beings, including their frustrations, their desires, their dreams, and their fears.

The line between deity and demon is also blurred in *Journey to the West* itself. Many characters, as well as the novel itself, defy easy categorization, with the Monkey King epitomizing the overall feature of multivalence. Adaptations in socialist China from the 1940s to the 1980s have redefined the difference between demons, humans, and gods. While the Monkey King in *Havoc in Heaven* represents the revolutionary and the people, the gods and deities become the subject of ridicule, symbolizing backward feudalist power. In *Sun Wukong Subdues the White Bone Demon*, Sun Wukong and his pilgrimage group stand for the Chinese people on the road of socialist construction, and the demons are the political enemies of socialist China. The mythical story is transformed into a discourse within which the demarcation of enemy versus friend, good versus evil becomes the major concern.

Although over time the differentiation between god and demon has changed from ambiguous to clear separation and back to ambiguity again, *A Chinese Odyssey* is not a simple return to the original *Journey to the West*. In the sixteenth-century text, Sun Wukong himself goes through the identity transformation from a demon (a king of monkeys who occupy a mountain and claim it as their territory without recognition from authorities), to a deity recognized by the Taoist authority (first as the imperial horse keeper, then as the Great Sage, Equal to Heaven), and finally a Buddhist pilgrim who eventually attains Buddhahood. This upward transformation from an outlaw to a recognized deity was deliberately overlooked by the socialist adaptations, which downplayed the importance of social recognition either from the Taoist or the Buddhist order but only emphasized the idea of rebel and the metaphor of the journey. Hence the Monkey King was simply represented as a heroic rebel of oppression or a devoted follower of the path for socialist construction. In contrast, Joker's transformation in *A Chinese Odyssey* moves in the opposite direction from Sun Wukong in *Journey to the West*. Refusing to return to the monkey-deity identity, Joker prefers to remain as an outlaw. In this film, for the first time, he is given the right to ask questions about who he is and what he is doing. His heroic halo taken away, the Monkey King once again becomes the down-to-earth nobody, a humanized antihero who speaks to the sympathetic audience.

REINCARNATION, REWRITING, AND THE STORY OF HONG KONG

The story of the Monkey King's reincarnation can be read as one of rewriting. Guanyin and Jade Emperor were official rewriters of Sun

Wukong's story: they dislike the version in which Sun Wukong rebels against Guanyin, and give him another chance by reincarnating him as Joker. Joker, however, after being reminded of his identity in his previous life, which he has completely forgotten, chooses to run away: he does not want to become Sun Wukong, the protagonist of the "Journey to the West" story already written. Instead, he makes as many revisions as he can and tries to lead the story in a direction of his own choosing. From this point of view, the entire movie is about the tension and conflicts of the two rewriting plans operating in opposite directions. Although Joker battles to be the writer of his own life, in the end he has to give in to the dominance of Guanyin's rewrite. Despite his resistance, in the end his memory and identity as the Monkey King is regained, or, more accurately, reconstructed.

Joker's own effort to rewrite his story can be seen from his repeated time travels. When he finds out that the Moonlight Box (*yueguang baohe*) can take people to other times, he uses it repeatedly, trying to go back in time to a particular moment in order to change what happens to Jingjing and hence change his own love story. But his time-travel plan never works out perfectly. After a few failed efforts, he travels back five hundred years by mistake and thus begins the unintended love story with Zixia.

Joker's plan eventually has to yield to divine intervention. Before his story reaches a happy ending, his life is taken by the spider demon, and subsequently his spirit faces Guanyin's master plan: the Monkey King's golden headband and golden rod are waiting for him. Although taking on the mantle of the Monkey King is presented as a matter of choice, there really is no alternative, and the film portrays this transformation as the saddest moment. Solemnly and ceremonially, Joker raises up and puts on the headband, repeating the lines he once insincerely spoke to Zixia: "Once there was a genuine love devoted to me, but I took it lightly. When I have lost it, I know it is too late to regret." It is as if he uses the last moment as Joker to redeem the lines that he performed badly before, but this time with complete sincerity. This sincerity in his last words about love proves the tragic nature of the unwilling transformation into Sun Wukong. Among all the *Journey to the West* adaptations, *A Chinese Odyssey* is probably the one that most emphasizes the tragedy of being the Monkey King.

The film contains many other disastrous transformations besides the exemplary case of Joker. Bull Demon King's sister, for instance, practices Body-Swapping Magic (*yi hun da fa*) twice. Unfortunately both occasions actually work against her own interest and create havoc. In the first switch, Bull Sister accidently swaps her body with that of Sandy, thus creating scenes of gender confusion in the film; in the second switch, which eliminates this gender confusion, she transmits her own soul into the body of a dog.

The film's demonstrated anxiety over transformation in general, and Joker's frustrated effort to work against the divine plan in particular, builds a significant link to the story of Hong Kong. The transfer of sovereignty over Hong Kong from the United Kingdom to China in 1997 had been a great concern in Hong Kong in the 1980s and 1990s. Whereas in mainland China the transfer was expected eagerly as Hong Kong's "return," in other parts of the world it is referred to as the "Handover." Anxiety and doubt about the Handover are expressed directly or indirectly in popular culture. The most forthright expressions about Hong Kong's future can be found in two songs by the Taiwanese songwriter and singer Luo Dayou (Lo Ta-yu), "Queen's Road East" (Huanghou Dadao Dong) and "Pearl of the Orient" (Dongfang zhi zhu), bookending a 1991 music album *Queen's Road East.* The story of this album, and its circulation in Hong Kong and mainland China, parallels the ways in which *A Chinese Odyssey* operates in these two distinct contexts.

"Queen's Road East" is named after Queen's Road, the first road in Hong Kong, built in 1841–43, which grew into an icon of the British colony. The lyric, written by Albert Leung (Lin Xi), plays with the names of different sections of the street and uses the changes of the route in the city to indicate the changes of political route. The song addressed the doubt and anxiety of Hong Kong residents so loudly that it was banned in the mainland. But even when it was finally available to mainland listeners years later, its meaning remained quite hidden behind the layers of camouflage and barrier formed by dialect and allegory. The song refers to the British government as a "noble friend" (*guizu pengyou*) and a "bosom friend" (*zhiji*), and the PRC government as a "great comrade" (*weida tongzhi*) and a "righteous friend" (*zhengyi pengyou*). The lyric offers no straightforward criticism but relies on uncertainty, uneasiness, and subtle satire. The music video for the song, on the other hand, sheds all subtlety, bringing the satire into sharp relief. The singers are dressed in blue and green uniform-like outfits, reminiscent of the pre-1980 socialist China. Pedestrians and cars are moving backward. Young people in the uniform group up in the poses of revolutionary statues, holding red flags, and on one occasion a red banner that reads "1997." The singers, Luo Dayou and Ram Chiang, who both act in the video, in one scene walk along the street while clapping their hands, imitating the style of political leaders on the mainland, although they both wear dark sunglasses, which possibly cover the sinister smiles on their faces.[14] The apprehension about the Handover is explicitly expressed by presenting the future as stepping backward into a status of monotonous and vicious ideological control.

Forming a contrast to the critical attitude toward the Handover in "Queen's Road East" and its banning in the mainland, "Pearl of the Orient" shows a more positive attitude toward Hong Kong's future and correspondingly enjoyed popularity across China. Originally written in 1986, with music composed by Luo Dayou and lyrics in Cantonese by the famous Cantonese lyricist Zheng Guojiang, the song has a very positive tone, addressing the turbulent past of Hong Kong and encouraging Hong Kong residents to strive for a brighter future. Luo Dayou wrote Mandarin lyrics for the song in 1991 and included it as the last song on his album *Queen's Road East*. To the earlier version written from Hong Kong's point of view, the Mandarin version adds a romantic note: the narrative voice addresses Hong Kong as "Pearl of the Orient, my love," thus positing the narrator outside of Hong Kong. It emphasizes the importance of the shared cultural tradition and Chinese identity between Hong Kong and the narrative voice, as the chord of the song repeats: "Standing in the sea wind for five thousand years / each teardrop is speaking of your dignity / together with the sea tide let me protect you / please do not forget my never-changing yellow face." Sung by Luo Dayou, and in another version by a group of popular singers from Taiwan,[15] the song arguably conveys the sympathy of Taiwan toward Hong Kong and the recognized common cultural root that the two areas share. But the lyric is ambiguous enough that it crossed the strait successfully and became a great success in the mainland. Or rather, the ambiguity of the subjective narrative voice makes it possible for the mainlanders to accept the song and transform its concern with Hong Kong's history into an embrace of the promise of a bright future.

The success of "Pearl of the Orient" in contrast to "Queen's Road East" demonstrates how the meaning of a cultural product can change when it travels from one subculture to another. Following a similar track, the reference to Hong Kong in the film *A Chinese Odyssey* is unnoticed when it travels north, despite its popularity and the abundance of discussion about the meaning of the story. The transformation of the "Journey to the West" narrative into a love story took *Dahua* fans by surprise and has been a major focus of their discussions. Furthermore, the fans have been busy relating the story to their own social reality and seem to have neglected the abundant references to the social transformations in Hong Kong either in the major theme or through specific scenes. For instance, against the backdrop of questionable transformations and failed efforts to make life revisions, the film has an allegorical scene of the entire group of pilgrims stranded in a town on an isolated piece of land that has been blown up by the Bull Demon King with his magic fan and is floating slowly toward the sun. The Monkey King, seeing the danger the island faces of being scorched and potentially exploding in the heat of the sun, tries to push the island back with his golden rod. But his individual effort cannot overpower the gusts created by the magic fan. For a few seconds the film freeze-frames on a distant shot of the blood-red sun (communist China), occupying almost the entire screen, with the small island (Hong Kong) floating irreversibly toward it, and the single Monkey King trying desperately to stop its motion. The scene poses an urgent question to the audience: Will the pilgrims be able to escape? The answer is yes, when the magic works: all pilgrims narrowly escape using the Moonlight Box, which transports them to a different time-space right before the island explodes.

As comparatist Ackbar Abbas has noted about films from Hong Kong, "almost every film made since the mid-eighties, regardless of quality or seriousness of intention, seems constrained to make some mandatory reference to 1997."[16] Even though *A Chinese Odyssey* is a spoof of a mythical story, the reference is quite clear. Joker's situation corresponds quite closely to the "floating" identity and the problematics of the "*déjà disparu*," as Abbas discusses; with the slipperiness and ambivalence of his true identity and the rapid changes of status, he is unable to see what is right in front of him, and when he does see it, it is "always already gone."[17] The desperate scene of the floating island moving toward the sun creates a pressing sense of crisis. Despite all of Sun Wukong's effort, the city disappears after all, indicating a quite pessimistic view of the future of the "floating city."

The image of the "floating city" (*fucheng*) is used frequently in popular culture as a reference to Hong Kong. For instance, Xi Xi, a female fiction writer whose stories examine the life and identity of Hong Kong, wrote a short story titled "Marvels of a Floating City" (fucheng zhiyi), a fairy tale–style allegory about the haunting uncertainty of the people living in a city floating on top of the sea, between the unreliable cloud overhead and the threat-ridden sea below.[18] Written in 1986, two years after the signing of the Sino-British Joint Declaration, the story quite obviously references Hong Kong.[19] *Floating City* is also the title of Yim Ho's 2012 film. A story of the transformations of a mixed-blood poor fisher boy on a small boat to the first native taipan of the Imperial East India Company, it simultaneously reflects on Hong Kong's changes in the recent past under British governance. With many historical references to the Handover, we see in this story the struggle of an individual as well as a story of Hong Kong.

CREATIVE MISREADING, POSTSOCIALIST HERO

The underlying themes concerning Hong Kong's identity are not explicit (or of great import) for mainland audiences. Because many *Dahua* fans are college students, the film resonates with those who struggle to find their own identities in an authoritative regime. Frequently discussed themes include impossible love, the struggle of the individual against society, and eventual submission to social pressure. The Joker with whom *Dahua* fans identify is the rebel who is doomed to fail but who nonetheless remains the rebel—that is, until he eventually has to give in to an indomitable external force. A common analogy discussed by fans is the comparison of Joker's resubmission to authority once he dons the golden crown of the Monkey King to the increased censorship of the Internet after 1997. When the actor portraying Joker, Stephen Chow, visited Peking University for a conversation with his fans, he was welcomed by three thousand college students, who recited aloud together the famous line that Joker speaks when he puts on the golden fillet of the Monkey King: "Once there was a genuine love devoted to me, but I took it lightly. When I have lost it, I know it is too late to regret."[20] Joker's resolute pursuit of his individual agenda, either love or other dreams, appears to resonate with fans of the story.

Thus, the same text, travelling from Hong Kong to the mainland, takes on a new meaning, even though the cinematic text remains the same. The creative misreading of *A Chinese Odyssey* has created a new image of the Monkey King for the mainland with Joker establishing himself as a "postsocialist" hero. This new hero replaces the images of Sun Wukong as "revolutionary" hero that were created and popularized in the 1960s in works such as *Havoc in Heaven* and *Sun Wukong Subdues the White Bone Demon*.

The term "postsocialism" was coined by historian Arif Dirlik before the Tiananmen Square massacre of 1989 and since then has been adopted by academics in various disciplines and has been defined in several different ways.[21] While Dirlik develops his idea of postsocialism in response to Deng Xiaoping's "socialism with Chinese characteristics," indicating that the Chinese socialism in practice is not exactly socialism (nor is it capitalism), scholars in Chinese studies adopt and adapt the concept for different purposes. Paul G. Pickowicz addresses the term from the domain of public perception: in terms of understanding China from the bottom up, "the socialist system is bankrupt," and although people may not know what kind of society they want, they know what they do not want: they "do not want what life has taught them to regard as socialism."[22] Michel Hockx supports his analysis of Internet literature in postsocialist China based on the understanding that the core socialist institutions in China had begun to disappear starting in the early 1990s.[23] The postsocialist nature of the image of Sun Wukong is evident from the relationship between the people and the system. If a socialist system means people have faith in the socialist discourse, it becomes postsocialist when this faith is lost, even though ideological control from the leadership is still strong and is currently getting stronger. There exists a discord and discrepancy between the expectation from above and grassroots-level practice. Instead of the kind of collective identification with common ideals established in the socialist period, the postsocialist hero is interested in his individual agenda, which often includes focusing on his personal struggle to challenge the authorities that want to control him.

A Chinese Odyssey indicates the postsocialist turn of *Journey to the West*: from here on, major adaptations of *Journey to the West* almost always present the Monkey King as a postsocialist hero (with one exception that will be discussed below). *A Chinese Odyssey* makes Sun Wukong a rebel again: he had already experienced the five hundred years of imprisonment and become a pilgrim following Tripitaka, but now he no longer wants to follow the prescribed narrative. And not only is he no longer willing to obey the command from above, but he also loudly lets the world know of his intention. This Wukong expresses a challenge to the ideological authority of the contemporary regime. Even though in the end his resubmission is unavoidable, his ridicule and rejection of authority is already enough for the audience to consider him a hero.

This heroic image in the beginning takes a double bootleg form, expressing his discontent in a borrowed package from Hong Kong, from the mouth of a fictional monkey. Soon after, the rise in *A Chinese Odyssey*'s popularity presents an opportunity to rewrite the story of Wukong as well as other main characters in *Journey to the West*. These new Monkey Kings represent a process of mythmaking from the popular culture of mainland China, in contrast to the top-down mythmaking that was prevalent forty years ago. This process begins with *Dahua* fans' interpretation of *A Chinese Odyssey* as well as their own retelling of the story, usually in shorter versions of *Journey to the West* located in a contemporary setting, using contemporary language, and focused on the challenges of contemporary life.[24] Following the example of *A Chinese Odyssey*, many newer images of Wukong are created. Although stories and styles vary, Wukong continues to stay on the postsocialist track. *Story of Wukong* and *Another Voice* are two outstanding examples.[25]

AND THE FIGHT CONTINUED: *STORY OF WUKONG*

The *Story of Wukong* is important both for introducing a new genre into the *Journey to the West* canon and for its success as a "born digital" Internet fiction. First, the *Story of Wukong* presents a new subgenre in which the stories of the characters in the *Journey to the West* form a fictional biography. Following the success of the *Story of Wukong*, various versions of "biographies" of the major characters of *Journey to the West* appeared on the Internet, many of which were subsequently published in print.[26] And, like the *Story of Wukong*, these works all bear the marks of the influence of *A Chinese Odyssey*—that is, the nonsensical humor and an independent retelling of the *Journey to the West* story that makes sense in a contemporary setting. Some characters that are created by *A Chinese Odyssey* and *Story of Wukong* also are found in the numerous other "biographies." More importantly, these figures are presented as heroic characters who rebel, each in their own ways, against authority, following the example of Joker. Even Bajie and Tripitaka are rewritten as strong-minded fighters against mind-controllers.

Second, the *Story of Wukong* has established its author, Jin Hezai, as one of the first writers to build his brand via Internet writing, becoming one of the trailblazers of Internet literature in China. Roughly from the time of *Story of Wukong*, Internet literature has become an important platform for literary production and consumption in China. As Michel Hockx states, "the postsocialist condition is nowhere more recognizable than on the Internet."[27] It therefore may not be mere coincidence that stories promoting the *Journey to the West* pilgrims as postsocialist heroes have flourished in and have contributed to the flourishing of this postsocialist space. Like *A Chinese Odyssey*, the success of *Story of Wukong* is not ephemeral. It enjoyed success when it first appeared on the Internet in 2000, and by the time it was published in print in 2001, it had already become quite famous.[28] Its influence reaches beyond that. In the comprehensive online literature review "Internet Literature Ten Year Review" co-organized by *Novel Offprint* (Changpian xiaoshuo xuankan) and 17k.com and supervised by China Writer's Association (Zhongguo zuojia xiehui) in 2008–9, *Story of Wukong* was voted one of the Top Ten Most Popular Works.[29]

The spirit of rebellion and confrontation is more apparent in *Story of Wukong* than in *A Chinese Odyssey*. The story presents an image of a Wukong who is more of a rebel than ever. Also a story of the Monkey King reborn with no memory of his previous life as a rebel, the life journey of the Monkey King in *Story of Wukong* is the opposite of Joker's in *A Chinese Odyssey*. In *Story of Wukong*, the gods in heaven want Wukong to forget about his rebellious previous life and to completely forget about who he really is. However, urged by an internal desire, Wukong seeks to recover his memory, continues his unfinished battle against all deities in his previous life, and prevails in the final combat, albeit at the sacrifice of his own life. If *A Chinese Odyssey* portrays a Monkey King who tries to reject his fate by running away, the Wukong in *Story of Wukong* dashes headlong against his predestination and the fate-making deities, branding himself as the ultimate rebel.

Wukong is not the only rebel in *Story of Wukong*. Tianpeng/Bajie, when deposed from heaven and reborn as a pig as punishment for disrespecting the Jade Emperor and the Empress, also chooses the hard way for the rest of his life. He refuses to forget about his past and continues his life as a pig with memories of his love for Chang'e the moon goddess and his hatred toward the heavens. Tripitaka, formerly a student of the Buddha, is punished to be reborn as a human as a result of his confrontation with Buddha. Yet he continues to seek the truth in this life. One of the best-known quotes from *Story of Wukong* is a line from Tripitaka: "I want the sky to no longer cover my eyes; I want the earth to no longer bury my heart; I want all sentient beings to understand my meaning, and all buddhas to disperse like smoke!"[30] Sha Monk in the story serves as an object of ridicule and a foil for the fighters. He sustains his loyalty to the gods in heaven even though he is treated as a slave. Being punished because of a broken glass bowl, he goes through hell just in order to return to the celestial court. However, even he is driven into a state of rebellion by the end of the story, unable to endure the oppressive treatment from heaven any longer.

The division and confrontation between demon (*yao*) and deity (*shen*) becomes a major driving force of the narrative of *Story of Wukong*. The journey to fetch sutras in *Journey to the West* is turned into a scheme by Buddha and Guanyin to deal with their uncontrollable agents, Tripitaka and Sun Wukong. This again is a predestined deal that leaves no opportunity for Monkey to win. Instead of following a chronological order, the narrative presents the two fiercest disorders that Monkey creates side by side: the havoc he creates in the sequence of "Havoc in Heaven" and the chaos raised by the true and fake Monkey in the sequence of the battle between Sun Wukong and the six-eared macaque.[31] In *Journey to the West*, the six-eared macaque is another capable monkey demon that has transformed into an image of Wukong. His masquerade is so real that no one except Buddha can tell the real from the fake. *Story of Wukong* presents the six-eared macaque as another Wukong, the part of Wukong that is "evil," to fight with the Wukong that is recognized as "good" while controlled by Buddha's headband. This means that Wukong the rebel has to defeat the deities as well as himself in order to win. This conflict appears to guarantee the victory of Buddha: after Wukong kills the other half of himself, he is left no choice but to succumb to Buddha, who announces that Wukong is actually the six-eared macaque and extends to him the opportunity to become his student once he accepts this identity. However, at this point Wukong has already recovered his memory of who he is. With his last breath, he declares war against Buddha and proclaims his real identity as the invincible Sun Wukong.[32] His action surprises Buddha himself, who admits that it is Wukong who has won—he has done something out of Buddha's expectation and therefore has jumped out of Buddha's control. In claiming his rebel identity, Wukong dies, but he also wins.

Both of the Wukongs in *A Chinese Odyssey* and *Story of Wukong* fit the model for a postsocialist hero: on the one hand, the "post" of postsocialism is reflected in the spirit of rebellion, the lack of belief in authoritarian control, and the challenge to authority; on the other hand, the "socialist" ideology and the government that represents it still maintain a strong presence. In contrast to the socialist revolutionary Monkey King produced during the 1950s and 1960s, who celebrates his victory in the end, both of the postsocialist Monkeys are doomed to lose. Joker has to fight hard for his right to disagree, and eventually he gives in. Wukong in *Story of Wukong* fights to the end, which culminates in his death. Although Buddha and other immortals acknowledge his victory in death, it is exactly because the victory is purely spiritual that the readers can relate the story of Wukong to the forms of compliance they have to endure in real life. The popularity of *A Chinese Odyssey* and *Story of Wukong* lies in the sympathy that the readers share with Wukong. They grieve over these sad stories just as they grieve over their own problems.

WHOSE BODY IS THIS?: *ANOTHER VOICE*

If both *A Chinese Odyssey* and *Story of Wukong* use a magical story to reflect on a realistic situation, in *Another Voice* the magic is lost. The only thing surreal in this story is Sun Wukong's long life and his body. Sun Wukong's body in *Journey to the West* is miraculous and is capable of seventy-two transformations without injury. In *A Chinese Odyssey,* his body is reduced to that of a normal person, and in *Another Voice*, his body becomes frozen in one of his transformations when the magic disappears. The figure originating in the fantasy world of *Journey to the West* walks into the real world of China, witnesses and experiences historical changes, and becomes a person just like everyone else. This story of Sun Wukong's journey through history bears a clear trace of national allegory.

The narrative of *Another Voice* starts when the journey to India is over. As if waking up from a dream, the pilgrims find no glory or magic as described in the legend. Instead, they return to harsh reality. Sun Wukong returns to his mountain and falls into a long sleep. When he finally wakes up after an unknown number of years, he realizes he has been forgotten by his monkey subjects in the kingdom and replaced by a new king. Seeing no point to a life in the mountain any more, he embarks on an aimless journey. At Bajie's place, Sun

Wukong loses his virginity by mishap and subsequently starts to lose his magic abilities.

When he continues his journey, sometimes adopting the form of a woman, he is stopped by a bandit gang and finds himself trapped in the body of a woman, named "He Cuihua," and can no longer transform himself. For hundreds of years, He Cuihua deals with the troubles of life the only way she knows: to endure until reality becomes history. She becomes a legendary courtesan, grows old and feeble, and loses her memory of who she is. Beginning another journey, she wanders alone until she meets Wu Cheng'en, the author of the book *Journey to the West.* Her memory and sense of identity gradually returns when she reads Wu's draft. After writing down "I am Sun Wukong," she sets off on the journey again for another few hundred years, her body growing stronger, until one day she transforms into a young man.

Thus, He Cuihua/Sun Wukong's journey through time—not via a time machine but by walking step by step through history—is accompanied by two transformations: first a transformation characterized by loss (of both power and memory), then a transformation characterized by rejuvenation and the regaining of memory. Significantly, the young man into whom He Cuihua transforms wears a Western suit, speaks about U.S. dollars, and chooses to take a taxi, instead of walking as she has been, to the city. He has transformed into a modern human being, as the last line of the story emphasizes: "Now he is exactly the same as the young taxi driver, as well as the pedestrians in the street."[33] The importance of Sun Wukong becoming human is earlier noted in the narrative when the He Cuihua–transformed young man walks across a forest, where all the animals bid him to stay: "He keeps walking without any stop, and only waves when he passes a host of monkeys playing in the trees. He feels none of them are his kind." When finally reaching the street with the city in his view, "he realizes that the human shapes walking along the street, the shapes that have long been familiar, for the first time feel dear to him."[34]

Sun Wukong walks through China's historical path, from the strong and glorious Tang era to the following weakened dynasties, until the modern age when China opens its door to Western cultures. This journey is rough and challenging, with no flying or somersaulting, only walking step by step through the years. The Monkey King's transformation from a monkey to a woman (a courtesan with a monkey tail), then finally to a young man, corresponds to the historical journey of the nation. Once a superpower in Asia and the world, it later becomes an old and impotent nation that is bullied and exploited by rising Western powers. The oppressed and dispossessed people of the ancient land slowly move forward in the process of modernization, like He Cuihua's journey on foot, which ends with her final transformation into a man, reflective of the dramatic social transformation in recent history. Significantly, this transformation does not take place by the time of the socialist revolution, which replaces the long-dominant feudalist system with a dramatically new socialist system. Instead, the young man transformed from He Cuihua walks into a postsocialist setting, a place clearly under strong influence from the West, a promising time-place that encourages looking forward instead of looking back. The socialist period, together with other previous eras, like the Qing dynasty, are bypassed by the narrative.[35] The purposeful negligence of the socialist period identifies this part of history as something to be endured and overcome, something that stays in the dark shadow in contrast to the bright ending of the story, when He Cuihua/Wukong walks to, and blends right into, the rapidly changing society that has opened up to other cultures.

Despite He Cuihua's apparent difference from the rebel Joker in *A Chinese Odyssey* and the Sun Wukong in *Story of Wukong*, the endurance of the dispossessed He Cuihua through several imperial dynasties and most of the twentieth century, and her final transformation into the young man Wukong, indicate the narrative's attitude toward the socialist restraint and toward postsocialist opportunities. The varied images of the Monkey King in these three cases represent the shared postsocialist desire of both the authors and the readers. The three adaptations are all engaged with the major contradiction of *Journey to the West*: why would Monkey, once a brilliant rebel, become a model Buddhist pilgrim? It is the ways in which the readers approach this contradiction that determines to a large extent their understanding of *Journey to the West.* One common theme shared by these three texts is the central issue of amnesia in relation to Wukong's identity as a rebel. In all three texts, the lack of memory is a rationale for his seeming complacency. Thus, looking for his identity is a major struggle for Wukong, and it is a lonely one. He is no longer presented as a member of the pilgrim team—only he himself can solve the problems he experiences, and only from within. In *A Chinese Odyssey*, Joker refuses to become the hero Sun Wukong, and in this action he remains the rebel. He Cuihua in *Another Voice* has lost his vitality and memory as the monkey, but he recovers his memory and identity as Sun Wukong by reading and participating in the writing of his own story. It is because of his own journey/pilgrimage that he is able to accomplish his recovery. Does the ending suggest that the time for Monkey to become a rebel and troublemaker has come again? The *Story of Wukong* is about how Sun Wukong finds his memory and identity as the once-notorious rebel—when this is accomplished, he is considered victorious even though he dies. Other new adaptations follow the same track in which variants of Wukong, though they may be presented with varying degrees of humor or seriousness, are always marked by a shared sense of loneliness. His struggle has turned inward: finding his identity and his inner strength.

"I AM SUN WUKONG": THE RETURN OF THE REBEL

The momentum that *A Chinese Odyssey* and *Story of Wukong* have started for a new Monkey image as a postsocialist hero is in full swing. Adaptation of *Journey to the West* continues, and those receiving public praise have a common theme: rethinking the transition of Sun Wukong from a rebel to a pilgrim, and depicting Sun Wukong rising up as a rebel again. Monkey's failure and dejection at the beginning and his ultimate transformation into a rebellious hero earns the audience's sympathy, and their identification with him ensures interest in the project of such revision.

Three other noteworthy examples of postsocialist-oriented adaptation are: *The Monkey King* (2014), *Monkey King: Hero Is Back* (2015), and "Wukong," as sung by Dai Quan on *Sing My Song* (2015). *The Monkey King* (Xiyou ji: Da'nao tiangong), directed by Pou-Soi Cheang, released during the Chinese New Year holiday of 2014, was a box-office success but a critical failure. Expectation for the film was very high, indicating the long-standing popularity of the "Journey to the West" theme among Chinese audiences. The "Havoc in Heaven" sequence it chooses as the main narrative is the first remake in the media since the influential 1964 animation by the Wan brothers. However, the film's rating on douban.com—4.2 out of 10, with 34.5 percent of the 94,951 reviewers giving it one star, and 32 percent giving it two stars out of five—demonstrates the audience's disappointment.[36] The top reviews on this site point to a central issue: Monkey is not presented as a rebel but rather as a naïve demon who is manipulated by Bull Demon King; he willingly admits his "mistake" and wants to help rebuild the palace for the Jade Emperor. One reviewer calls the writer of the story "a Wu Cheng'en who works for the Propaganda Department," and *The Monkey King* is seen as an educational film promoting the mainstream theme of cooperating with deities.[37]

The 2015 animation film *Monkey King: Hero Is Back* (Dasheng guilai, hereafter *Hero Is Back*), directed by Tian Xiaopeng, was a success both at the box office and in critics' reviews.[38] Audiences were excited by the prospect of a quality animation film after a long stagnant period for Chinese animation, and they also liked the image of Sun Wukong created by the film. The film focuses on the moment when Monkey has just been released from the mountain after five hundred years of imprisonment. A dejected Monkey who cannot find his power all through the film, he is irritated, instigated, and finally inspired by a little boy named Jiangliu (Tripitaka's boyhood name), who believes in the greatness of the Great Sage he knows from legend. At the very last moment, Monkey rediscovers his magic power and defeats the demon Hundun. The short moment of Monkey regaining his magic in the end, lasting for only two minutes, wins the audience's heart. Many popular reviews note Monkey's repeatedly yelling throughout the film, "I can't do it, I can't do it," a frustration that aligns his character with normal human beings, in contrast to the radiant hero he finally becomes.[39] The most popular review on douban.com states: "Every Chinese will fall in love with Sun Wukong. Each generation has its own Sun Wukong. I think this film can serve as a good first Monkey King film for children of the new century."

Why does the audience respond to the Wukong in this 2015 film *Hero Is Back* so positively while regarding the 2014 film *The Monkey King* as a failure? The different attitudes toward these two films point at the significance of the rebellious quality of a postsocialist hero. The Monkey King in *The Monkey King* accepts what is offered him from both deities and demons, including evil plans that masquerade as friendly help and that eventually result in the havoc in heaven. The Great Sage in *Hero Is Back*, however, does not just accept. He searches, he questions, and he fights against his limits, echoing the examples of Monkey in *A Chinese Odyssey* and *Story of Wukong*. Significantly, although the animated *Hero Is Back* is adapted from the sequence when Sun Wukong meets Tripitaka, it is not about how Monkey pledges allegiance to his Buddhist master. What it highlights is Wukong's struggle against the seal from Buddha that still controls him, preventing him from using any magic power. This struggle persists until the last minutes of the film, when he finally breaks free and becomes the glorious hero once again. If the reason that audiences resisted the 2014 film *The Monkey King* is because it transformed the heroic Sun Wukong portrayed in the now classic 1964 animation *Havoc in Heaven* into a subservient capitulator, the 2015 animation returns another hero to the audience. But this is a different hero, one whose purpose is not so much breaking down the old (feudalist) structure and building a new (socialist) one. His interest, rather, is in his own individual agenda of breaking free from the seal so that he can fight as before.

The third example is the song "Wukong," written by Dai Quan, who performed it on the stage of *Sing My Song* in 2015, a reality talent show where contestants must perform their own compositions. The identification with Sun Wukong is explicit: when performing, Dai wears Wukong's signature tightening band over his wrist. The lyrics describe Wukong's internal journey and struggle from a first-person point of view. Explaining the reasons he wrote this song, Dai says his identification with Sun Wukong is due to what he believes is the "spirit of Wukong" (*Wukong jingshen*): rebelliousness, variability, optimism, and persistence, which has encouraged him in his life as an artist.[40] While "variability" (*duobian*) can be a translation of multivalence, a primary feature of the Sun Wukong character discussed in chapter 1, "rebelliousness" is a quality that is particularly developed and emphasized in the twentieth century, both during the socialist and postsocialist phases. The bitterness and loneliness that Dai Quan's Wukong experiences in his individual struggle, and the freedom this Wukong seeks, are particular traits of the postsocialist Monkeys. Audiences associated this Wukong with *Story of Wukong*. A few months after Dai's song was aired, when *Hero Is Back* was screened, fans of both the film and the music saw a distinct connection of this song with the film—various versions of fan-made music videos that combined edited movie clips with the song "Wukong" appear online, all claiming that "Wukong" would have fit the film better than its actual theme song.

"Wukong" sings at the refrain, "What is the use of my Iron Rod and my transformations? There is no cure to the anxiety and frustration. Golden band on my head, unspeakable pain." But when it repeats at the end, the message turns positive, a victorious Wukong singing the last line: "Watch my rod—it reduces all problems into ashes."[41] The conflict between the golden band and the rod is notable in this short song. These few lines represent the major theme of the postsocialist Monkeys: engaging with this major conflict, Sun Wukong tries to use his rod to break free from the limitations of the headband. This is a clear contrast to the socialist Wukong: the revolutionary who is invincible, and the loyal party supporter who does not complain about the golden band. After all his failures and frustrations, the postsocialist Monkey in the end manages to find something to celebrate, a sense of accomplishment for himself, as Dai Quan indicated in his statement: "In the end, every monkey can become Sun Wukong." The monkey becomes Sun Wukong when he finds his lost ability to use his rod again.

New adaptations of *Journey to the West* in recent years thus share several common features. The first is a clear individualist bent, as Wukong invariably goes through a personal struggle, the solution for which lies in himself, not in any external agency. Second, Monkey is no longer the filial protector of Tripitaka or true follower of Guanyin's teaching. The once-suppressed rebellious spirit is back. And third, although Monkey still has to submit to heavenly authority, he is allowed to think, to search, and even to challenge. His signature headband, which is transformed into a bracelet in both *Hero Is Back* and "Wukong," reflects this change.

CHAPTER 5

Chronotope and Orientalism

Time Travel between China and America

While the Monkey King has been an iconic and much-beloved figure in China's literary and popular cultures for centuries, his appearance in global media is more recent, earning him a steadily increasing audience. *Journey to the West* enjoys a long-standing popularity in China's neighboring countries including Japan and Korea, and it is via Japanese adaptations, often titled *Saiyūki*, that the Monkey King has gained audiences in the West. An example is the Japanese TV show *Saiyūki* (1978–80), known as *Monkey* by its English title, dubbed in English and Spanish and broadcast in countries including the United Kingdom, India, Australia, and Mexico.

Although *Monkey* was not released in the United States, another *Saiyūki* was: a 1960 musical anime based on Osamu Tezuka's manga adaptation of the Chinese classic, created under the influence of the Chinese animation *Princess Iron Fan*. American International edited and dubbed it, and titled it *Alakazam the Great* (1961). After the Japanese revision of the story and the American editing and dubbing, the Monkey King Alakazam (echoing the then-popular TV magician show *The Magic Land of Allakazam*) is portrayed as a brave student magician who becomes arrogant but subsequently learns lessons about humility, mercy, and love through his punishment. For the first time in the adaptations of *Journey to the West*, the monkey is given a girlfriend in the story. *Alakazam the Great* is among the first Western adaptations of Japanese animation, released two years before *Astro Boy* (considered the first successful export of anime to the West); thus, the greatest concern of *Alakazam the Great* is the American audience rather than the original story. It is therefore not surprising that many of the details of the story were adapted for American tastes.

Following *Alakazam the Great*, American audiences next encounter the Monkey King through the *Dragon Ball* series of anime and feature films. Although the *Dragon Ball* series was originally inspired by *Journey to the West*, and the protagonist's name, "Goku," is the Japanese version of "Wukong," the series had developed its own story, and Goku became famous as a character distinct from the Monkey King, becoming an iconic image in his own right. Two other recent adaptations, however, focus more on introducing *Journey to the West* to the American audience, and present the Monkey King as Sun Wukong from the Chinese classic: *The Lost Empire* (2001), aka *The Monkey King*, and *The Forbidden Kingdom* (2008), or *King of Kung-Fu* (Gongfu zhi wang) in Chinese.

The Lost Empire is a television miniseries produced by NBC and the SciFi channel, directed by Peter McDonald and written by Asian American playwright David Henry Hwang. Asian American audiences were unhappy with the show's stereotypical representation of Asian people and culture, and *The Forbidden Kingdom*, directed by Rob Minkoff, disappointed audiences familiar with the *Journey to the West* story despite its appeal as the first film pairing of martial arts superstars Jet Li and Jackie Chan. These examples raise a series of questions about adaptation: How do we address the question of adaptation of traditional stories when loyalty to the original is not a concern? How may our concern change if this adaptation is an effort that involves both the East and the West? How do we deal with adaptations that cross media and that cross wide chronological and cultural gaps?

Of relevance here is the Russian philosopher Mikhail Bakhtin's concept of literary chronotope: "the intrinsic connectedness of temporal and spatial relationships," or the configurations of time and space as represented in literary discourse, literally translated as "time-space." [1] This concept is useful for analyses of cross-cultural and transmedia adaptations, as it not only "defines genre and generic distinctions" but is a formally constitutive category that determines to a significant degree the image of a character in literature, because "the image of man is always intrinsically chronotopic."[2] Second, a chronotopic approach offers a channel for cross-media and cross-cultural comparison. Modern retellings of the *Journey to the West* take all varieties of form, but whichever medium is chosen, however variant their plots are from one another, their *chronotopic* pattern and style promise something comparable. Juxtaposing the chronotope of the original text and the adapted texts enables the comparison of a text such as *The Forbidden Kingdom* to other adaptations. The chronotopic approach examines the patterns of time-space where the characters operate, the spatiotemporal world that they live in and travel to, and the nature of the travel itself.[3] Third, an examination of chronotope facilitates analysis of texts about travel and time travel, both featured in the original text and the two adapted texts discussed in this chapter. Travel, a movement from place to place, crossing borders of space and time, is a natural focal point for the study of chronotope. A particular type of boundary crossing, time travel usually means sudden and extreme change of chronotope in the story, additionally enacted through dramatized changes of social and cultural environment. Although time travel was not a concern for Bakhtin when he developed his theory of the chronotope, it has become a popular theme in modern literature, and it is certainly a major theme in many rewritings of the Monkey King narrative. In these cases, focusing on the spatial and temporal indicators facilitates the analysis of characters who travel across time and space.

BIOGRAPHICAL TIME AND MAGICAL TIME IN *JOURNEY TO THE WEST*

The spatiotemporal world of *Journey to the West* is full of magic, although normal human beings live and travel in it. Time in *Journey to the West*, much like what Bakhtin describes of the chivalric romance, becomes miraculous: "There appears a hyperbolization of time typical of the fairy tale: hours are dragged out, days are compressed into moments, it becomes possible to bewitch time itself. . . . We begin to see the peculiar distortion of temporal perspectives characteristic of dreams."[4] The chronotope of the miraculous world of the chivalric romance is characterized by the subjective playing with time as well as subjective playing with space, featuring an emotional and lyrical stretching and compressing of time and space.[5] Although *Journey to the West* does not fit in the category of the Western chivalric romance that Bakhtin writes about, the miraculous world it describes does also feature such malleable time and space. Time and space not only appear to be "bewitched," but their malleability also varies depending on the characters and the spheres of which *Journey to the West*'s world is composed. Major characters demonstrate different degrees of mastery of space and time, and different spheres of the world also have their own spatiotemporal structures.

The Monkey King is a master of travel, well-known for his mastery of the "somersault cloud" that can take him more than 108,000 *li* (33,554 miles) in moments, flying easily across all spheres. The first seven chapters of *Journey to the West* deal with the monkey's extension of his sphere of activity from his mountain, to the seas, the underground hell, and finally to the heavens. After he becomes a disciple of Tripitaka, because he travels faster than everyone else, he functions as the messenger of the team and the seeker of information and help, as well as being the primary fighter. Like Sun Wukong, all gods and demons in *Journey to the West* can travel at magical speed, to different degrees.

The head of the pilgrim team, Tripitaka, on the other hand, travels within his natural biographical time. Although he has been appointed by Bodhisattva Guanyin to fetch sacred sutras from the Western Heaven, and is the master of Monkey, Pigsy, and Sandy, Tripitaka's ability to travel in terms of speed and sphere is nonetheless the most limited of the group. Born and raised as a normal human, he can only walk as a human, relying on the dragon-transformed white horse during the journey to make the travel easier.

While Monkey flies around at his magical speed, the journey itself has to proceed at a human historical speed. All disciples of Tripitaka have to follow Tripitaka's pace. There thus exists a tension between the time of Tripitaka and the time of the immortals: while Monkey and other immortals enjoy much freedom within their miraculous chronotope and can fly from the Land of East to the Western Heaven within the time it takes to brew a cup of tea, when it comes to the journey itself they are bound to the historical time of Tripitaka, walking from China to India in as many years as Tripitaka needs.

Although the difference between Tripitaka's human time and the disciple's magical time forms a major tension in the chronotopic system and determines the form and pattern of the journey, it is not a problem that needs to be solved as far as the narrative is concerned. On the contrary, it is a decided necessity of the narrative. The tension of chronotopes exists throughout the journey as an accepted reality. Such questions as why it is necessary for the disciples to follow Tripitaka's human speed, or why they cannot simply finish the pilgrimage via a jump of Sun Wukong, have been brought up a few times among the disciples, only to be brushed away each time by a simple explanation that the journey has to be accomplished by the chosen human. Sun Wukong at one point explains to Pigsy that it is impossible for immortals to carry a human when they fly, but this explanation sounds rather facile, indicating only the narrative's need to hold the chronotopic pattern together. On the other hand, the narrative does take time to pause and tease out the contrast between the two kinds of journeys. For instance, in chapter 22, when the pilgrims arrive at the side of the Flowing Sand River (Liusha he), Tripitaka and his disciples hold a small discussion about the possibility of crossing the river that is as wide as 800 *li* (249 miles). The monkey jumps into the air, looking forward beyond the raging waves of the river, and comments: "If Old Monkey wishes to cross this river, he need only make one twist of his waist and he will reach the other shore. But for you, Master, it's impossible to get across."[6] The numerous jokes such as this testify to the tension between the two conflicting time frames as a basic and essential element of the narrative, without which the story would not hold together.

In the universe of *Journey to the West,* time also varies within each sphere, depending on whether it is human space or magical space. The narrative of *Journey to the West* comments on a few occasions on such difference: one day in the world of the immortals equals one year or longer in the human world. For instance, when Sun Wukong returns from heaven to his Flower-Fruit Mountain after a trip he experiences as but a few days, the monkeys in his kingdom ask him about his years in the heaven palace and remind him that one day in heaven equals one year on earth. The time ratio between the Buddha's palace and the human world is even greater. In chapter 77, when the Monkey King reports to the Buddha about the three monsters from the Mountain of Spirits (Lingshan), the Buddha realizes that the monsters have left the mountain for seven days, and seven days in the mountain equals a few thousand years in the human world. It seems that time is bewitched to a larger degree in the heaven of Buddhist divine beings, who are depicted as more powerful than the Taoist gods.

The universe of *Journey to the West* is thus composed of patches of worlds of different chronotopic nature. Although Sun Wukong travels frequently between these patches, somehow he can always return to the spot of Tripitaka's journey within a reasonable time, as if he has been travelling within homogeneous time. One can say that the journey of Tripitaka and his disciples is set in two sets of interfacing chronotopes, with the magical one of the Monkey King and other immortals developing around the straight line of Tripitaka's historical journey, departing temporarily from the line, darting around it, but always coming back to it. In addition, Tripitaka's travels in a different chronotope notwithstanding, he is staying in the same world with the immortals, demons, and deities, being an important member of it, and becoming an immortal himself at the culmination of the journey. In other words, in the end the historical transforms into the magical. Thus the contradictory patterns of time-space manage to nevertheless coexist, together forming a multivalent type of chronotope.

Within this multivalent chronotopic pattern, Sun Wukong, with his larger and more capable chronotope, is inevitably assigned most of the actions that the narrative needs. In this sense, Sun Wukong has to be the protagonist of *Journey to the West* because his chronotope is more powerful. Further, the inconsistency between his higher level of chronotope and his lower level of social status, that is, as the disciple of a rather incapable master, from time to time becomes the driving force for the development of the plot.

A THRESHOLD OF FIVE HUNDRED YEARS

"Five hundred years" is a phrase that recurs in *Journey to the West* and has become a point with which many adaptations play.[7] Before creating the famous turmoil in heaven, Sun Wukong has lived for about five hundred years. After the turmoil and consequently being subdued by the Buddha, the monkey spends another five hundred years under the Five Phases Mountain, before becoming Tripitaka's disciple. The narrative of *Journey to the West* uses the first seven chapters to cover the monkey's story in the first five hundred years, in which he has been growing his power, completing heroic deeds, and causing trouble. About the five hundred years under the mountain, however, the narrative says nothing. Instead, it shifts from the miraculous encounters of the monkey in the mythical world to a six-chapter account of the historical world of the Tang emperor and Tripitaka, followed by the seventeen-year journey to India, which occupies the rest of the hundred-chapter book.

The five hundred years of captivity suspend Sun Wukong's miraculous deeds and set off the historical yet legendary story of the human Tripitaka, which, developing along its own biographical chronotope, intersects with the story of the Monkey King five chapters later. In other words, the five hundred years are important because it is there that the two types of chronotope braid together to form the ambivalent chronotopic structure of the book. In effect, the five hundred years under the mountain formulate a "threshold chronotope" for the Monkey King. Identified by Bakhtin as a motif chronotope of crisis and break in life, the threshold chronotope usually appears at a breaking point of life, occurring with a life-changing decision, during events such as falls, resurrections, and renewals. It presents a tightly circumscribed space, such as the threshold, staircase, the front hall, and corridor, literally or metaphorically a transitional space between two worlds. In the threshold chronotope, time is suspended, detached from the normal flow of biographical and historical time, and the threshold transition of what appears to be a long period always turns out to have lasted for only a few moments.[8] It is quite peculiar in this sense that the threshold transition from the magical to the historical in *Journey to the West* lasts for five hundred years. These five hundred years, however, are referred to but not discussed by the Monkey King, important but dismissed by the narrative—all the better to show how time is suspended in the threshold chronotope. In another light, the five-hundred-year threshold can be considered as an instance of time travel effected by the narrative.

It is no surprise that the five-hundred-year gap in Monkey's life becomes a place where almost all modern rewritings of the Monkey King story expand the narrative. In the two adaptations to which we will soon turn, the five-hundred-year threshold is connected to the portal of the protagonists' time travel. As the transitional stage of Sun Wukong's life and the liminal time-space between two worlds, it is a crucial bridge of the miraculous and the historical.

JOURNEY TO THE EAST/PAST: *THE LOST EMPIRE* AND *THE FORBIDDEN KINGDOM*

Both *The Lost Empire* and *The Forbidden Kingdom* are loosely based on the "Journey to the West" narrative, keeping the major characters and the basic plot, but the world where the story takes place is modernized. These two examples indicate that changes in the chronotopic framework can transform the meaning of the story altogether. While the modernization of the chronotope enables the story to speak more directly to its audience, it also alters the story significantly, and the authorization of such change reveals much about the sociohistorical world that allows such significant change to the narrative.

Significantly, the modernization of the chronotopic world in both texts is only partial. In both adaptations, while the Monkey King story remains in the past, a modern framework is added to the Monkey King—a change that showcases a white American protagonist. Thus, in both texts, a stark contrast between modern Western culture and the ancient Eastern culture is constructed. Both texts feature a contrast between a realistic and historical chronotope of the West and a stagnant mythical chronotope of the East.

The Lost Empire presents Nick Orton (played by Thomas Gibson) as the Tripitaka figure of the story. A "China scholar" turned businessman, Nick is recruited by Bodhisattva Guanyin (played by Bai Ling) to travel to a mythical China, which is located in Emperor Qin Shihuang's tomb, where he can release the Monkey King and help rescue the original copy of the book *Journey to the West.* Believed to be the only person who can defeat the demons who have been trying to destroy the original copy for the past five hundred years, Nick is tasked with bringing the book back to the modern world and, by doing so, saving the entire modern world. Although it is claimed that this is a world where all immortals and spirits of historical and literary figure of China forever stay, conveniently the historical Tripitaka, Xuanzang, does not, and the Monkey King and his team are desperately waiting for Nick to act as their teacher and leader in undertaking their important task. With the help of Guanyin and the team, Nick eventually accomplishes the mission and returns to his world.

Two significant diegetic transformations effected by Hwang in *The Lost Empire* are of interest. First, the American spatiotemporal framework bracketing the Monkey King story transposes the protagonist of the story: the white American Tripitaka takes center stage, overshadowing the Chinese Monkey King. Second, the modern framework of the story throws Chinese culture represented by the Monkey King story into the past, remaining static within a mythical chronotope. The combination of the superimposed chronotopes thus forms a new chronotope that operates according to an imperialist logic.

Nick's first accomplishment in the mythical China is to set free the Monkey King, who for five hundred years has been passively waiting for his help. Although the action of this part of the story comes from the original, in which Sun Wukong also passively waited for the help of Tripitaka, the relationship between Tripitaka and the Monkey King is reversed because of the change of the chronotopic framework. In the traditional *Journey to the West* narrative, Tripitaka is repeatedly rescued from peril by the Monkey King. In *The Lost Empire*, the monkey-saving-monk episodes are excluded, and the narrative focuses on Nick's heroic actions, setting the tone for the glorification of Nick instead of the Monkey King. In terms of the chronotope, the relationship between the chronotope of the human and that of the immortal is reversed. Instead of the magical universe framing the human Tripitaka's trip, in this version it is the human's trip bracketing the fictional and mythical world of Sun Wukong. In this new structure of time, Nick's action is effectively miraculous: in a few moments, Nick is able to correct a mistake that in the past five hundred years no one in the mythical world can deal with, not even the gods and goddesses. The ambivalent structure of the peaceful coexistence of the two chronotopes is replaced by a structure that demonstrates a clear hierarchy, with Nick's chronotope bestriding that of the Monkey King.

It is ironic to consider that *The Lost Empire* is also titled "The Monkey King," when all the Monkey King does in the miniseries is wait, complain, watch Guanyin teaching Nick kung fu, and fight alongside Nick as his backup. The Monkey King's transformation into a sidekick is completed by the change of purpose and means of the journey. In *Journey to the West*, the journey is a pilgrimage to retrieve the religious sutras, and at the end of the journey all five members of the team attain enlightenment. *The Lost Empire* turns this pilgrimage into a journey of a single man in the mystical oriental world: a dreamlike experience, a break from the ordinary routines of his everyday life. Whereas in *Journey to the West,* Tripitaka travels along his biographical trajectory at a human pace, in *The Lost Empire* Nick becomes the figure who takes the magical trip, a miraculous transition from one world to another.

Nick's adventure takes on the chronotope of "adventure time." According to Bakhtin, adventure time in the ancient literary genre of the Greek romance features an extratemporal hiatus between two moments of biographical time. The adventure itself takes place in the gap, or the hiatus, between the two adjacent biographical moments, so the entire story is not contained in the biographical time-sequence. Instead, "it lies outside biographical time; it changes nothing in the life of the heroes, and introduces nothing into their life. . . . All the events . . . that fill this hiatus are a pure digression from the normal course of life; they are excluded from the kind of real duration in which additions to a normal biography are made."[9] This is almost an exact description of Nick's trip, a detour from the normal progress of his life, and yet it does not affect the time and progress of his life. When he returns from his trip to China, his life goes on and is even improved.

As Bakhtin states of a typical Greek romance, "No matter where one goes in the world of the Greek romance, with all its countries and cities, its buildings and works of art, there are absolutely no indications of historical time, no identifying traces of the era."[10] It is in a legendary, nonhistorical place where the detour trip for the hero and heroine of Greek romance takes place. Nick's trip resembles what Bakhtin describes as typical of Greek romance, except the China in which that Nick travels is at the same time extratemporal *and* historical. It is as if the narrative of the story needs China to be an extratemporal world, yet it gives in to the strong temptation of the idea of the exotic oriental country staying in the past.

Nick's trip starts when Nick follows Guanyin into Emperor Qin Shihuang's tomb through a secret gate. Surviving booby traps thanks to his knowledge of Chinese classics, he falls into the world right in front of the Monkey King locked underneath the mountain. The "fall" indicates both a spatial and temporal relationship between where Nick comes from and where he travels to. Temporally, although no time machine is involved, apparently he has fallen to a place in the past. There exists a clear contrast between Nick the modern person and his noncontemporaries in the mythical world—located in a tomb, an indicator of death and the past. Modern figures and figures from near history cannot be found here. When Nick has just arrived, the world in the tomb should also be set in the twenty-first century, as Guanyin has told Nick that the evil immortals have been trying to destroy the sixteenth-century book for five hundred years. However, no trace of the present is present. Nick is the only person to be seen in contemporary clothes, which strengthens the contrast between Nick as the only white man and the surrounding world. In addition, there is also a lack of historical differentiation between characters from different historical periods; time has collapsed as a dimension. Gods, spirits, or fictional characters from historical times thousands of years apart are all living together simultaneously, or extratemporally, residing in buildings and clad in clothing both ancient and ahistorical. As an example of the extratemporality, the film has confused Emperor Qin Shihuang and Emperor Huangdi as the same person, although historically there is about two thousand years between the legendary creator of Chinese culture Huangdi and the first emperor of China Qin Shihuang.[11]

Nick's descent into the tomb clearly indicates the spatial and hierarchical relationship between the two worlds. The moment he falls into the mystical world, he is addressed as the "scholar from above" and considered also the saver of modernity and the entire world because, according to the narrative, modernity will collapse if the book is destroyed. His "fall" from the status of an ordinary businessman to the savior of the world also indicates a hierarchical structure between the above and below. During the journey, he enjoys the special honor of Goddess Guanyin's company, as well as a special audience with the Jade Emperor to determine the fate of the book. Returning to his own world, he still remains the businessperson/China scholar, while the goddess, one of the most important religious figures in China and other Asian countries, is transformed into a professor of literature to be his companion, someone of equal social standing with Nick.

The relation of the two temporal spaces—present versus past, above versus below—is also indicated by a short intrusion of Shu and other demons in the human world. Via this trip from below to above, Shu, one of those who have been working on destroying the book, was trying an alternative way to destroy modernity: breaking everything modern so that the world could return to the past. Shu's intrusion is vanquished by Nick with the help of Guanyin. Apparently, the threat from the ahistorical world of the mythical China to stop the progress of time in the modern world is absolutely not allowed by the narrative, while on the other hand, Nick is invited for a trip into the ahistorical world, to join the play with time there. Evidently, between the two chronotopes, the order of time in one world (the realistic world) is treated with great respect, while in the world down below time is compressed entirely, its (dis)order suppressed. In short, the past, the below, the backward, the unenlightened, untimely, nonmodern, and unprogressive, should be sacrificed for the sake of modernity.

A "threshold chronotope" is clearly at work to maintain this logic. Nick's journey started at a time when the demons were already partially successful in interfering with time in his biographical world: buildings started to fall apart and clocks clicked backward. At the critical moment, he takes the trip to defeat the demons in defense of modern civilization. When he returns, both his personal problems and the world crisis are solved. The narrative has all the features of the "threshold chronotope" discussed earlier. The secret doorway that

Guanyin shows to Nick located in the tomb of Qin Shihuang with the terra-cotta warriors is the liminal space in which Nick undergoes a radical transformation of his identity, from a businessman to a rescuer of the world. One can also say that the China within the tomb itself is the threshold, both temporally (via collapsed time) and spatially (within the enclosed tomb). *The Lost Empire* has in this sense transformed the entire "Journey to the West" narrative as the threshold chronotope for Nick, making the journey into a critical moment for his transformation and fulfilment.

This threshold chronotope accomplishes the imperial hierarchy between the two worlds discussed. Nick's trip follow the same pattern as many characters in nineteenth-century European literature, such as Honoré de Balzac's Charles Grandet, who leaves home at a time of personal crisis and returns home rich by means of exploitation in the Third World. For Nick, his personal crisis is his recent divorce and his lost confidence in his career as a professor of literature. His trip to China and to the Tombs of Qin Shihuang was originally intended as cultural exploitation: making money by means of transforming the tombs into a theme park. The encounter of Nick with Guanyin changes the nature of the journey, which establishes Nick as the savior of the world. In the end, Nick returns to his world with honor and recognition of his contribution to the world of literature, as well as a new love, found when he meets Guanyin's double, a college professor specializing in *Journey to the West*. At his first sight of her, when Nick addresses Professor Liu as "Goddess," the latter expresses her appreciation to Nick by likening him to a "scholar from above."

Besides creating a transformative opportunity for Nick by making a threshold chronotope of an entombed China-in-stasis, the imperialist logic also features a channel and direction where objects and subjects are transmitted, exemplified by the romantic relationship between Nick and Guanyin that develops during the adventure, and Guanyin's migration from the mythical China to the human world at the end. Nick's adventure is actually twofold: the adventure to save the book becomes intermingled with the romantic adventure involving a goddess who holds an important position in this other world. The romantic connection between Guanyin and Nick develops from the very first moment that the two meet, when Guanyin quickly gets drunk and initiates an intimate encounter with Nick. This romantic and sexual feeling plays an important role in Nick's world-saving adventure, as it is owing to this connection that Nick dares to follow

Guanyin through the portal to the China within the tomb. The film structures it in such a way to seem as if only via sexual attraction can Guanyin earn Nick's trust, and only through a romantic relationship can they solve the problem of both worlds. The relationship between Guanyin and Nick, in this sense, represents the relationship of the two worlds for which they each stand. Therefore at the end, when the highly sexualized figure of Guanyin migrates from the mythical world to Nick's world, the hero of the story only needs to sit back and enjoy the victory in incorporating the other world into his own empire. Incidentally, the sexualized representation of a bodhisattva contradicts the central Buddhist belief that desire is the root of suffering and therefore should be abandoned. Nick has succeeded in converting a most influential goddess of Buddhism into a believer in love, and thus while rectifying the catastrophic situation he has also imposed a new order upon the other world.

Speaking in an interview about the motivation to include white leads in ethnic films, Hwang stated that "producers and studio executives feel that Caucasian audiences are better able to 'relate' to a Caucasian character," but he also admitted that such a point of view is "increasingly less emphasized in recent years, as audiences become increasingly diverse, and foreign income represents a larger percentage of a film's total income."[12] Ironically, in 2008 when another Monkey King film, *The Forbidden Kingdom,* was made, a white male was chosen as the lead once again, and he accomplishes a lot more than the "stand-in for the viewer." Exactly like Nick Orton, Jason Tripitakas in *The Forbidden Kingdom* is the savior of the Monkey King, a rescuer of the catastrophic situation in that world, and by means of the trip has fixed his own problems and developed a romance on the side. Although the characters in this film are less Fu Manchu–like in their appearance, the chronotope shares the same imperialist logic as in *The Lost Empire.*

Showcasing the first collaboration of Jet Li and Jackie Chan, *The Forbidden Kingdom* predictably devotes much attention to the fight scenes, but the role of the American teen Jason is unquestionably that of the lead. Resembling *The Lost Empire*, the movie also adds a modern historical chronotopic bracket to the Monkey King story and by changing the chronotope has transformed the "Journey to the West" narrative into a chapter in Jason's bildungsroman.

Jason Tripitakas is a kung fu–obsessed white American teenager from Boston who is sent to a mythical China to deliver a golden staff he has found in a pawn shop to its proper owner, the Monkey King. His last name, Tripitakas, reveals his role in the mythical world. Although unprepared, unwilling, and appearing to be incompetent in every aspect, like Nick in *The Lost Empire*, Jason is nevertheless the chosen one, the "Seeker" according to the prophecy, the only person who can save the world from a devastating situation. The trip also engages liberating the Monkey King as well as developing a romantic relationship with the female lead from the other world, Golden Sparrow.

The Monkey King is put in an even more inert position in this movie. Transformed into a stone statue by the Jade Warlord five hundred years earlier, he has been passively waiting for Jason to bring the golden staff back to him. It is only when Jason, with the help of the Silent Monk (Jet Li) and Lu Yan (Jackie Chan), throws the golden staff at the statue that the Monkey King is able to break free from the curse and become an activated fighter again. The motionless stone statue of Monkey, reactivated by the magic touch from Jason, forms a chronotopic image that is exemplary of the idyllic spatiotemporal world of China where Jason travels.

Jason's idyllic China presents beautiful scenery and a world that clearly exists somewhere in the past, even though there is no time indicator except the mentioning of the five hundred years that the Monkey King has waited as a statue. It is as if time stopped moving forward when the Monkey King was frozen into a statue. Bakhtin's explanation of the idyllic chronotope features an organic fastening-down of events to a place. In an idyll, the life of generations displays a unity of place and lack of boundaries between individual lives and various phases. The imaginary China in *The Forbidden Kingdom* features exactly such a fastened time-space. Compared to the dead time in the world of the tomb in *The Lost Empire*, time in Jason's China is tied up, frozen like the statue of the Monkey King. When the magic touch of the magic staff reactivates Monkey near the end of the movie, the world that has been interned within the unseen walls of time and space is set back in motion. The idyllic world in *The Forbidden Kingdom* demonstrates a clearly confined chronotope even though it is not located in a tomb as in *The Lost Empire*.

In terms of the spatial and temporal hierarchy, the idyllic China is also structured as staying below and behind, indicated by Jason's entry to this world via falling. Running away from hooligans chasing him in Boston's Chinatown, Jason jumps down from the top of a building and finds himself waking up in a bed in a farmhouse, with an old couple in old-time attire speaking a language unknown to him; thus starts his journey. Upon finishing the task of his journey, ready to go home, Jason requests help from the Jade Emperor, who gives him a magic blow of air. Jason then floats, passing high clouds, and wakes up lying in a street in Boston's Chinatown, exactly where he jumped down a moment earlier. The falling down to China and flying back to Boston suggests the higher location of Jason's home world relative to the imaginary China, although the entry and return also resembles that of a dream.

Just like Nick's trip in *The Lost Empire*, Jason's journey to the exotic other world is again in the name of doing a favor for that world, but at the same time it is a big favor for himself. Jason loves Chinese kung fu movies but has no actual fighting skills; he is bullied by the bigger Hispanic boys and timid in front of the girls. The journey is an experience by means of which he grows as both fighter and lover. In the imaginary China he finds the Silent Monk and the "immortal" Lu Yan both to be his kung fu teachers, who train him and assist him in fighting against the evil Jade Warlord. At his eventual return, Jason finds himself a kung fu master, defeating the hooligans with the skills he has obtained in the other world. Jason's "threshold chronotope" takes place during the fall, through which he finds his resurrection. It is in the seemingly open but actually tightly circumscribed time-space of China that he accomplishes the important task of destroying the Jade Warlord for the other world and simultaneously changing his own life for himself.

Parallel to *The Lost Empire*, Jason's romantic connection with Golden Sparrow is intertwined with his mission as rescuer and learner. This interaction is actually predicted by the owner of the pawn shop in Chinatown at the beginning of the film: "[You are] another white boy learning kung fu: kick the ass, get the girl." The double mission of kicking the ass and getting the girl has been too daunting for Jason until after his trip in the fantasized China, where he has acted as their hero, fixing their problem. When his status as the hero is established, he has also earned the heart of the girl. In fact, Jason's interaction with Golden Sparrow has changed the girl's sense of subjectivity altogether. Throughout the journey, she refers to herself in the third person, yet at the last moment of her life, when Jason has fulfilled her wish to kill the Jade Warlord with her jade hairpin, Golden Sparrow utters her final and only words in the first person: "I thank you." This formation of her subjective view of self is realized because of Jason and in relation to Jason. The expression "I thank you" can also represent the relationship between the fantasized China and Jason's home world. At the end of the film, after Jason defeats the hooligans, "Golden Sparrow" is introduced into Jason's biographical world. The girl comments on his courage, ready to see a relationship develop. Whereas Nick's journey in *The Lost Empire* results in transformation, Jason's experience in *The Forbidden Kingdom* serves as an initiation.

In short, the above versus below, present versus past relationship between the worlds and the prominent savior's role shifting from the Monkey King to the white American protagonist demonstrates the same imperialist chronotope in *The Forbidden Kingdom* as is seen in *The Lost Empire*. The important changes in the protagonists' lives are accomplished and only accomplishable by means of an exploitive journey in a mythicized other world, which leads to personal and material success upon their return to their original Western contexts.

The chronotope as lens is a useful tool for analyzing cross-cultural adaptations, as the focus on space-time allows a direct comparison that does not rely heavily on culturally specific forms or tropes. For free adaptations like *The Lost Empire* and *The Forbidden Kingdom*, in which direct comparison of the major characters and the story with the original source material is seemingly impractical, the chronotopic approach shows its strength. As we have seen, the change in chronotope in these texts is closely related to the altered image of the character, and the transformed message of the story. The switching of roles between the Monkey King and Tripitaka in these texts represents the change of position of their spatiotemporal worlds in relation to each other. These changes reveal the politics of representation behind these adaptations, pointing out the dangerous imperial and orientalist messages behind the seemingly benign portrayal.

CHAPTER 6

Of Monkey, Human, and God

The Performance of Asian American Identity

The Monkey King has been a favorite of Asian American writers and artists, who have created new fictional, graphic, musical, and cinematic stories based on this character to represent the difficulties that Chinese Americans encounter as a marginalized social group in the United States. The relationship between the trickster and ethnic self-representation is a topic that has long been explored by literary scholars. There is a recognized analogy between the trickster and writers of marginal social positions, as they both share the task of positively negotiating between multiple cultural systems.[1] While the trickster and writers at the margins may be comparable, it is difficult to know the extent to which trickster strategies can be used successfully to create spaces in cultural borderlands or even outside white patriarchal authority.[2] When considering rewritings of the Monkey King as representations of the mediation between and among conflicting value systems, one cannot overlook the fact that Sun Wukong is subjugated by the Buddha and has become a loyal follower of Tripitaka. Sun Wukong's submission and conversion is crucial for the adaptation and also a central issue for the examination of the role of this particular trickster in Asian American self-representation.

Since the 1950s, the study of "performance" has expanded from theatrical performance alone to a broader field that includes cultural performances such as rituals, dance, and political events.[3] Sex, gender, and sexuality are described as performative instead of being predetermined essences.[4] Following gender theorist Judith Butler's *Gender Trouble*, scholarly works have developed a performative approach to deessentialize identity formation, demonstrating that identities such as race, gender, and class are historically and politically formulated rather than biologically based.[5] The use of the Monkey King image in self-representation is also a performance of one's identity, with the Monkey King as a mask. In addition to taking place onstage, this performative action can be expressed through media such as graphic novel or films, using the Monkey King to tell one's own story.

Stage and ritual performances of the Monkey King story raise complicated issues related to adaptation as performance. For instance, ritual performances were used by the Boxers during the Boxer Rebellion (Yihetuan) to invite gods such as Sun Wukong to enter their bodies in order to acquire his power. One contemporary example is the play *Day Job, Opera Dreams* produced by the Chinese Theatre Works Ensemble, which combines the tale of the Monkey King with the experiences of Peking Opera artists in the United States.[6] During the performance, the actor who plays the Monkey King, while still in costume, narrates the story of his personal experience as a new immigrant, recently moved to New York City. Other actors also share their stories about immigrant life, as trained traditional opera performers who must work day jobs at nail salons and takeout restaurants to feed themselves.[7] Such interweaving of personal narrative with the traditional opera performance borrows power from the Monkey King figure while using the transformative story of the monkey to represent the performers' experiences.

Asian American artist Fred Ho has also used the image of Monkey King in his creative work. He composed a score to accompany what would become a synthesized stage musical production called *Journey beyond the West: The New Adventures of Monkey*, a fusion of Chinese folk music and opera, African American music, martial art dance, and allegorical reinvention of the *Journey to the West.* The creative development of *Journey beyond the West* resulted in the formation of the Monkey Orchestra (formerly the Journey beyond the West Orchestra) and two albums, *Monkey: Part One* released in 1996 and *Monkey: Part Two* released in 1997.[8] In the liner notes, Ho admits that he has freely adapted the Chinese classic and has "conceived of some very new story/plot twists and conceptually refashioned it to be a radical allegory about the struggles of Chinese Americans and oppressed nationalities."[9] The most striking difference is in the ending, "Act 4: The Journey Home—The Struggle for Heaven on Earth." The titles of the music speak volumes. After their "Arrival in

India," the pilgrims learn that heaven has colonized and corrupted the monkeys of the Flower-Fruit Mountain. In "Monkey Decides to Return Home 'to Right the Great Wrongs,'" Monkey finds that his home has been transformed into a veritable hell. He works to assist and lead uprisings and rebellions, and soon "The Revolution Begins/ The Liberation of Flower and Fruit Mountain" follows. With the help of his allies, including "Pig with Coyote (the Native American Trickster), Eshu (the African trickster monkey), and guerrilla gorillas and other tricksters from many cultures, Tang Seng with a contingent of Buddhist Shaolin monks and nuns, and the Ogre with a group of wretched humans including the white-haired woman warrior and a troop of witches," Monkey wins the victory of "The Mighty Battle (the Struggle of All Struggles)!"[10] The carnivalesque stage with clear reference to Maxine Hong Kingston's *The Woman Warrior* and Henry Louis Gates Jr.'s *Signifying Monkey* speaks to the nature of this Afro-Asian "trickster jazz."[11] Ho admits the ambiguity of the allegorical meaning of the revolution, but there is no doubt that he is making use of the multivalent nature of Monkey and his story to compose the musical story that he calls "Chinese American."[12]

Maxine Hong Kingston is another signifying artist. Her novel *The Woman Warrior* (1976) retells the Mulan story as well as other traditional Chinese tales to relate to Asian American experience, while the protagonist of *Tripmaster Monkey: His Fake Book* (1989), Wittman Ah Sing, considers himself the Chinese Monkey King in America. Set in the 1960s, the novel narrates the encounters of a college graduate in the San Francisco area seeking to produce a stage show of his own. The book is replete with allusions to American pop culture, Western literature, and Chinese tradition, and it is from a mixture of all these elements that Wittman brings forth his own show in the end. The performance, directed by Wittman at a local community center, is not a one-man show, although it ends with Wittman's monologue on the closing day. The lengthy epic show is a carnivalesque play, performed by everyone he met along the way, a hodgepodge of his retelling of classical works including *Romance of Three Kingdoms* and *Water Margin*, together with exhibits of Asian American history and culture. Performing his play onstage is the means for Wittman to create community, and it is by means of performing Asian American identity and enacting community that he can deal with the problems he has with his identity, developing a panethnic consciousness.[13] Wittman's identification with the Monkey King well fits with this inclusive identity.

AMERICAN BORN CHINESE

Gene Luen Yang's graphic novel *American Born Chinese* (2006) illustrates the identity struggles of a Chinese American schoolboy through a retelling of the Monkey King story and resculpting of the Monkey King image. In addition to being the first graphic book ever nominated for the National Book Award in the young people's literature category, it won numerous book awards, including the 2007 Michael L. Printz Award for young-adult literature. In 2016, Yang was also awarded a MacArthur Fellowship, or "Genius Grant," for his contribution in "confirming comics' place as an important creative and imaginative force within literature, art, and education."

Although Yang's adaptation is only loosely based on the well-known Chinese source material, a comparative approach helps understand the complex issues of cross-ethnic representation, Asian American identity, and ethnic autobiographical writing. Adaptations can be seen as double-voiced discourses. In this case, Gene Yang's Monkey King story takes into account and refers to the *Journey to the West* story, and although the latter remains outside of Yang's text, it nonetheless influences Yang's story, questions it, negotiates with it, and determines to some degree its meaning. Without fully acknowledging the double-voiced nature of the retelling, and giving due consideration to both voices and their relationship, the meaning of Yang's story may not be fully appreciated.

The new Monkey King image in Yang's version evokes questions related to stereotype. In *The Location of Culture*, when discussing the concept of "fixity" as a mode of representation in the discourse of colonialism, postcolonial theorist Homi Bhabha identifies a process of ambivalence that is central to stereotype. Fixity always "connotes rigidity and an unchanging order as well as disorder, degeneracy and daemonic repetition," while stereotype likewise "vacillates between what is always 'in place,' already known, and something that must be anxiously repeated . . . as if the essential duplicity of the Asiatic or the bestial sexual license of the African that needs no proof, can never really, in discourse, be proved."[14] This process of ambivalence is central to the stereotype, and the recognition of "the stereotype as an ambivalent mode of knowledge and power" suggests that the point of intervention in reading colonial discourse "should shift from the ready recognition of images as positive or negative, to an understanding of the *processes of subjectification* made possible (and plausible) through stereotypical discourse."[15]

What Bhabha has listed as ambivalent is not strictly a process of ambivalence, for the fact that the stereotype is "already known" is not contradictory to the fact that it needs to be "always repeated." Rather, because it has been always repeated, it is therefore always "in place," with no need for proof. Repetition is the mode in which stereotype functions, and it is precisely through repetition that the stereotype remains and works as a stereotype. In *American Born Chinese*, the character of Chin-Kee—as well as the Monkey King—created by Gene Yang in its own way repeats stereotypes, but this repetition is not intended to ensure that the stereotype stays "in place"; instead, this image is created in an effort to understand the effectiveness of the stereotype and hence to replace it.

American Born Chinese is comprised of three distinct story lines that intertwine throughout the graphic novel. The first narrative is a retelling of the Monkey King stories, based on, but distinctly altered from, *Journey to the West.* The Monkey King narrative is broken up by the other two narrative arcs: the fictionalized autobiography of the author's own coming-of-age story, here narrated by the character Jin, and an allegorical description of a Caucasian boy, David, who is haunted by a Chinese cousin, Chin-Kee, who represents all of the negative stereotypes attributed to Asians in American culture. The three story lines eventually converge, as the reader discovers that Chin-Kee is actually an incarnation of the Monkey King and David is a transformation of Jin.

Discussing the origins of *American Born Chinese*, Yang states: "Like most Chinese children, I first heard the Monkey King's exploits as bedtime stories from my mom. Almost before I started drawing comics, I knew I wanted to do a comic book adaptation of the Monkey King. . . . I eventually came up with the idea to use the Monkey King as a lens through which to reflect on my own experience as an Asian-American."[16] To the author, the Monkey King is part of the Chinese culture in which he grew up, the heritage he would like to take over and pass on. However, the story he loved as a child, in order to better reflect the experience of the Asian American, had to go through the process of rewriting, taking the form of a different story, with new attributes such as the parallel structure between the story lines of the Monkey King and Jin, the shared theme of transformation among all three lines, and the intricate relationship between the major characters of the book.

The three narrative lines of *American Born Chinese* braid into one another. The book alternates between the three lines, beginning with a section about the Monkey King and ending with the Chin-Kee story merging into the Jin narrative line, when the Monkey King walks into the picture, lining all three stories up. The Monkey King serves as the central figure of the entire book and has either direct or metaphorical /metonymical presence in all three lines.

The most conspicuous digression from *Journey to the West* might be the reconstruction of the Buddha figure. The Buddha is the highest authority, or a god on the highest level of the hierarchy of beings in *Journey to the West*, and the most apparent metaphorical meaning of the original book has to do with the conversion to Buddhism. Yang has changed the Buddha into the Western Judeo-Christian God, given him the name Tze-Yo-Tzuh ("Zi You Zhe" in standard pinyin spelling), and thus has changed the mythological framework of the entire story.[17] The transformation of the Buddha into the Judeo-Christian God indicates the author's emphasis on the social significance of this change in the context of the new story. Accordingly, the Monkey King's religious identity is changed from that of a Buddhist monk to that of a Christian convert. As confirmed by Yang himself, the purpose of this change is to better represent the Asian American experience, to "give the entire story an Asian-American mythological foundation": "I did this to draw out the similarities and differences between the two worldviews. I hope that to someone who is familiar with the original story, my version offers a contrast that says something meaningful about the similarities and differences between Asians and Asian-Americans." [18] Yang's approach confirms the importance of juxtaposing the original and the rewriting in the study of adaptations, to point out the "similarities and differences between the Asians and Asian-Americans," or between the two "worlds" to which the original and rewriting "discourses" respectively refer, in the Bakhtinian sense. Yang intends his rewriting as a "double-voiced discourse," so that the two voices of the original Monkey King story and this new story create tension and new meaning.

THE DOUBLE-VOICED MONKEY: THE IDENTITY CONCERN

Yang's Monkey King story is loosely based on the first fourteen chapters of *Journey to the West,* including events such as Monkey's birth, the havoc in heaven, the subjugation of Monkey by the Buddha, and Monkey's conversion by Tripitaka. In *Journey to the West*, the turning point of Monkey's story—his subjugation—occurs in the seventh chapter, when the Taoist deities turned to the Buddha for help in subduing the monkey demon. The Buddha proposes a wager with Monkey: should the monkey be able to somersault clear of the Buddha's palm, he will be granted what he wants, which is to replace the Jade Emperor. Accepting the offer, Monkey jumps with his entire capacity and finds himself at the end of the world, where there is nothing but five massive pillars. Having left his personal marks there, Monkey jumps back to the Buddha's hand, only to find that the five pillars are actually the Buddha's fingers. At this point the Buddha transforms his hand into the Five Phases Mountain and suppresses Monkey underneath it.[19]

The contest of escape and reach between the Monkey King and the Buddha remains unchanged in *American Born Chinese*, but besides the replacement of the Buddha figure by an old man who introduces himself as "Tze-Yo-Tzuh," the relationship of the two opposing figures is also altered. Although it is still a game about whether Monkey can run away from the reach of Tze-Yo-Tzuh, it is no longer a wager, and the exchanges between the two become stressful conversation rather than the humorous boasts and mockery in *Journey to the West.* The conversations become the focus of the incident, despite the graphical form of the book, informing the nature of the battle: one that is of discursive importance.

The first meeting of the Buddha and Monkey in *Journey to the West* begins with the latter questioning the former's authenticity. When the Buddha gives an order for the two sides of the battle to cease so that he could talk to Monkey,

> [The Great Sage] approached [him] angrily and shouted with ill humor, "What region are you from, monk, that you dare stop the battle and question me?" Thatagata laughed and said, "I am Sakyamuni, the Venerable One from the Western Region of Ultimate Bliss. I have heard just now about your audacity, your wildness, and your repeated acts of rebellion against Heaven. Where were you born? When did you learn the Great Art? Why are you so violent and unruly?"[20]

Apparently, in this exchange it is Monkey (identified as the Great Sage in the quotation) who has initiated his challenge to the patriarch, and the latter replies only very briefly before he turns back to the Great Sage to ask about his origin. The Monkey King's response becomes a formal declaration of his rebellion to the existent order in heaven, of his intent to upset the hierarchy:

> The Great Sage said, "I was
> Born of Earth and Heaven, immortal magically fused,
> An old monkey hailing from the Flower-Fruit Mount.
> I made my home in the Water-Curtain Cave;
> I sought friend and teacher to gain the Mystery Great.
> Perfected in the many arts of ageless life,
> I learned to change in ways boundless and vast.
> Too narrow the space I found on that mortal earth;
> I set my mind to live in the Green Jade Sky.
> In Divine Mists Hall none should long reside,
> For king may follow king in the reign of man.
> If might is honor, let them yield to me,
> Only he is hero who dares to fight and win!"[21]

In replying, the Buddha "laughed aloud in scorn," addressed the Monkey King as "only a monkey who happens to become a spirit," essentially in the monkey's own words, and reproached him for his blasphemy. Undaunted, the Monkey King boasted of his powers, prompting the Buddha to propose the wager.[22]

A few points in this part of *Journey to the West* should be underscored for the purpose of comparison. When the Monkey King declared his battle against heaven, his purpose was no less than attaining the highest seat in the heavenly empire. Although the heavens did not want to give the Monkey King real power, they had been quite generous when assigning him titles, first "Supervisor of Imperial Stables" and then "the Great Sage, Equal to Heaven." Though demanding to be no less than the Jade Emperor himself, Sun Wukong also admitted, in good humor, that he was an "old monkey." In other words, he was at the same time the Great Sage and a monkey. Although the Great Sage is a self-proclaimed "hero," the style of his speech is humorous and lighthearted, which is in agreement with the style in which the whole story is narrated.

The Monkey King story in *American Born Chinese,* also focusing on the havoc in heaven and the monkey's conversion, diverges from *Journey to the West* in all of these aspects. In Yang's version, the Monkey King is not so much declaring a war against heaven as claiming himself as "The Great Sage, Equal of Heaven." The "Great Sage" in this case is only a self-proclaimed title, never one assigned to the monkey. By asserting himself as the "Great Sage" and assuming a large form, the Monkey King refuses to accept the fact that he is a monkey and will not allow others to call him a monkey either. Tze-Yo-Tzuh's purpose is to convince the Monkey King that he is indeed a monkey, and he proves this to be so by defeating the Monkey King's challenge and imprisoning him under the mountain. However, it is by the transformation into a much larger form that the Monkey King is restrained underneath the mountain. To himself, he is still the Great Sage over the five-hundred-year period. It is only when he ceases using the false form and referring to himself as the Great Sage that he is able to win his freedom from the rock. The Monkey King is portrayed, both verbally and visually, as a warrior who is dealing with a matter as important as his own identity. The entire encounter between the Monkey King and Tze-Yo-Tzuh is depicted as a solemn and serious battle about the essential nature of the Monkey King.

In brief, all the changes made to the Monkey King story in *American Born Chinese* are related to the Monkey King's identity as monkey or not-monkey. The identity concern can be traced to the very beginning of the book, with a new story of the havoc in heaven. Trying to enter a dinner party for deities in heaven, the Monkey King finds himself rejected at the front gate by the guard, who claims, "You may be a king—you may even be a deity—but you are still a monkey."[23] Being called a "monkey" by the guard humiliates the Monkey King deeply. In response, he creates an upheaval, unsettles the party, and beats up the guard and guests. The human-versus-monkey division and confrontation is much sharper than that in *Journey to the West*, where Monkey's dissatisfaction in heaven is based on his social status rather than his monkey identity itself. In the Chinese classic, the upheaval that he produces in heaven is more an unintended mistake than a purposeful action, all beginning from the mischievous theft of the celestial wine and food from the banquet and then of Laozi's elixir when he was drunk. Waking up from his intoxication and realizing the severity of his mistakes, he returns to his Flower-Fruit Mountain but nevertheless continues his drinking party there with his guests, apparently planning to continue as Monkey King in style while giving up the position of "Great Sage."[24] In contrast, in *American Born Chinese*, the Monkey King's rebellion starts immediately at the moment when he is ejected from the party owing to his monkey identity. Subsequently, when he returns to his kingdom, he starts a reform, taking measures to refine the social behavior of the monkeys, such as getting rid of the smell of monkey fur and commanding all monkeys to wear shoes. He also trains himself in magical powers, including the ability to change his form freely. He adopts a giant form and issues an announcement that the Monkey King no longer exists but instead is now "the Great Sage, Equal of Heaven."[25] The encounters that follow with the Dragon King, Laozi, Yama, and the Jade Emperor are all to convince them that he is not a monkey but rather the "Great Sage."

The identity battle reaches its climax when the Monkey King and Tze-Yo-Tzuh meet. When the problem between the monkey and all other deities is relayed to Tze-Yo-Tzuh, the latter approaches the Monkey King, addressing him as "Little Monkey." The words strike at the core of the problem—this is exactly what the Monkey King could not accept. Replying, "I am not—a monkey," he sizes up Tze-Yo-Tzuh and, realizing that he is only half as large, adopts an even more gigantic form to match that of Tze-Yo-Tzuh. Tze-Yo-Tzuh responds to the Monkey King's denial by proclaiming his own authority:

> Silly little monkey.
>
> I created you. I say that you are a monkey. Therefore, you are a monkey.
>
> It was I who formed you within that rock.
>
> I am Tze-Yo-Tzuh. All that I have created—all of existence—forever remains within the reach of my hand. You I have created. Therefore, you can never escape my reach.[26]

Without the lubrication of humor, the relationship between the two is heated in comparison to that in *Journey to the West.* The Monkey King has no choice but to stand against Tze-Yo-Tzuh if he insists on the identity he is assuming. In response, the Monkey King takes action: he tries to fly from Tze-Yo-Tzuh's "reach," an effort to prove Tze-Yo-Tzuh's statement wrong. The wager between the Buddha and Monkey in *Journey to the West* here turns into a firm assertion of the power over a subject's identity on one side and denial and challenge of that power on the other. In this "double-voiced" text, with the "voice" of Monkey in *Journey to the West* pointing in a different direction, the "voice" of the Monkey King in the new story asserts, with more emphasis, his identity. Interestingly, the Monkey King shows his concern about his identity through action, in contrast to Tze-Yo-Tzuh, who demonstrates his power over the monkey's identity through words. The end of the battle makes clear that it is the one who dominates through the power of words and discourse who wins.

TZE-YO-TZUH: THE RELIGIOUS AND SOCIAL PATRIARCH

Tze-Yo-Tzuh's domination through the power of words indicates that he represents the dominant social discourse in American culture. Therefore, the conversion of the Monkey King not only means a change from Buddhism to Christianity, but it also refers to the suppression of minority social groups by the mainstream culture. In *American Born Chinese*, Tze-Yo-Tzuh has power over the Monkey King's identity, determining his place within society.

The role of Tze-Yo-Tzuh becomes clearer when we compare Monkey's failure to fly from the palm of Tze-Yo-Tzuh to the same scene in *Journey to the West*. In contrast to the benign character of Buddha, who tolerated the monkey's ignorance before giving him a serious lesson, Tze-Yo-Tzuh does not hesitate to spell out cruel reality to the Monkey King. In chapter 7 of *Journey to the West*, two short paragraphs state matter-of-factly how the Buddha put the monkey under the mountain of his palm, and how he put up a sign with the mantra "Om mani padme hum" on the mountain to secure the monkey's imprisonment. In *American Born Chinese*, however, what follows the Monkey King's fiasco is a prolonged moment of recognition of his failure and a lengthened celebration of Tze-Yo-Tzuh's victory, as pages 76 to 84 relate the ceremonially long moment when the Monkey King is named once again as a monkey, now confined under a mountain, representing the ultimate power of Tze-Yo-Tzuh, with His name sealed on top.[27]

Central to the new adaptation of the story is the question of why the Buddha is replaced by Tze-Yo-Tzuh, and what Tze-Yo-Tzuh stands for. As the ultimate authority to which all other deities have recourse through their emissaries, Tze-Yo-Tzuh, meaning "He who is," in the graphic novel takes the appearance of an old man in a maroon-red gown, with white hair, long beard, and a big cane, almost always accompanied by large speech balloons.[28] In contrast, the Monkey King never has much to say, especially when in front of Tze-Yo-Tzuh. With his words taking almost a bigger visual form than his physical figure, even more so than the figure of the monkey, Tze-Yo-Tzuh exists as a loud voice in the graphic book. The voice is depicted as deafening at the point when the monkey comes back from his trip "through the boundaries of reality itself." The voice of Tze-Yo-Tzuh here has taken over the physical form of Tze-Yo-Tzuh. It is also freed from the limits of a speech balloon. So what the monkey finds when he returns from the trip is the hand of control, and the voice that decides his fate: "The five pillars of gold you found at the end of all that is—those were the five fingers of my hand. Silly monkey. You were never out of my reach. You only fooled yourself." This stark white voice carved in the dark reality, together with the hand from which the monkey has never escaped, weigh heavily over the monkey's head, which in turn is squeezed into small squares and suppressed underneath.[29] The same flabbergasted face of the monkey appears five times on this page and continues onto the next page, emphasizing the strength and effect of the voice, which in the end wakes him up, admonishing the monkey to "walk with me."[30]

The authorial function of Tze-Yo-Tzuh is immediately evident: on the following page we see the monkey following Tze-Yo-Tzuh onto a narrow bridge, with the latter's speech balloons dominating each panel:

> "I am Tze-Yo-Tzuh. I was, I am, and I shall forever be. I have searched your soul, little monkey. I know your most hidden thoughts. I know when you sit and when you stand, when you journey and when you rest. Even before a word is upon your tongue, I have known it. My eyes have seen all your days.
>
> "Where did you think you could hide from me? Where can you flee from my presence?
>
> "I am in the heights of heaven—and the depths of the underworld. Even at the end of all that is, my hand is there, holding you fast. It was I who formed your inmost being, I who knit you together in the womb of that rock. I made you with awe and wonder, for wonderful are all of my works.
>
> "I do not make mistakes, little monkey. A monkey I intended you to be. A monkey you are."[31]

The weight of Tze-Yo-Tzuh's words is significant both in visual form and in content. The resemblance between these words and those of the Bible, together with the fact that his emissaries are the lion, the ox, the human, and the eagle, the "four living creatures" that in Christian tradition are connected to the authors of the four Gospels, identifies the ultimate authority in *American Born Chinese* as the Christian God instead of the Buddha in *Journey to the West*.[32] Later in the book, when the Monkey King appears before Jin as an emissary of Tze-Yo-Tzuh, the image treats the "Journey to the West" as

Figure 6.1. The Monkey King and the pilgrimage group meet with Baby Jesus. From *American Born Chinese* © 2006 by Gene Luen Yang. Reprinted by permission of First Second, an imprint of Roaring Brook Press, a division of Holtzbrinck Publishing Holdings Limited Partnership. All Rights Reserved.

a Christian experience recorded in the Bible: the search for Buddhist sutras becomes a tribute to the Child by the wise men from the East (figure 6.1).

In the bottom panel on page 215, the pilgrims from the East are seen bowing toward a baby child and his parents, a family that represents the Holy Family. The Monkey King is holding a large gold ingot in his hand, with both Pigsy and Sandy standing behind him and also holding presents. Interestingly, in the picture Baby Jesus is stretching out his hand, toward which the Monkey King reaches his arm. It seems that the completion of the journey is finalized by the touch of their hands, after which ceremonial gesture the Monkey King is entitled to "[stand] in His holy presence."[33] The two hand gestures on these two individual pages form a contrast. If Tze-Yo-Tzuh's hand, which catches the Monkey King and suppresses him under the mountain, signifies repression and domination, the hand of Baby Jesus represents acceptance and possibly gestures toward social uplift. The change from Tze-Yo-Tzuh's hand-mountain to Baby Jesus's gentle touch is tightly bound with the Monkey King's own transformation.

The establishment of Tze-Yo-Tzuh as the Judeo-Christian God as well as his performative words invite us to read the Monkey King's conversion allegorically. Besides religious conversion, the Monkey King's transformation also points at social and cultural adjustment. Social and cultural elements and codes permeate the book, represented through images of shoes, hairstyles, and meals. After the completion of the pilgrims' conversion, for example, a multicultural quality is indicated by the images in the panel of the pilgrims standing together with Tze-Yo-Tzuh.[34] In the picture, Tze-Yo-Tzuh stands in the middle, two of his Christian emissaries, the human and the lion, standing on the left, and the monk Wong Lai-Tsao (*American Born Chinese*'s version of Tripitaka) and Pigsy on the right, and the Monkey King in front. The images of the emissaries all strongly suggest Chinese culture. The monk remains in his monk attire. The lion emissary resembles a typical Chinese stone lion, and the human emissary, standing with palms together, resembles Guanyin, the Goddess of Compassion, or Avalokitesvara. The multicultural visual references point clearly to the multicultural aspect of the world, mythical, religious, and cultural, that Gene Yang chooses to represent.

REPRESENTATIONS OF THE CHINESE IN AMERICA

By replacing Buddha with Tze-Yo-Tzuh, Yang's story represents the Asian American experience in the pluralistic U.S. religious, cultural, and social environment. The Monkey King image well suits the representation of Chinese Americans, in both historical and contemporary contexts. Tze-Yo-Tzuh's treatment of the Monkey King echoes the simianization of the image of Chinese immigrants and Chinese Americans in U.S. popular culture, and the repressed/repressing relation between the monkey and the dominant discourse parallels the history of Chinese experience in the United States. Chinese immigrants to the United States, although an integrated part of the growth of economy and the empire, were rejected as demonic others, a process vividly characterized by the representation of the Chinese in American popular culture of the nineteenth and twentieth centuries, especially around the time of the Chinese Exclusion Act of 1882.[35] As with other ethnic groups in the United States, such as Irish immigrants, the Chinese image was simianized and demonized in propaganda cartoons, fiction, and other popular media. Yet in comparison to the image of the Irish, the representation of the Chinese was far more complex. The Chinese immigrant could be depicted as a huge nefarious monster, a baby-sized youngster, or a tiny unrecognizable figure with a long pigtail. He could be sickly, smart, or purely stupid. Always evil in nature owing to the otherness of his image, whether a monster or an incomprehensible dehumanized creature, the various "Chinaman" images are nonetheless dissimilar to one another.

Historical cartoons in the *Wasp* magazine are typical of how Chinese were represented in the late nineteenth century. The cartoons "What Shall We Do with Our Boys?" (*Wasp* 1882) and "The Coming Man" (*Wasp* 1881) are illustrative of the fear of Chinese monopoly of manufacturing industries.[36] In the former image (figure 6.2), the yellow-faced Chinaman with octopus hands is dealing with multiple businesses at the same time: tobacco, shoemaking, match, clothing, and printing, etc. The Chinaman takes over the low-paying, bottom-rank jobs, which makes him a lesser man, yet the excess arms and ability with which he handles these jobs render him superior, with powers that normal human lack. Because of the demonic ability of the Chinaman, the normal human-looking white workers outside on the right-hand side of the picture have lost their jobs. A police officer, taking one of these boys toward the jails in the distance, looks back at the idle white laborers with concern. The monstrous Chinese image, occupying two-thirds of the page, provides an overt explanation for the social problem that forms the title of the cartoon.

"The Coming Man" (figure 6.3) is a close-up of the same Chinaman, a monster in size, the bucktooth sticking out, "monopoly" imprinted in the huge hand, and of course the iconic pigtail flying in the air. His evil eyes look at all the industries he has safely covered under his grasp, a viperous smile at his mouth. In contrast to the yellow-faced Chinaman in Chinese clothing, putative white workers in normal work clothing are protesting at some distance, not even reaching his knee in size. Both of the images of the Chinese in these two cartoons, more than ten years apart in time, dehumanize the

Figure 6.2. Chinese man with multiple arms taking over every industry; idle white laborers are depicted on the right side, with jails in the distance. George Frederick Keller, illus., "What Shall We Do with Our Boys?," *Wasp*, March 3, 1882. Chinese in California Virtual Collection: Selections from the Bancroft Library, F850.W18 v. 8, Jan.–June 1882, No. 292: 136–37. Courtesy of The Bancroft Library, University of California, Berkeley.

Chinese, emphasizing the superhuman/nonhuman industrial ability as well as the animal connotation.

Besides being represented with monstrous features, the Chinese image is also often associated with that of a child. "The Three Troublesome Children" (figure 6.4) is such an example. In this cover illustration of an 1881 issue of the *Wasp*, Lady Columbia, representing the American people, is busy with three kids: the Chinese and the Mormon each sitting on her lap and the Indian at her feet. Apparently, these children are creating trouble for Columbia, who appears to be tired and lacking means, while the figure of Law, sitting in a rocking chair with the "Politics" column, does not provide any help. The three babies in this cartoon each represent political problems related to these ethnic groups, serious topics of discussion at the time. Like the Mormon and the Native American, the Chinese is here an uncivilized child who needs to be educated and tamed, a burden to Columbia, while his long pigtail taking a wild curl at the end gives a strong nonhuman connotation.

Figure 6.3. Giant figure of Chinese man spreading hand of monopoly over various industries. George Frederick Keller, illus., "The Coming Man: Allee samee 'Melican Man Monopoleeee," *Wasp*, May 20, 1881, 336. Chinese in California Virtual Collection: Selections from the Bancroft Library, F850.W18 v. 6, Jan.–June 1881 No. 251. Courtesy of The Bancroft Library, University of California, Berkeley.

Figure 6.4. Columbia trying to juggle the Chinese, Mormon, and Indian questions. George Frederick Keller, illus., "The Three Troublesome Children," *Wasp*, December 16, 1881. Chinese in California Virtual Collection: Selections from the Bancroft Library, F850.W18 v. 7, July–Dec. 1881, No. 281. Courtesy of The Bancroft Library, University of California, Berkeley.

Figure 6.5. Judge Lorenzo Sawyer of the U.S. Circuit Court dumping a barrel of Chinese men at the feet of California. Solly H. Walter, illus., "There's Millions in It," *Wasp*, 1888. Chinese in California Virtual Collection: Selections from the Bancroft Library, F850.W18, v. 21, July 21, 1888. Courtesy of The Bancroft Library, University of California, Berkeley.

In "There's Millions in It" (figure 6.5), Judge Lorenzo Sawyer of the U.S. Circuit Court is dumping a barrel of Chinese coolies at the feet of California, who holds her hands up in protest. The Chinese from the barrel are identically sketchy in feature—they are all tiny creatures wearing the same uniform. Minuscule sizes are often related to huge numbers in representations of Chinese of the time. Here, each Chinaman is pictured only as an infinitesimal part of the threatening whole, lacking human features and individuality.

These representations of Chinese—either as huge monsters or miniature figures—deform and dehumanize the Chinese so that they look starkly distinct from the image of a normal human. Such stereotypical images of the ethnic others on the one hand keep the social "others" alienated and rejected as outsiders from the normal human category, and on the other hand justify the suppression of the "others" should they try to cross the boundary. These images together point to an interesting feature of the demonization of the Chinese image in the United States: it is at the same time huge and small, supercapable and inept, holding contradictory qualities in one. It would not be hard for readers to build a visual connection between these historical caricatures and the Chin-Kee figure in *American Born Chinese*, who is created as a conglomerate of Chinese American stereotypes. However, there are similarly conflicting characteristics between Chin-Kee and the multivalent Monkey King.

The connection between the Chin-Kee image and that of the Monkey King is noticeable before the disclosure at the end of the book. Not only does the Monkey King's story resemble the experiences of the Asian American, but the fact that he is denied human identity and the problems he has over his body size also relate to Chinese images in historical popular culture. If the image of Chin-Kee is a representation of the racial stereotype inscribed by the dominant discourse, the Monkey King in this context is a self-representation with an effort to both reflect such racial representation and to reflect its influence over the subject.

CHIN-KEE: FIXITY AND TRANSFORMATION OF STEREOTYPE

In his discussion of the character's development, Yang notes that Cousin Chin-Kee is "yanked . . . straight out of American pop culture."[37] He gives examples such as a 2001 six-panel strip by American political cartoonist Pat Oliphant, the 1984 film *Sixteen Candles*, and

Figure 6.6. Gene Yang's drawing of a character resembling Chin-Kee in his second-grade notebook. From notebook by Gene Yuen Yan, which appeared online at http://firstsecondbooks.com/uncategorized/gene_yang_origi_2/. All Rights Reserved.

a 2007 *American Idol* performance. In Yang's words, "Every time Asian America thinks it's finally time to breathe easy, the doorbell rings and we find Cousin Chin-Kee on the doorstep with a piece of take-out box luggage in each hand."[38]

The Chin-Kee image is so powerful that he exists not only in pop culture, in the mainstream representation of the Asian American, but he also lives in Yang's own life, under his own pen. He first drew a cartoon image resembling Chin-Kee while in the second grade (figure 6.6), apparently picking the story up from the cultural environment. A schoolboy at the time, unaware of racial discrimination in the stereotypical image targeted at himself, he drew the image because it was "funny."

Comparing his early creation of Chin-Kee to Jeff Smith's *Fone Bone and Company*, which was first created when Smith was in kindergarten, Yang states: "In many ways, Cousin Chin-Kee is my Bone. He's a character conceived in childhood who's stayed with me ever since, consciously or not. . . . *American Born Chinese* is an exploration of WHY Cousin Chin-Kee is my Bone."[39] Thus the creation and exploration of the Chin-Kee image has an autobiographical element for the author, similar to that of the Monkey King image. One might say that the author created a new Monkey King in order to fully understand Chin-Kee. The Monkey King is on the one hand a self-portrait and on the other hand related to Chin-Kee, a distorted mirror image. Chin-Kee, a seemingly anachronistic Chinaman stereotype with a yellow face, exists as a living example of the pejorative representation of the Chinese in America, a part of the heritage that main character Jin has tried to reject, and above all a contrast to the Monkey King image.

An amalgamation of racially offensive stereotypes, Chin-Kee wears a nineteenth-century Chinese outfit and is portrayed as slant-eyed, bucktoothed, pigtailed, and yellow-faced. He is the smart Asian student in the classrooms but speaks with a strong accent that regularly inverts *R*s and *L*s when speaking English; he is a kung-fu master who announces each of his strikes with the name of a Chinese dish. Even the name "Chin-Kee" itself is a revival of a racial slur. In short, the idea of "fixity" is demonstrated exemplarily in Chin-Kee. He is an example of the historical stereotype living yet today, with both historical and contemporary references inhabiting one body.

When *American Born Chinese* was run as a webcomic on *Modern Tales*, Yang would receive comments about how hilarious the Chin-Kee character was. To some extent, the reception of Chin-Kee as a hilarious character by some readers points to the danger of perpetuating a stereotype despite the purpose of the author. Yang nevertheless continued his project because the majority of responses understood the author's anger "seething beneath Cousin Chin-Kee's toothy smile."[40] He believed the book contributes more to ending the stereotype than otherwise. Indeed, the portraiture of the stereotypical image of Chin-Kee in the book, by means of a turn of the image in the Monkey King, helps to positively transform the stereotype.

Chin-Kee is a major figure in one of the three story lines of *American Born Chinese*. A cousin of the Caucasian schoolboy Danny,

Chin-Kee is a bad dream that has haunted Danny for years. Chin-Kee visits Danny regularly, accompanying him like a shadow during his visits. Suffering tremendously at school because of Chin-Kee's appearance and behavior, Danny is in the end determined to chase his cousin away. He fights with Chin-Kee and ultimately decapitates him. At this moment, beheaded yet still standing in front of Danny, Chin-Kee reveals his true form: he is the Monkey King.

As a transformation of the Monkey King, the significance of Chin-Kee's existence is reflected on at least two levels. At the story level, as Chin-Kee/Monkey King explains to Jin himself, he "came to serve as [Jin's] conscience—as a signpost to [his] soul."[41] Even though Danny (who is a transformation of Jin) hates his influence and rejects him, Chin-Kee persists. One may say that he visits and stays with Danny/Jin because he represents the fixed stereotypes that Jin cannot shake off from himself as a Chinese American and/or that he stands for the unhappy history that Jin should not forget. At the level of narrative structure, the revelation of the Monkey King's transformation of Chin-Kee accompanies the revelation of Danny's true identity as Jin and brings the three story lines together, merging the three separate stories into one. Instead of pointing to a conclusion of the story, this dramatic moment of fusion sets off many questions regarding ethnic identity. The beheading of Chin-Kee discloses the purpose of the author's depiction of this character—to eventually eliminate this stereotype, uncover the hidden layer of the meaning of the Monkey King story, and reveal the complicated identity problem of Jin/Danny. It is exactly through transformation that the beheading of Chin-Kee, or the annihilation of the stereotype, is set in motion.

PERFORMING THE EXECUTION: FIXITY VERSUS TRANSFORMATION

The beheading of Chin-Kee and the disclosure of his Monkey King identity demonstrates the significance of the Monkey King myth in the text as the metaphoric frame of reference of the Chinese experience in America. Jin/Danny's identity is also brought into focus at the same time. The dual transformations highlight the issue of identity as the central theme of the book, and the question of "true self" unanswered in the Monkey King narrative line is returned here. At this point, transformation has been highlighted too many times to be neglected as essentially relevant to the "true self."

The transformation of Chin-Kee/Monkey King is a reflection of the transformation of Jin/Danny, indicating that the end of stereotype lies not in simple removal but rather in transformation—the replacement of negative representations with positive ones—introduced as a way to end the stereotype. With transformation, the arrested discriminatory stereotype is replaced with images of new meaning that could be used for positive self-representation.

The return of the Monkey King upon the execution of Chin-Kee indicates a positive turn of identity construction in *American Born Chinese*. For Jin/Danny, this means a positive performance of ethnic identity. Danny was never successful in chasing away the haunting influence of Chin-Kee. The cartoon page showing Danny in the final fight with Chin-Kee, however, indicates that the stereotypical image could be terminated—not through a simple removal but by means of a replacement.[42] When Chin-Kee's head is punched off and flies into the air (page 212), the head of the Monkey King is already standing upon Chin-Kee's shoulders (figure 6.7). In addition, on the following page, it is the hybrid of the Monkey King's head upon Chin-Kee's body that is speaking to Danny. The polymorphic existence of the Monkey King and Chin-Kee highlights the fact that Chin-Kee does not simply disappear; he can only be transformed into something else, replaced with a new image. This transformation, furthermore, does not come from an external social force; instead, it is from a force within Jin/Danny himself.

There is a moment of recognition at the death of Chin-Kee when the Monkey King sits with Jin (page 221). In the lower-left plate of the page, Jin looks from the page directly at the reader, creating a mirror-image eye contact. In the plate to the right, Chin-Kee's puppet head lies on the ground, with the quirky smile frozen on his dead face. The juxtaposition of the two images indicates that Chin-Kee's head is the object of Jin's gaze. It is also the object of the reader's gaze. The merged gaze is invited to contemplate the replacement of the stereotype. At this moment, the Monkey King is also looking at the same object, saying, "I came to serve as your conscience—as a signpost to your soul." Referring to Chin-Kee as "I," the Monkey King points to his transformation as the ability to fuse together different images and identities.

Although a very unrealistic image of the Chinese, Chin-Kee is supposed to be a realistic figure in the Danny story line, just as the stereotype is supposed to be realistic in American society. Stereotyping

Figure 6.7. Danny knocks Chin-Kee's head off. From *American Born Chinese* © 2006 by Gene Luen Yang. Reprinted by permission of First Second, an imprint of Roaring Brook Press, a division of Holtzbrinck Publishing Holdings Limited Partnership. All Rights Reserved.

adopts the form of realism, as pointed out by both Edward Said and Homi Bhabha. When speaking of *Orientalism*, a study of the semiotics of stereotypes, Said argues that orientalism is "a form of radical realism," in that anyone who is employing orientalism talks about the objects in ways as if what they are speaking and thinking about is the truth.[43] Relevant to Said's discussion of stereotypes, Bhabha observes that colonial discourse "employs a system of representation, a regime of truth, that is structurally similar to realism."[44] In the case of the stereotypical Chinese image of Chin-Kee, although far from a true and realistic representation, it has gone through so many repetitions that it has been accepted as such. This explains why in *American Born Chinese* Danny and his parents had never questioned the story that Chin-Kee was the cousin of Danny, even though he really had no relationship with either side of the family.

The repetitive use of the stereotype builds an arbitrary connection between the Chin-Kee image as the signifier and the Chinese American as the signified, to use Saussure's semiotic terms. When in use,

Chin-Kee the stereotype is treated as if equal to the real image of the Chinese American. Although many aspects of society have gone through development and changes, the stereotype remains the same and the connection between the signified and the signifier has not been severed. The beheading of Chin-Kee, and the revelation of his true nature as a transformation of the Monkey King, is an effort to sever the connection between the signifier and the signified of the stereotype by revealing the unrealistic nature of the image. By transforming Chin-Kee into the Monkey King, *American Born Chinese* subverts the realistic strategy of stereotype, points toward its imaginary nature, and suggests to use the Monkey King as a replacement.

JIN'S TRANSFORMATION: THE MONKEY KING AS AUTOBIOGRAPHY

Gene Yang has acknowledged the autobiographical nature of his graphic novel.[45] The story itself reveals the connection between Jin (standing for Gene) and the Monkey King. Moreover, the problems that Jin experiences resemble those that the Monkey King went through. In both metaphorical and metonymical senses, Jin is the Monkey King. In other words, the story of the Monkey King is a trope of Jin's own experience, written as a form of autobiography.

Transformation is one of the signature attributes of the Monkey King, a well-known trick he plays and a method he uses most frequently with his friends or against his enemies in *The Journey to the West*. In *American Born Chinese* it is the social significance of transformation that is stressed. No longer merely a simple trick, transformation becomes a major theme in all three story lines. Physical form in the book has been used ubiquitously as a metonym for identity, hence transformation stands for identity shifting. Of critical significance is the role that transformation plays in the identity shifts between Jin and Danny, Chin-Kee and the Monkey King.

In the Monkey King story line, in order to resist the category of monkey, the Monkey King assumes a large form as well as a new name, "Great Sage, Equal of Heaven." Transformation in this case is used as a strategy to fight discrimination against monkeys, as well as to identify with deities that are not monkeys. In parallel, Jin also uses transformation to change his form and hence his identity. In fact, images of transformers, in some cases a monkey transformer, appear in the panels repetitively, reminding the reader of the constant, although at times submerged, theme of transformation. Corresponding to the Monkey King's use of transformation in crossing the boundary between human and monkey, Jin's metamorphosis attempts to cross the racial border. In order to compete for Amelia, who is close to Greg, a Caucasian, Jin perms his straight black hair to make it curly, like Greg's (page 97). Jin's failure in such transformative efforts pushes him to go further in shape-shifting, until he has transformed himself into another person altogether in Danny.

The later transformation of Jin is also comparable to the Monkey King's experience. The giant form the Monkey King assumes for five hundred years fails to bring him recognition from others as either a human or the "Great Sage." It only serves as a cage that imprisons him, within which the monkey forgets about his true form and "true self." Jin's permed hair in no way equalizes him with Greg; it is merely the first step as Jin gives up on his own form/identity and acquires a forged one. When Danny/Jin meets the Monkey King as his spiritual guide, Danny is told to give up the fake form and change back to Jin. This move suggests that total assimilation is not recommended, but it also seems to recommend that in order not to lose one's true identity one has to forsake transformation altogether.

TRANSFORMATION: CAPTIVITY VERSUS FREEDOM

Transformation in the *Journey to the West* tradition is appreciated as an ability to shift freely between various forms, whereas in many other mythical traditions it can also mean a one-dimensional switch from one form to another, or the loss of the original form. Besides Sun Wukong, many other beings in *Journey to the West* are able to transform freely, without being locked into one form and losing avenues to others. In contrast, some transformation stories in Greek and Latin traditions focus on metamorphoses of a rigid kind, wherein a being after transformation is permanently locked in the adopted form, unable to return to the original. This form of transformation is seen as a loss, or a suffering. Daphne's transformation into a laurel as described in Ovid's *Metamorphoses*, for instance, is depicted as a loss of motion along with the loss of human form. Lucius in Apuleius's *The Golden Ass* goes through pains and tribulations because of his transformation, and his entire journey as a donkey is in seeking the return to his original form, which, when achieved at the end, is celebrated as a salvation. It is the free kind of transformation (one that is reversible) that the new Monkey King myth here advocates.

In *American Born Chinese*, both the Monkey King's giant form and Jin's Danny form are depicted as one-dimensional transformations for as long as they refuse to change back, and this rigid transformation represents their loss of freedom to return to their original forms or to shift to other forms. As explained by the monk Wong Lai-Tsao, the Monkey King can only be "freed" when he returns to his "true form."[46] In this sense, staying in the giant form for five hundred years means being held captive in that fixed untrue form, because he has lost his flexibility, his transformative power. The importance of the "true form" is not because it is the original, but that only by sustaining the ability to return to this form will one be able to attain any freedom in form-choosing. Under the guidance of the monk, the Monkey King in the end is transformed back to himself, regaining his ability to shift forms and fight with demons, and thereafter becoming a missionary of Tze-Yo-Tzuh. The return of the Monkey King to his monkey form does not indicate that he has given up his fight against social discrimination. Instead, by attaining the ability to choose forms and thus the freedom to shape identity, his return works as a denunciation of rigid social norms regarding the identity formation of marginalized social groups.

TRANSFORMATION AND AMBIVALENT ASIAN AMERICAN IDENTITY

Chin-Kee's existence in the book argues for the "fixity" of stereotype, as Homi Bhabha contends in his discussion of discriminatory stereotypes in "The Other Question." The contradictory characters that Chin-Kee as well as the "Chinaman" images discussed earlier in this chapter carried with them also resonate with what Homi Bhabha describes as the "splitting" and contradictory nature of the stereotype. When relating colonial discourse to fetishism, Bhabha describes the stereotype as "a form of splitting and multiple belief," and because it contains these contradictory elements, it requires being continually repeated and also "a continual and repetitive chain of other stereotypes" for its signification to be successful.[47] Pointing at the "contradiction and heterogeneity" in the construction of stereotypes as well as their strategic fixations, Bhabha then describes stereotype as suturing and ambivalent: "My concept of stereotype-as-suture is a recognition of the *ambivalence* of that authority and those orders of identification. The role of fetishistic identification, in the construction of discriminatory knowledges that depend on the 'presence of difference,' is to provide a process of splitting and multiple/contradictory belief at the point of enunciation and subjectification."[48] Bhabha then relates his idea of the splitting and contradictory stereotype with Fanon's discussion of the splitting of ego, meaning the triple split between the incongruent knowledge of body, race, and ancestors, as well as Freud's analysis of fetishism as a knowledge that allows for multiple contradictory beliefs.

Bhabha's move from split and contradiction to "suture" and "ambivalence" leaves the "suturing" of the contradictions undiscussed. Juxtapositions might suggest a suture, but it also suggests the want of a suture. Real suture happens in Asian American self-representation, in the multivalence discovered from mythical archetypes and from the community of the marginalized group. It is the emphasis on "valence," in transformation, in the ability to alloy, that makes the difference between fixity/split and multivalence. In *American Born Chinese*, the powerful fusion takes place in the performance of the execution of Chin-Kee, in the revelation of the power of the Monkey King's transformations. The Monkey King is an exemplary multivalent character who represents a type of image that fuses dualistic contradictions and contains possibilities of constant change. Calling for transformation is to refuse to be forced into any one category and to advocate for diversity and multivalence. For the Monkey King, this means his denial of being called a little monkey, as well as the rejection of his huge monkey form that he adopted later to compete with the deities. For Jin, it means neither staying in the Chin-Kee tradition nor remaining arrested in the Danny image. The capacity to contain "both/and" rather than "either-or" in the concept of transformation negates the dichotomy in the contrasting position of the Asian and the American.

About the ambivalence of identity for immigrant American writers, Shirley Geok-lin Lim states that the naturalized American is always partly American, with another part always remaining non-American: "In a nation of immigrants, there must always be already that straining against the grain, the self that is assimilated and the self that remains unassimilable."[49] In this ambivalence she sees hope for American culture, for it is a dynamic process of renewal, a process of the "remaking of American civilization."[50] However, human sight cannot see the contradictory sides of the ambivalence simultaneously, and immigrants, while "both simultaneously alien and American," are "conscious of only one or the other at any one time."[51]

The ambivalence of ethnicity is apparent not only related to immigrants—it is evident in Asian American as well as other ethnic American identities in general, although branding the assimilated and unassimilable as the contradictions for every case would be an oversimplification. The Monkey King story in *American Born Chinese* serves as a model of positive ambivalence, or "multivalence," that fuses the seemingly unresolvable conflicts. Although even the Monkey King's life requires enduring tribulations before arriving at the stage of multivalence, it is a model that suggests the attainment of a status where one does not have to be caught or split between the assimilated and the unassimilable.

This stance echoes what David Palumbo-Liu explains in the use of the solidus in the term "Asian/American": "As in the construction 'and/or,' where the solidus at once instantiates a choice between two terms, their simultaneous and equal status, and an element of indecidability, that is, as it at once implies both exclusion and inclusion, 'Asian/American' marks *both* the distinction installed between 'Asian' and 'American' *and* a dynamic, unsettled, and inclusive movement."[52] What Yang demonstrates by "transformation" in *American Born Chinese* might not have reached the simultaneity and equality between "Asian" and "American," but it clearly argues for an inclusive and dynamic motion between the different "forms" between which the Monkey King and Jin have traveled. Transformation as the crossing of racial frontier means not a one-way crossing but rather a constant movement, a crossing so large that no effort for each individual crossing is needed anymore. The effortless constant liaison between "Asian" and "American" seems to lie in the model of transformation that emphasizes the whole entity, including both constituent parts instead of stressing the importance of either part.

Multivalence, then, is a crucial quality for maintaining transformability. A transformation with integrity is the one that remains fluid, in which an identity may transform itself back and forth freely. Instead of making a choice among different forms, it contains all. The multivalent and dynamic transformation is an answer to the split and contradiction of the stereotype. In this sense the "true form" or true identity does not really refer to the original form of the Monkey King or Jin; it refers to a form or identity that is "dynamic, unsettled, and inclusive." When the Monkey King is locked in his giant form and has lost the ability to transform, a victim of the "split" identity, he has forgotten about his multivalent quality. The moment he casts off the false form, he also shakes off the split and arrested identity and resumes his ability to change forms, such as transforming into Chin-Kee.

Jin's fault in transforming himself into Danny is that Danny is only one form of the Jin complex. This form, albeit the favorite one for Jin because it enjoys privileges, reflects only one aspect of the "soul." Sticking to this one form, Jin forgets about the richness of his identity and his culture. The paradoxical revisiting by Chin-Kee is necessary for Jin to return to the richness of his self because Chin-Kee represents the forms of Jin that he has problems containing. Interestingly, it is only when he finally stands strong enough against Chin-Kee that is he able to cope with the coexistence of the two, no longer having to chase away one form in order to become another. Chin-Kee in this sense becomes the "signpost" to Jin's "soul." Drawing this image does not mean reactivating the stereotype; on the contrary, it is a revision of the stereotype that has never ceased to exist. Instead of pretending that the stereotype is no longer among us, the creation of Monkey King/Chin-Kee image points out the fixated and split nature of the discriminative representation and suggests an alternative representation.

REPRESENTING THE SUBJECTLESS SUBJECT

Kandice Chuh's *Imagine Otherwise: On Asian Americanist Critique* conceives of Asian American studies as a "subjectless discourse" and questions the insistent discussion of identity in the field. From a deconstructive approach, Chuh's discussion reminds us that a subject is always an epistemological object since a "subject" cannot become recognizable and act as such without conforming to certain regulatory matrices.[53] Instead of focusing on Asian American subjectivity, we should question "'Asian American' as the subject/object of Asian Americanist discourses and of U.S. nationalist ideology, and Asian American studies as the subject/object of dominant paradigms of the U.S. university."[54] "Subjectlessness" is recommended as a conceptual tool and a discursive ground for Asian American studies to avoid simplified understandings of subjectivity in U.S. American culture and politics.

Chuh's deconstructive approach toward subjectivity in no way suggests that identity politics should be ignored. Her book itself is indeed a discussion about identity and subjectivity, albeit the undecidability of identity and subjectivity as a construct. Chuh quotes Gayatri Spivak to clarify her point of questioning instead of discarding identity politics: "Deconstruction does not say there is no subject, there is no truth, there is no history. It simply questions the privileging of identity so that someone is believed to have the truth. It is not the exposure of error. It is constantly and persistently looking into how truths are produced."[55] Chuh's critique, based on close reading of literary texts, offers alternative frames such as transnationalism instead of nation and citizenship for Asian American studies.

The model of the Monkey King image in representing the Asian American aligns well with the lines of such deconstructive argument about identity. As *American Born Chinese* showcases, the image of the Monkey King directs attention to the discursive constructedness of subjectivity and to the problems and constraints in "Asian American" as both object and subject. It problematizes the achieving of social assimilation and upward movement of the "model minority." The trickster image of the Monkey King is self-deconstructive, disallowing its own image to solidify, which results in fundamental multivalence and the capability for positive transformation.

Transformation can be viewed as corresponding to Chuh's approach to transnationalism. It is the power of the constructive discourse in society that transforms Jin into a "Chinaman" with "buck teeth."[56] Although born an American, Jin is changed into a stereotypical Asian by such a transformative conception, in reaction to which Jin transforms into Danny, someone who looks all-American. Besides the problematization that the transnational approach brings, multivalent transformation also provides a positive alternative: instead of remaining a captive citizen of one nation, it should be possible to be recognized as a "citizen" of multiple nations simultaneously. This, however, goes against the very concept, as well as practice, of modern nation-states, which is perhaps why it takes a mythical story to make such a suggestion.

The strength of the Monkey King image in *American Born Chinese* lies in its function as a deconstructive image used constructively to represent the subjectless subject of Asian Americans. The deconstructive approach that Chuh introduces in her book can and should be viewed constructively. After all, since coming to the conclusion of

Asian American subjectlessness, Asian Americans still need to live as acting subjects in all occasions in society, and these actions, of subjectless subjects, or of subject/object, are still being represented, and the ways of representation still need to be discussed. The concept of identity is still useful in discussing such representation, especially when the discussion is conducted as a way of questioning the mode of representation of otherness. The Monkey King image suggests that "identity" does not have to negate plurality; it offers an option of enriching the meaning of "identity" as an alternative to giving up on the concept or using concepts such as "unification" in its stead.[57]

Conclusion

Like all trickster characters and despite the best efforts of researchers like myself to analyze him, the Monkey King remains a footloose figure, and one who will leave his mark on cultural texts that reflect the ever-changing and flowing multiplicity of global cultural currents. Moreover, he serves as a mask for the performance of diverse politics, bodies, and identities, yet simultaneously remains a character that is distinctly and indelibly Chinese. This volume has certainly not exhausted the range of narratives that the Monkey King has inhabited across time and space, but I hope it points the way toward an understanding of what this figure can represent for future narratives.

This inquiry works at the intersection of Chinese studies, Asian American studies, film studies, and translation and adaptation studies. Asian American tropes of identity continue to evolve from the Monkey King story, accentuating the concept of transformation. The aim of this book has been to provide a renewed understanding of the Monkey King character as a trickster, as well as to demonstrate the link between the Monkey King character and the Chinese self-conception of national identity. By using a broader conceptualization of the notion of performance when studying cultural texts, and by bringing the concept of time and chronotope into transcultural representations, the preceding chapters build the connection between rewriting and the performed identity of ethnic and marginalized social groups.

This work is a first step toward expanded studies of Asian diasporic cultures within a trans-Pacific frame. The current volume focuses on one representative case—Sun Wukong. Other narratives of transformation—such as that of the butterfly lovers, Lady White Snake, Mulan, Avalokitesvara, and Guan Gong—reveal their own patterns as they travel across time and culture. Trans-Pacific cultural themes such as that of the dragon, Chinese food, and kung fu can also join this larger project of diasporic cultural studies.

The original plan for this work included a cross-cultural comparative study of the Monkey King from China and Hanuman from India. Although both originated as monkey figures in the traditional legends and beliefs, Sun Wukong turned into a trickster figure, whereas Hanuman remained a hero with serious and upright values. The difference between the two monkeys is especially interesting when the possible genealogical connection between them is considered as a transcultural experience of one monkey and its rewriting. This comparative plan, although too ambitious to be included in the current project, points to another area into which this work could grow in the future.

A similar transcultural comparison can also be imagined between Sun Wukong and the Signifying Monkey. While both monkeys are characters in the stories of translators, the vocal plays a central role in tales of the Signifying Monkey, whereas in *Journey to the West* language as a cultural factor is forgotten, as if the authors/storytellers are deliberately neglecting it. This aspect of the narrative echoes other, more contemporary Chinese fictional and media works featuring time-travel themes that have been popular in recent years—all of which stubbornly overlook the language factor. This leads us to ask whether the deemphasizing of the diversity of language is a specifically Chinese cultural tendency, perhaps rooted in its early development of a common written language that overlooked differences in spoken dialect, or in the concept of "all under heaven" (*tianxia*) that is still prevalent today. Such disinterest in problematizing linguistic diversity or language differences in a narrative may also explain the popularity of complex stories of time travel.

Journey to the West has become "part of the rich background texture of Chinese thought, speech, and behavior; it is to the present day an inexhaustible archive for role modeling, argumentative wit, and political innuendo."[1] Beyond that, it is also worth our attention that the "Journey to the West" has increasingly become a trope for East-West relations. The "West," referring to India or the movement toward the Buddha in and before *Journey to the West,* refers in many contemporary rewritings to the West of today's global economic structure. For instance, since the late 1990s, an Internet forum named "Weiming kongjian" has been popular among overseas Chinese, mostly Chinese students who study in the United States and those who remained abroad.[2] "Dahua Xiyou," originally the title of Jeffrey Lau's film duology and loose adaptation of *Journey to the West* (discussed in chapter 4), became in the forum the name of a discussion group focused on all issues related to going to the "West," referring in this case to the United States and Europe. The popularity of both the film *Dahua Xiyou* and the online discussion group point to the correspondence in popular culture between "Journey to the West" (the West where Buddhism originated) and the idea of going "west" (the Euro-American West). In the texts discussed in this book, "West" frequently carries such double meaning. Gene Yang's Monkey King still refers to his journey to the West as a religious pilgrimage, but it is one toward Jesus, not the Buddha (chapter 6). In *The Lost Empire* and *The Forbidden Kingdom* (discussed in chapter 5), the journey is replaced altogether with a different one, that between the China of the past and the modern West. In contrast, Li Feng's *Another Voice* presents the journey as one of China itself progressing toward modernization/Westernization (chapter 4). The replacement of the concept of "West" works as a central trope for this project, which explains to some degree the reasons that the Monkey King is so closely related to issues of the representation of Chineseness.

Only in retrospect does it emerge that the adaptations of *Journey to the West* focused on in this project are all based on the episode of "Havoc in Heaven" (Da'nao tiangong). Besides the fact that it is one of the most well-known episodes of *Journey to the West*, this coincidence points to a probable explanation of the reasons for the common usage of the Monkey King in self-representation. The "Havoc in Heaven" episode takes place in the period of Sun Wukong's life when he arrives at the borders of his growing self, a transitional and transforming period of his life. At the significant event of boundary crossing, he has to battle with and negotiate between the conflicting values of rebellion and submission. The trope of this battle, when taking on different forms, can be applied to quite different situations. Not only does it stand as a sound analogy for the social struggles and inner battles that Asian Americans experience in *American Born Chinese*, or for the real war or "revolution" that the Chinese have experienced in the mid-twentieth century, but with a twist it can also stand for the midlife crisis of an American citizen or the growing pains of a kung fu–loving teenager. The transitional stage in which the havoc (*nao*) is located can be found at various times and in various cultures; thus the image of the Monkey King reaches across wide geographical and temporal gaps. When we get a better idea of what this monkey is creating havoc against in a particular rewriting, we begin to know what is at stake.

The transitional status of havoc fundamentally links up the Monkey King as the trope of transformation (between the monkey and the human/god), and the Monkey King as the trope of translation/adaptation (in terms of transcultural experience between East and West). As such the Monkey King suggests the connections between transformation and translation. Despite the neglect of the language factor in *Journey to the West*, one can easily see Sun Wukong as a transformer and a translator. On the other hand, because translation always involves a transformational aspect, it ultimately makes sense to have the trickster monkey replacing the monk in the "Journey to the West" narrative. The transposition of the narrative's protagonist accounts both for this link between translation and transformation and for the monkey's ability to rebel (*nao*). In this sense, the trope of transformation in Sun Wukong not only connects the rebelliousness against racial stereotypes and a flexible position toward ethnic identity, but it also informs and explains the trope of translation. As discussed in chapter 1, the preferred transformation is not the accomplishment of change from one form to another. It is the freedom to transform into any form needed and to achieve two-way transformations. The same can be said of translation. What is important is not the successful translation from China into United States, or from West to East, but the free two-way flow of ideas between different places, different genres, and different chronotopes. *Another Voice* is an example of this. I hope this book has at least pointed to this possible connection between transformation and translation, a subject to which I hope to return in a future project.

In the retelling and rewriting history of the Monkey King, performance brings history and the mythical/fictional together. The historical journey of the monk Xuanzang is brought into the fictional realm through oral performances. Although how the Monkey King has joined the journey is never clearly explained, it is agreed that it is the result of the Indian and/or Chinese religious or legendary figure(s) joining the "Journey to the West" narrative via performances. The Monkey King in the story and the Monkey King god in popular belief have developed and evolved side by side, interwoven with each other. The Monkey King is thus found in real life and written in history, such as in the records of the Boxer Rebellion. One can also argue that the popularity of the Monkey King in real life and the popularity of "Journey to the West" have promoted each other. In our recent examples, when Sun Wukong is linked to real historical figures such as Mao Zedong and to national or social groups such as the Chinese or Asian Americans, the connection between history and myth is made evident. It is through this connection that this project of the Monkey King becomes a vehicle, its moving window enabling us to observe the history of various periods.

NOTES

INTRODUCTION

1. See Andrew H. Plaks, *The Four Masterworks of the Ming Novel* (Princeton, NJ: Princeton University Press, 1987).

2. The Xinhua.net report on the mascot selection process has been circulating widely on the Internet: http://news.xinhuanet.com/focus/2005-11/11/content_3767361_5.htm.

3. For a summary of the debate, see http://media.people.com.cn/n1/2016/0128/c40606-28090913.html.

4. See Robert E. Hegel, "Traditional Chinese Fiction—The State of the Field," *Journal of Asian Studies* 53, no. 2 (May 1994): 394–425; and Anthony C. Yu, introduction to *Journey to the West*, trans. Yu, 10–96 (Chicago: University of Chicago Press, 2012) for the span of studies on traditional Chinese fiction in general and on this novel in particular.

5. For more about the accretive history of *Xiyou ji*, see Glen Dudbridge, *The Hsi-yu chi: A Study of Antecedents to the Sixteenth-Century Chinese Novel* (Cambridge: Cambridge University Press, 1970); Anthony C. Yu, introduction; Zheng Zhenduo, "*Xiyou ji* de yanhua" (Evolution of *Journey to the West*), in *Zhongguo wenxue yanjiu xinbian* (Chinese literary studies new edition), 263–99 (Taibei: Wenguang, 1973); and Huang Yongnian's preface to *Xiyou zhengdao shu*. *Xiyou ji zhuan* is also known as *Tang Sanzang chushen quanzhuan* (Complete biography of Tang Sanzang).

6. Since Lu Xun identified Wu Cheng'en as the author of *Xiyou ji* in his *Zhongguo xiaoshuo shilue* (A brief history of the Chinese novel) (Beijing: Renmin Wenxue Chubanshe, 1973), and Hu Shih confirmed this authorship in "*Xiyou ji* kaozheng" (Textual criticism of *Xiyou ji*), in *Hu Shih gudian wenxue yanjiu lunji* (Shanghai: Shanghai Guji Chubanshe, 1988), this conclusion has been generally accepted, but it is challenged by many scholars. For a summary of studies on the work's authorship, see Anthony C. Yu, introduction, 17–31. Andrew Plaks in *The Four Masterworks of the Ming Novel* suggests that there might exist an earlier "urtext" that Wu Cheng'en revised or merely edited into the Shidetang edition of *Xiyou ji*. The existence of some urtext is also supported by the fragment of a *Xiyou ji* story in *Yongle dadian*, and fragments of *Xiyou ji* stories in *Pak t'ongsa onhae*, as examined

by Dudbridge. But none of these theories can exclude other sources that the author may likely have consulted and included in his writing. This is discussed further in chapter 2.

7. There have been many discussions about where the monkey figure comes from. Studies have pointed at a large variety of sources, both from Chinese culture and Indian culture. For lack of solid proof, a lot of these studies are outlines of possibilities, and none of them can exclude the other possibilities. I discuss more of the development of the monkey's image in chapter 2.

8. Sarah Cardwell, *Adaptation Revisited: Television and the Classic* (Manchester, United Kingdom: Manchester University Press, 2002); Linda Hutcheon, *A Theory of Adaptation* (London: Routledge, 2013); Julie Sanders, *Adaptation and Appropriation* (London: Routledge, 2016).

9. See, for instance, Martin M. Winkler, ed., *Classical Myth and Culture in the Cinema* (New York: Oxford University Press, 2001); Margaret Jane Kidnie, *Shakespeare and the Problem of Adaptation* (London: Routledge, 2009); and Caryl Emerson, *Boris Godunov: Transpositions of a Russian Theme* (Bloomington: Indiana University Press, 1986).

10. As an instance, Ping Shao's PhD dissertation, "Monkey and Chinese Scriptural Tradition: A Rereading of the Novel *Xiyou ji*" (Washington University in St. Louis, 1997), started as a study of all pilgrims but changed into an exclusive study of Monkey because as she examined the relationship between Monkey and other pilgrims, she found out that Monkey is the single protagonist and other characters are manifestations of the same character.

11. André Lefevere, *Translation, Rewriting and the Manipulation of Literary Fame* (London: Routledge, 1992).

12. Edwin Gentzler, *Translation and Rewriting in the Age of Post-Translation Studies* (New York: Routledge, 2017); Siri Nergaard and Stefano Arduini, "Translation: A New Paradigm," *Translation*, inaugural issue (December 2011): 8–17; Sherry Simon, *Translating Montreal: Episodes in the Life of a Divided City* (Montreal, Quebec: McGill-Queen's University Press, 2006).

13. Zuojia Chubanshe (Writer's Press) was part of Renmin Wenxue Chubanshe (People's Literature Press) during 1953–58. After publishing *Xiyou ji* under the imprint of Zuojia Chubanshe, Renmin Wenxue Chubanshe reprinted the same edition a few more times (see Dong Qiang, "The Branches and Development of Renmin Wenxue Chubanshe," www.thepaper.cn/newsDetail_forward_1449360).

14. See Hu, "*Xiyou ji* kaozheng"; Zheng Zhenduo, "*Xiyou ji* de yanhua"; Dudbridge, *The Hsi-yu chi;* Victor Mair, "Suen Wu-Kung = Hanumat?: The Progress of a Scholarly Debate," in *Proceedings of the Second International Conference on Sinology* (Taipei: Academia Sinica, 1989), 659–752; and Miyoko Nakano, *Sun Wukong de dansheng: Hou de minjian wenxue yu Xiyou ji* (The birth of Sun Wukong—Monkey folklore and *Xiyou ji*) (Beijing: Zhonghua shu ju, 2002) for discussions of the origin of the Monkey King figure. I engage at more length with this issue in chapter 2.

15. For instance, in *Monkey King Subdues the White Bone Demon*, an influential adapted episode of *Xiyou ji*, the monk is portrayed as deceivable

yet stubborn, following his blind assumptions to incorrect conclusions. The Monkey King, on the other hand, is the one who has true insight and fights against the mistake with determination (see chapter 3).

16. Henry Louis Gates Jr., *The Signifying Monkey: A Theory of African-American Literary Criticism* (New York: Oxford University Press, 1988), 3–64.

17. Ibid., 21.

18. Ibid., xxiv.

19. Ibid., 88.

CHAPTER 1

1. Wu Cheng'en, *Journey to the West,* translated by Anthony C. Yu (Chicago: University of Chicago Press, 1977–83), 1:68.

2. For example, in describing Subhūti's lecture, the text goes: "For a while he lectured on Tao. For a while he lectured on Zen. To harmonize the three schools was a natural thing" (ibid., 1:83).

3. Ping Shao's study of *Journey to the West* from the point of view of Taoist religion finds that the religious framework of the novel corresponds well with Zhang Boduan's critique of the traditional Taoist conception of the elixir. The dynamics of Five Phases Mountain is the driving force behind the cycles of life and death, and Monkey's experience at the Five Phases Mountain stands for his death and reincarnation. Thus, before and after Five Phases Mountain, Monkey's life represents respectively the two steps of the quest for the gold elixir according to Zhang Boduan: the cultivation of the elixir and the realization of the Buddha-nature. See Ping Shao, "Monkey and Chinese Scriptural Tradition: A Rereading of the Novel *Xiyou ji*" (PhD diss., Washington University in St. Louis, 1997).

4. In *Understanding Comics* (Northampton, MA: Kitchen Sink, 1993), Scott McCloud calls the space between the panels of a comics the "gutter." The two images on both sides of the gutter seem to be unconnected or even unrelated, but the reader's imagination can transform them into a single coherent idea. The mental process that brings seemingly unrelated parts together and perceives them as a whole is the "closure."

5. The historical journey of Xuanzang from China to India is described in *Xiyou ji* as a journey from Chang'an of Tang, located in the South Jambudvipa Continent, to "Western Heaven," the land of Buddha in the West, located in the West Aparagodaniya Continent. I refer to it as a journey from China to India in order to avoid the ambiguity of the legendary place-names.

6. Wu Cheng'en, *Journey to the West,* trans. Yu (1977–83), 4:159.

7. Ironically, "the Monkey King" has become the name that is known in the West, which is an example of the effects of cross-cultural translation.

8. Wu Cheng'en, *Journey to the West,* trans. Yu (1977–83), 1:82.

9. Ibid., 3:347.

10. Ibid., 1:352.

11. Claude Lévi-Strauss, "The Structural Study of Myth," in *Structural Anthropology*, trans. C. Jacobson and B. Schoepf (Garden City, NY: Anchor, 1967), 226.

12. Ibid., 229.

13. See, for instance, analysis of Susa-no-o as a Japanese mythic trickster in Robert S. Ellwood, "A Japanese Mythic Trickster Figure: Susa-No-O," in *Mythical Trickster Figures: Contours, Contexts, and Criticisms*, ed. William J. Hynes and William G. Doty, 141–58 (Tuscaloosa: University of Alabama Press, 1993).

14. William J. Hynes, "Mapping the Characteristics of Mythic Tricksters: A Heuristic Guide," in *Mythical Trickster Figures: Contours, Contexts, and Criticisms*, ed. Hynes and William G. Doty, 33–45 (Tuscaloosa: University of Alabama Press, 1993), 34.

15. Ibid., 35. In his brief study, William J. Hynes encompasses Claude Lévi-Strauss's view of the trickster as the epitome of binary oppositions, and echoes Robert Pelton's observation that the trickster "pulverizes the univocal" and symbolizes the ambivalence of life (Pelton, "West African Tricksters: Web of Purpose, Dance of Delight," in *Mythical Trickster Figures: Contours, Contexts, and Criticisms*, ed. William J. Hynes and William G. Doty, 122–40 [Tuscaloosa: University of Alabama Press, 1993]).

16. For the unavoidable question of where the "and" function comes from, Laura Makarius explains that the ambivalence originates from the practice of magical violation of taboos in tribal societies by magicians, owing to the belief that in certain situations these violations can bring protection to the violator. The trickster, like the magician, takes upon himself the culpability of the group for breaking taboos for the sake of mankind. She further posits that the "ambivalence and contradictions that impregnate the accounts of the trickster do not . . . derive from an incapacity to differentiate the true from the false, the good from the evil, the benignant from the malevolent—but from a situation generative of ambivalence and contradictions that has shaped itself in the society, and of which the myth of the trickster is the expression" (Makarius, "The Myth of the Trickster: The Necessary Breaker of Taboos," in *Mythical Trickster Figures: Contours, Contexts, and Criticisms*, ed. William J. Hynes and William G. Doty, 66–86 [Tuscaloosa: University of Alabama Press, 1993], 86).

17. Wu, *Xiyou ji*, chaps. 50–53.

18. Anthony C. Yu, introduction, 73. The *locus classicus* of *shou fang xin* is from Mencius, meaning the retrieval of the original heart. My interpretation differs from that of Mencius, viewing the term as two separate functions: *shouxin* and *fangxin*.

19. Wu, *Xiyou ji*, chaps. 27–31, 56–58, the episodes of the White Bone Demon and the episodes of the real and fake Wukong.

20. For instance, in chapter 17 he transforms into a cinnabar pill and in this way gets into the Black Bear. In chapter 59, he turns himself into a tiny mole-cricket and hides in the tea bubble, and is then drunk by Raksasi (Princess Iron Fan). In chapter 82, after his first effort of being drunk along with the tea failed, he turns into a red peach and is eaten by the white-haired rodent demon.

21. Plaks, *Four Masterworks*, 257–58.

22. Wu, *Xiyou ji*, chap. 7.

23. Wu Cheng'en, *Journey to the West,* trans. Yu (1977–83), 3:115.

24. A recent rewriting of Monkey's story, *Wukong zhuan* (Story of Wukong) by Jin Hezai (Beijing: Guangming Ribao Chubanshe, 2001), is aligned with this interpretation. In eliminating himself, Wukong supposedly achieved ultimate freedom. See chapter 4 for a discussion of this work.

25. See Andrew H. Plaks, "Allegory in Hsi-Yu Chi and Hung-Lou Meng," in *Chinese Narrative*, 163–202 (Princeton, NJ: Princeton University Press, 1977)"; and Anthony C. Yu, introduction, for comments on three religions.

26. Robert Campany, "Demons, Gods, and Pilgrims: The Demonology of the *Hsi-yu Chi*," *Chinese Literature: Essays, Articles, Reviews* 7, no. 1/2 (1985): 106.

27. However, Robert Campany's taxonomy of demons largely overlooks the difference and hierarchy between different mythical systems. Also, his paradigm overlooks another level of the hierarchy, the heavenly gods, and neglects the complex roles that the pilgrims play between the demons and the gods.

28. Campany, "Demons, Gods, and Pilgrims," 113.

29. Ibid., 114–15; Plaks, *Four Masterworks*, 243. Stating some problems of an allegorical reading of the book, Plaks points out some doubts over the necessity of the entire journey. He later resolves the doubts by taking the journey as internal pilgrimage of the mind.

30. See, for instances, chapters 23 and 44 of *Journey to the West.*

31. Campany, "Demons, Gods, and Pilgrims," 107–8.

32. Plaks, "Allegory," 167–78.

33. Ibid., 168.

34. Makarius, "The Myth of the Trickster," 66–86.

35. Compare to Andrew Plaks's translation: "The bodhisattvas and the demons are all manifestations of a single concept" (*Four Masterworks*, 245).

36. Wu Cheng'en, *Journey to the West,* trans. Yu (1977–83), 1:363.

37. In the chapter "Metapictures" of his book *Picture Theory*, W. J. T. Mitchell discusses examples of different types of metapictures, including Saul Steinberg's *The Spiral*, Alain's "Egyptian Life Class," the classic "Duck-Rabbit," Velazquez's *Las Meninas*, and Rene Magritte's *Les trahison des images.*

38. Ibid., 45.

39. Ibid., 50.

40. Ibid., 53.

41. Ibid., 48.

42. Ibid., 48.

CHAPTER 2

1. Dudbridge, *The Hsi-yu chi*, x.

2. Although scholars tend to accept that the author of *Zaju* is Yang Jingxian, this is not without challenge, and some argue that the text dates to the Ming era, after Yang's time (ibid., 76–80).

3. Scholars such as Chen Dakang view *Xiyou ji* as a rewriting of previous texts. Chen in his *Mingdai xiaoshuo shi* compares *Xiyou ji* with the

Korean book *The Interpreter Pak* (Pak tongshi) of the Yuan period, and sees *Xiyou ji*'s revision as a further development of the "Xiyouji" narrative (see Chen Dakang, *Mingdai xiaoshuo shi* [A history of the Ming novel] [Shanghai: Shanghai wenyi chubanshe, 2000], 404–29).

4. Mei Chun, *The Novel and Theatrical Imagination in Early Modern China* (Leiden, Netherlands: Brill, 2011).

5. The Kozanji version refers to two texts that essentially tell the same story despite the minor linguistic discrepancies between them and that originally belong to the monastery Kozanji in Japan: *Xindiao Da Tang Sanzang Fashi qujingji* and *Da Tang Sanzang qujing shihua*. Both texts were printed in China during the early twentieth century, with the latter being reprinted a few times. I am using the 1997 Zhonghua Shuju reprint of *Shihua*, annotated by Li and Cai.

6. On dating of *Shihua*, see Dudbridge, *The Hsi-yu chi*, 26–29.

7. See Li Shiren and Cai Jinghao, "*Datang Sanzang qujing shihua* chengshu shijian kaobian" (Investigation on the composition date of *Datang Sanzang qujing shihua*), *Xuzhou shifan xueyuan xuebao* 3 (1982): 22–30. See Cai Tieying, *Xiyou ji de dansheng* (The birth of *Xiyou ji*) (Beijing: Zhonghua Shuju, 2007) for an account of the history of the dating of *Shihua*.

8. Li and Cai in their article argue that the word *chu* (place, spot) that appears in the title of many sections (*jie*) indicates the transition from the text to the picture, as the storyteller needs to point to certain pictures at certain points of the story. This feature is similar to the *bianwen* from Dunhuang (Li and Cai, "Datang Sanzang qujing shihua," 22–24).

9 See Zhang Jinchi "*Datang Sanzang qujing shihua* chengshu niandai kaolun" (A discussion of the date of *Tale of the Grand Tang Sanzang Seeking Buddhist Sutra*), *Xueshu jiaoliu* 4 (1990): 108–14. Relating to literary history, art history, religion, and other scholars' work, Zhang set an upper limit and lower limit for the book's publication date (both in the Song dynasty) and narrowed the most likely date down to end of the Northern Song. Chen Yinchi confirmed this stance by focusing on the rhyme style of *Shihua*. See Chen Yinchi, "*Datang Sanzang qujing shihua* shidaixing zaiyi: yi yunwen tizhi de kaocha wei zhongxin" (A revisit of the time of *Monk Xuanzang of the Tang Dynasty on a Pilgrimage for Buddhist Scriptures*: Focus on rhyme style), *Fudan Journal (Social Sciences)* 5 (2014): 69–80.

10. For a more detailed discussion of the change of the journey's nature in *Datang Sanzang qujing shihua* and the 1592 novel, see Anthony C. Yu, introduction, 53–59.

11. Dudbridge, *The Hsi-yu chi*, 29–47.

12. Ibid., 35.

13. Zhang Chengjian, "Datang Sanzang fashi qujingji shishi kaoyuan."

14. Lu Xun, *Zhongguo xiaoshuo shilue* (A brief history of the Chinese novel) (Beijing: Renmin Wenxue Chubanshe, 1973), 228.

15. For summaries and theories about the origin, see Anthony C. Yu, introduction; Dudbridge, *The Hsi-yu chi*; Cai Tieying, *Xiyou ji de dansheng* (The birth of *Xiyou ji*) (Beijing: Zhonghua Shuju, 2007); and Miyoko Nakano, *Sun Wukong de dansheng*: *Hou de minjian wenxue yu Xiyou ji*

(The birth of Sun Wukong—Monkey folklore and *Xiyou ji*) (Beijing: Zhonghua shu ju, 2002).

16. Ji Xianlian, "Luomo yanna zai Zhongguo" (Ramayana in China), *Zhongguo bijiao wenxue* 3 (1988): 13, 17, 22 (Hangzhou: Zhejiang Wenyi Chubanshe).

17. See Cai Tieying, *Xiyou ji de dansheng.*

18. These images are reprinted in many columns, e.g., in Cai Tieying, *Xiyou ji ziliao huibian* (A collection of materials on *Xiyou ji*) (Beijing: Zhonghua Shuju, 2010); Dudbridge, *The Hsi-yu chi*; and Nakano, *Sun Wukong de dansheng.*

19. *Datang Sanzang qujing shihua jiaozhu,* section 2, p. 12. I am using the print that is annotated by Li Shiren and Cai Jinghao (Beijing: Zhonghua shuju, 1997).

20. Dudbridge, *The Hsi-yu chi,* 31–32. Although Dudbridge here states that the *xiucai* title implies a junior academic qualification with no automatic official status, depending on the time of *Shihua*, the term does not necessarily mean those who have passed any qualification exams.

21. *Datang Sanzang qujing shihua jiaozhu*, section 11, pp. 31–32.

22. See Dudbridge, *The Hsi-yu chi*, 37–38, for an account of the development of the story of the Queen's peaches.

23. *Datang Sanzang qujing shihua jiaozhu*, section 10, p. 28.

24. Many of the episodes detailed in *Zaju* are mentioned in the fragments of the Korean book *The Interpreter Pak* (Pak tongshi) of roughly the same time of the Yuan period. See Dudbridge, *The Hsi-yu chi,* for detailed introduction and the text.

25. Sui, *Yuanqu xuan waibian*, *Zaju* scene 10, 659. I am using the edition of *Zaju xiyouji* in Sui Shusen and Zang Maoxun, eds., *Yuanqu xuan waibian* (Additional selected works of the Yuan *qu*) (Beijing: Zhonghua Shuju, 1959). For a summary in English of each scene of the *zaju,* see Dudbridge, *The Hsi-yu chi*, 193–200.

26. Sui, *Yuanqu xuan waibian*, *Zaju* scene 9, 654.

27. Ibid. He introduces himself as having "brass tendon, iron bone, golden eyes, diamond asshole, and tin penis."

28. Ibid., *Yuanqu xuan waibian*, *Zaju* scene 10, 659. [Xingzhe aside] "Such a plump monk. I may as well eat him up to my heart's content, and then return to Flower-Fruit Mountain."

29. Ibid., scene 10, 669.

30. Ibid., scene 10, 660.

31. Ibid., scene 9, 654–57.

32. Ibid., scenes 13–16, 665–76.

33. Ibid., scene 10, 659.

34. Ibid., scene 21, 687.

35. J. I. Crump, *Chinese Theater in the Days of Kublai Khan* (Ann Arbor: Center for Chinese Studies, University of Michigan, 199), 182–83; Wang Guowei, *Song Yuan xiqu shi*, 95.

36. Sui, *Yuanqu xuan waibian*, *Zaju* scene 9, 657.

37. Ibid., scene 15, 671.

38. Ibid., scene 15, 674.

39. Ibid., scene 17, 679.

40. See Dudbridge, *The Hsi-yu chi*, 129–38, for a discussion of a number of *zaju* related to the monkey figure or Erlang shen, the character who captures Monkey in some *zaju* and in *Xiyou ji.*

41. Dudbridge, *The Hsi-yu chi*, 82.

42. Ibid., 82–83.

43. *Mo* is one of the four main role categories of *zaju*: *mo* (male), *dan* (female), *jing* (villain), and *chow* (clown).

44. Qian Zhongshu lists as many as seven records, including *Zaju*, as one following previous examples, about monkeys abducting women (see Qian, *Guanzhui bian* [Compilations of tubes and awls] [Shanghai: Zhonghua shuju, 1979], 2:546).

45. See the preface and commentary in the Shibun edition of the drama printed in Japan in 1928. The preface is dated "Wanli jiayin," which is 1614.

46. The Ming printer of the drama considers Wu Changling as the author. Presently Yang Jingxian is considered as the author.

47. Yang Jingxian, *Yang Donglai xiansheng piping Xiyou ji,* (*Xiyou ji*: Annotated by Yang Donglai). Tokyo, Japan: Shibun, 1928), i–ii.

48. Yan Dunyi, "*Xiyou ji* he gudian xiqu de guanxi" (The relationship between *Journey to the West* and classical drama), in "*Xiyou ji*" *Yanjiu lunwen ji* (Collected essays on the study of *Xiyou ji*) (Beijing: Zuojia Chubanshe, 1957), 147.

49. *Zaju* scene 15, 671. It is in a song that Sun delivers the message from Pei Haitang to her father.

50. Dudbridge, *The Hsi-yu chi*, 63–74; see 179–88 for the Chinese text and an English translation.

51. Ibid., 63.

52. Ibid., 180.

53. There has been much study and discussion of the allegorical meaning of *Xiyou ji*, including by Chinese scholars of Qing and later time, and contemporary scholars in China and the West (see Plaks, "Allegory"; Plaks, *Four Masterworks*; and Anthony C. Yu, introduction).

54. For instance, in chapter 2 of *Xiyou ji*, a poem describes Subhūti's teaching of three religions: "For a while he lectured on Dao; For a while he spoke on Chan—To harmonize the Three Parties is a natural thing" (Wu Cheng'en, *Journey to the West*, trans. Yu [1977–83], 1:116). In chapter 47, Sun Wukong told the King of the Cart-Slow Kingdom to respect all three religions: "I hope you will honor the unity of the Three Religions: revere the monks, revere also the Daoists, and take care to nurture the talented. Your kingdom, I assure you, will be secure forever" (ibid., 2:316)

Many Ming and Qing scholars talks about the message of three religions in one. Yuan Yuling of Ming summarizes it as "three religions in one volume" (sanjiao yi kuo yu yibu); Zhang Hanzhang of Qing speaks of "three religions of one source" (sanjiao yiyuan); Liu Yiming and Feng Yanggui of Qing "three religions of one family" (sanjiao yijia); Zhu Dunyi "three religion with one principle" (he sanjiao er qi kui yi) (see Zhu Yixuan and Liu

Yuchen eds., *Xiyou ji ziliao huibian* [Research materials for *Xiyou ji* study] [Henan: Zhongzhou Shuhua She, 1983], 210, 240, 246, 262, 266). Contemporary scholars also comment on the teaching of three religions (see Lu Xun, *Zhongguo xiaoshuo shilue*; Plaks, *The Four Masterworks*; and Anthony C. Yu, introduction).

55. Anne E. McLaren, "Constructing New Reading Publics in Late Ming China," in *Printing and Book Culture in Late Imperial China*, ed. Cynthia J. Brokaw and Kai-Wing Chow, 152–83 (Berkeley: University of California Press, 2005), 152.

56. For readings of the book as mainly a work for fun, see Hu, "*Xiyou ji* kaozheng"; Lu Xun, *Zhongguo xiaoshuo shilue,* 310; and Yan Liang, "When High Culture Embraces the Low: Reading *Xiyou ji* as Popular Fiction in Chinese Society" (PhD diss., University of California, Santa Barbara, 2008).

57. In *Shihua*, however, there is a mention of a cudgel that Hou Xingzhe uses to beat the dragon he fights when the pilgrims pass the Nine-Dragon Pond. However, the mention of this is strange, since there is no description of Hou Xingzhe carrying any weapon, except using the three gifts from Vaisravana (see section 7, *Da Tang Sanzhang qujing shihua*).

58. In chapter 3, after obtaining the cudgel from the dragon palace, Sun Wukong explains to his little monkeys back at his kingdom: "Everything has its owners. This treasure has presided in the ocean treasury for who knows how many thousands of years, and it just happened to glow recently. The Dragon King only recognized it as a piece of black iron, though it is also said to be the divine rarity which fixed the bottom of the Heavenly River. After I struck it once and expressed my feeling that it was too large, it grew smaller" (Wu Cheng'en, *Journey to the West*, trans. Yu [1977–83], 1:137–38).

59. In chapter 51, having lost his cudgel to a demon, Sun Wukong visited the Jade Emperor to ask for help, using a styled language that sounds strange out of the mouth of the monkey. An immortal at the court asked why he has become so humble all of a sudden, to which Wukong responded, "I'm not acting haughtily at first and humbly afterwards, but right now I'm a monkey who has no rod to play with" (ibid., 3:3).

60. Ibid., 2:15–42.

61. Plaks, *Four Masterworks*, esp. 240–76.

62. Anthony C. Yu, introduction, esp. 63–76.

63. Qiancheng Li, "Transformations of Monkey: *Xiyou ji* Sequels and the Inward Turn," in *Snakes' Legs: Sequels, Continuations, Rewritings, and Chinese Fiction*, ed. Martin W. Huang, 46–74 (Honolulu: University of Hawai'i Press, 2004).

64. Robert E. Hegel, *The Novel in Seventeenth-Century China* (New York: Columbia University Press, 1981), e.g., 232; Andrew H. Plaks, "After the Fall: Hsing-shih yin-yüan chuan and the Seventeenth-Century Chinese Novel," *Harvard Journal of Asiatic Studies* 45, no. 2 (1985): 553. I have changed the title *Xiyou bu* from Wade-Giles style into Pinyin.

65. For a detailed reading of *Xiyou bu,* see Robert E. Hegel, "Picturing the Monkey King: Illustrations and Readings of the 1641 Novel *Xiyou*

bu," in *The Art of the Book in China*, 175–91 (London: London University School of Oriental and African Studies, 2006).

66. Although traditionally the author is believed to be Dong Yue, there are also scholars who argue that the author is Dong Yue's father, Dong Sizhang (see Fu Chengzhao, "*Xiyou bu* zuozhe Dong Sizhang kao" [On Dong Sizhang, author of *Xiyou bu], Wenxue yichan* 3 [1989]: 120–22; Gao Hongjun, *Xiyou bu* zuozhe shi shei" [Who is the author of *Xiyou bu*?], *Tianjin shida xuebao* 6 [1985]: 81–84; Hegel "Picturing the Monkey King," 176–78; Li Qiancheng, "*Xiyou bu* de zuozhe ji Ming Qing banben" [On the authorship of *Xiyou bu* and its Ming and Qing editions], *Chuantong Zhongguo yanjiu jikan* 7 [2009]: 306–21; and David Rolston, *Traditional Chinese Fiction and Commentary: Reading and Writing between the Lines* [Stanford, CA: Stanford University Press, 1997], 276–78).

67. Qiancheng Li, "Transformations of Monkey." Steven Moore in *The Novel: An Alternative History* 1600–1800 compares *Xiyou bu* to Joyce's *Finnegans Wake* and states that the writing reminds one of Carroll, Freud, Kafka, Jung, Joyce, and Borges (449–50).

68. See Liang's reading of sequels as allegorical interpretation, *When High Culture Embraces the Low*, 242–67.

CHAPTER 3

1. The Wan brothers—including Wan Laiming, Wan Guchan, Wan Chaochen, and Wan Dihuan—are considered the pioneers of Chinese animation.

2. Qtd. in Marie-Claire Quiquemelle, "The Wan Brothers and Sixty Years of Animated Film in China," trans. Claire Beliard, in *Perspectives on Chinese Cinema*, ed. Chris Berry (London: BFI, 1991). The article gives a history of the Wan brothers' animated films since the 1930s, most of which are educational and patriotic.

3. Laiming Wan and Guohun Wan, *Wo Yu Sun Wukong* (Sun Wukong and I) (Taiyuan: Beiyue Wenyi Chubanshe, 1986), 50.

4. Ibid., 90.

5. Mao Zedong, "Talks at the Yan'an Forum on Literature and Art," in *Modern Chinese Literary Thought: Writings on Literature*, 1893–1945, ed. Kirk A. Denton, 458–84 (Stanford, CA: Stanford University Press, 1996), 464–68.

6. Li Tianwang, in *Antian hui.*

7. Wang Hecheng, *Xinzhu Sun Houzi nao tiangong quanqu* (Monkey creates uproar in heaven, new complete script), printed by Zhuyou zhai, 1880, p. 9, copy in National Library of China, Beijing.

8. Anonymous, *Antian hui* (Tranquilizing heaven), hand-copied transcript, produced by Baiben Zhang bookshop (ca. 1850, Rare Book Division, National Library of China, Beijing.)

9. Weng Ouhong, *Weng Ouhong bianju shengya* (Weng Ouhong as a playwright) (Beijing: Zhongguo Xiju Chubanshe, 1986), 430.

10. Weng Ouhong, *Weng Ouhong bianju shengya* (Beijing: Tongxin chubanshe, 2008), 430–32. The emphasis on Tianxi xingjun, a figure that does

not exist in any of the traditional versions of *Xiyou ji*, reflected the government's disrespect for intellectuals. The case of Tianxi xingjun can be compared with the case of Liu Sanjie (see Lydia Liu, *Yuji shuxie: xiandai sixiangshi xiezuo gangyao* [Shanghai sanlian shudian, 1999]).

11. Ouhong Weng, *Da'nao tiangong.*

12. Ibid.

13. Mi Gu and Jiang Fan, "Youyi zhihua chuchu kai" (Friendship blooms everywhere), *Manhua yuekan*, November 18, 1955, 6.

14. Wan and Wan, *Wo Yu Sun Wukong,* 85–87.

15. Ibid., 136.

16. Ibid., 137.

17. Ibid., 140.

18. Ibid., 129.

19. Ibid., 128–53.

20. Ibid., 161.

21. Wu, *Xiyou ji,* chap. 31.

22. Ibid., chap. 32.

23. Ibid., chap. 27.

24. Rudolph G. Wagner, *The Contemporary Chinese Historical Drama: Four Studies* (Berkeley: University of California Press, 1990), 139–235.

25. Guo's poem, titled "Watching the Shao Play *Sun Wukong Subdues the White-Bone Demon*," goes as follows:

"Confounding humans and demons, right and wrong, / The monk was kind to foes and vicious to friends. / Endlessly he intoned "The Incantation of the Golden Hoop," / And thrice he let the White Bone Demon escape. / The monk deserved to be torn limb from limb; / Plucking a hair means nothing to the wonder-worker. / All praise is due to such timely teaching, / Even the Pig grew wiser than the fools."

In *Mao Tsetung Poems* (Beijing: Foreign Languages Press, 1976), 42. This version translated the difficult phrase *Dasheng mao* into a vague "wonder-worker." For Wagner's interpretation of this poem and of the phrase "Great Sage Mao," see Wagner, *The Contemporary Chinese Historical Drama*, 148–50.

26. Mao's entire poem goes: "A thunderstorm burst over the earth, / So a devil rose from a heap of white bones. / The deluded monk was not beyond the light, / But the malignant demon must wreak havoc. / The Golden Monkey wrathfully swung his massive cudgel / And the jade-like firmament was cleared of dust. / Today, a miasmal mist once more rising, / We hail Sun Wukung, the wonder-worker" (*Mao Tsetung Poems,* 41).

27. In the White Bone Demon episode, before dispelling Sun Wukong from the band, Tripitaka used the Tightening Fillet repeatedly in an effort to control him and stop him from beating the demon. Despite the serious distrust and misunderstanding, Monkey returned to Tripitaka's rescue when he learned that he was in need.

28. Carma Hinton, *Morning Sun* (Independent Television Service and the National Asian American Telecommunications Association, the BBC, and ARTE, 2003). Lei Feng (1940–1962) was a soldier of the Chinese army, a

subject of a nationwide propaganda campaign in 1963, in which he was characterized as a model soldier who selflessly devoted himself to the Communist Party and to the cause of communism in China.

29. Wagner, *The Contemporary Chinese Historical Drama*, 198.

CHAPTER 4

1. Hou Zhenwei, "Wangluo + xiaoyuan + daoban: Nairen xunwei de Dahua Xiyou xianxiang" (Internet + campus + bootleg: The intriguing *Dahua Xiyou* phenomenon"), *Bejing wanbao* (Beijing Evening News), August 24, 2000.

2. SMTH (Shuimu Tsinghua) BBS, based at Tsinghua University, and YTHT (Yi Ta Hu Tu) BBS, based at Peking University, were the largest and most influential BBS communities in China active during the turn of the twenty-first century.

3. Although few of the BBSes in China remain in existence, the BBS site at Massachusetts Institute of Technology is much less influenced by Internet censorship and is still a popular site for overseas Chinese students. Today, one of its forums is still named as *Dahua Xiyou* (Go West), devoted to topics related to study abroad.

4. See Li Zeng, "Adaptation as an Open Process: *Dahua* Fandom and the Reception of *A Chinese Odyssey*," *Adaptation* 6, no. 2 (2012): 187–201, for a review of how the audience response has changed the reception of *Dahua* in mainland China.

5. Zhang Lixian et al., eds., *Dahua Xiyou baodian* (Bible for *A Chinese Odyssey*) (Beijing: Xiandai Chubanshe, 2000), 141.

6. Hou, "Wangluo + xiaoyuan + daoban" (Internet + campus + bootleg).

7. See the list of audience reviews at https://movie.douban.com/subject/1292213/?from=subject-page. Many of these reviews carry hundreds of responses from other viewers.

8. "Ni lijie *Dahua Xiyou* pianwei naju 'Ta haoxiang yitiao gou' ma? Ruguo buneng lijie, na jiushi mei kandong" (Do you understand "He looks like a dog"? If not, You did not understand *Dahua Xiyou*), http://movie.douban.com/review/5199026/, posted by id Miao Hanzi on December 4, 2011.

9. "Women suo buneng kangju de zhiyou ai yu si" (What we cannot resist is only love and death), http://movie.douban.com/review/1385038/, published by id Wo Dui Ni de Wuyu Jianzhi Neng Chenmo Zhengge Yuzhou, May 21, 2008. The narrative voice of the review speaks of love from a woman's point of view.

10. "Gongzuo liangnian hou ganwu de *Dahua Xiyou*" (The *Dahua Xiyou* in my eyes two years after graduation), http://movie.douban.com/review/1427613/, reposted by id Dengdai Geduo, July 3, 2008. This review was circulated on the Internet, author unknown.

11. See, for instance, chapters 19, 23, 27, and 72 of *Xiyou ji*.

12. See chapter 1 of *Xiyou ji*. The pun of "*xing*" can function on multiple levels. In the original context of *Xiyou ji*, it means surname, nature, and temperament, but today the meaning of this word is extended to include sex/

sexuality. Although it may not be intended by the original text, Monkey's statement can work as a pun about his lack of sexuality—as he has never had sex in the *Journey to the West*, while a lot of contempary adaptations choose to focus on sexuality as a theme.

13. In relation to *Xiyou ji*, *xin* is traditionally translated as "mind," and the repeatedly used term *xinyuan*, referring to Sun Wukong, is translated as "mind monkey," since in Chinese the function of *xin* includes feeling and thinking. But in my discussion here I prefer to translate the term *xin* as "heart" for two reasons: First, *xin* does not correspond entirely to "mind." Although as the functionally defined entity in Chinese *xin* includes the function of mind, Chinese medicine does locate the organ of *xin* at the heart. Second, some Chinese adaptations of the Monkey King's story, such as *A Chinese Odyssey*, play with the concept of *xin* as both the heart-as-organ and the entity that is in charge of love, feeling, and memory. Referring to *xinyuan* as "heart monkey" facilitates our comparison in this context.

14. See the music video for "Queen's Road East," directed by Kuang Yongkang. There is also a video made for karaoke, in which the image is much more subtle, switching between the singer Luo Dayou and shots of daily life in Hong Kong.

15. The 1991 disc presents "Pearl of the Orient" sung by Luo Dayou. The other version is sung by a group of Taiwanese singers including Jonathan Li, Sarah Chen, Wakin Chau, Michelle Pan, Wawa, and Chao Chuan.

16. Ackbar Abbas, *Hong Kong: Culture and the Politics of Disappearance* (Minneapolis: University of Minnesota Press, 1997), 24.

17. See Ackbar Abbas's discussion about the cultural space of disappearance and the *déjà disparu* in Hong Kong ibid., chaps. 1 and 2.

18. Xixi, "Fucheng zhiyi" (Marvels of a floating city and other stories), in *Fucheng zhiyi: Xianggang xiaoshuo xinxuan* (New selected Hong Kong stories), ed. Ai Xiaoming, 24–36 (Beijing: Zhongguo Renmin Daxue Chubanshe, 1991).

19. Wang Dewei, "Xianggang: Yizuo chengshi de gushi" (Hong Kong: A story of a city), in *Ruhe xiandai, zenyang wenxue: 19–20 shiji zhongwen xiaoshuo xinlun* (The making of the modern, the making of a literature: New perspectives on 19th and 20th century Chinese fiction), 279–306 (Taipei: Rye Field, 1998).

20. Zeng, "Adaptation as an Open Process," 187.

21. Arif Dirlik, "Postsocialism? Reflections on 'Socialism with Chinese Characteristics,'" in *Marxism and the Chinese Experience*, ed. Dirlik and Maurice Meisner, 362–84 (Armonk, NY: M. E. Sharpe, 1989). For a summary of the discussions around this term, see Michel Hockx, *Internet Literature in China* (New York: Columbia University Press, 2015), 12–18. See also Sheldon Lu, "Postscript: Answering the Question, What is Chinese Postsocialism?," in *Chinese Modernity and Global Biopolitics: Studies in Literature and Visual Culture*, 204–10 (Honolulu: University of Hawai'i Press, 2007); Paul G. Pickowicz, "Huang Jianxin and the Notion of Postsocialism," in *New Chinese Cinemas: Forms, Identities, Politics,* ed. Nick Browne et al., 57–87 (Cambridge: Cambridge University Press, 1994); Chris Berry,

Postsocialist Cinema in Post-Mao China: The Cultural Revolution after the Cultural Revolution (New York: Routledge, 2004); Xudong Zhang, *Postsocialism and Cultural Politics: China in the Last Decade of the Twentieth Century* (Durham, NC: Duke University Press, 2008), 10; and James McGrath, *Postsocialist Modernity: Chinese Cinema, Literature, and Criticism in the Market Age* (Stanford, CA: Stanford University Press, 2008).

22. Pickowicz, "Huang Jianxin and the Notion of Postsocialism," 61–62. This view is expanded by Chris Berry in *Postsocialist Cinema in Post-Mao China.*

23. Hockx, *Internet Literature in China*, 16–18.

24. These stories are often circulated online with the authorship unknown. *Dahua Xiyou baodian* includes some examples of such retellings in the third section of the book.

25. Jin Hezai, *Wukong zhuan* (Story of Wukong) (Beijing: Zuojia chubanshe, 2000); Li Feng, "Ling yizhong shengyin" (Another voice), in *Jinye wuren rushui* (No one sleeps tonight), 45–71 (Wuhan: Hubei jiaoyu chubanshe, 2002).

27. For instance, *Tangseng zhuan* (Story of Tripitaka), by Mingbai Ren (Chengdu: Bashu shushe, 2001); *Xiyou Tangseng zhuan* (Xiyou—Story of Tripitaka) by Mo Nianjing (www.qidian.com); *Tangseng qingshi* (Love story of Tripitaka), by Murong Xuecun (Tianjin: Tianjin renmin chubanshe, 2003); *Tianpeng zhuan* (Story of Tianpeng), by Huoji (Beijing: Guangming ribao chubanshe, 2002); *Xiyou Bajie zhuan* (Xiyou—Story of Bajie) by Wangtian Yaomingyue (www.anzhuowang.net); *Shaseng zhuan* (Story of Sand Monk), by Xu Zhengkang (www.qidian.com); *Xiyou Shaseng zhuan* (Xiyou—Story of Sand Monk), by Qingtian Shangxian (www.qidian.com); and *Shaseng riji* (Sand Monk's diary), by Lin Changzhi (Changsha: Hunan wenyi chubanshe, 2002).

27. Hockx, *Internet Literature in China*, 17.

28. On the cover of the book, *Story of Wukong* is promoted as a winner of the Second Internet Writing Competition, and Jin Hezai as one of the top-ten Internet writers voted by bookuu.com, a large online bookstore.

29. "Wangluo wenxue shinian pandian luoxia weimu" (The curtain falls for Internet Literature Ten Year Review). See news.xinhuanet.com, June 26, 2009.

30. Jin Hezai, *Story of Wukong*, 56.

31. The two sequences are the focus of chapters 5 and 58 of *Xiyou ji.* The titles of these chapters name these actions as *luan* (chaos), indicating that these actions are marked as against the cosmic/social order. In historical language, *luan* is used to refer to military insurrections.

32. Jin Hezai, *Story of Wukong*, 182–83.

33. Li Feng, "Ling yizhong shengyin," 71.

34. Ibid., 70.

35. Ibid., 70–71.

36. See reviewer evaluation and reviews at https://movie.douban.com/review/ 5317291/. The count had been updated when I accessed the site on April 3, 2016.

37. See the review and other audience responses at https://movie.douban.com/review/6530776/.

38. See, for instance, "Ouran yu biran" (Coincidence or inevitability) by Ma Yong in *People's Daily* on July 24, 2015, which expresses hope that the success of the film will bring a return to the glory of Chinese animation, just like the return of glory of the Monkey King at the end of the film (http://culture.people.com.cn/n/2015/0724/c87423-27353338.html).

39. See popular reviews at douban.com: https://movie.douban.com/review/7520681/; and https://movie.douban.com/review/7513217/.

40. *Panni, duobian, leguan,* and *jianchi*. Dai further explains that by "rebelliousness" he does not mean the immature disobedience of a child but rather the spirit of breaking through the limitations of a grown-up. And by "variability" he means the ability to try different artistic style (see *Zhongguo hao gequ* [Sing my song], season 2, episode 5).

41. Dai Quan, "Wukong," *Zhongguo hao gequ* (Sing my song), season 2, episode 5.

CHAPTER 5

1. M. M. Bakhtin, *The Dialogic Imagination*, trans. Caryl Emerson and Michael Holquist (Austin: University of Texas Press, 1981), 84.

2. Ibid., 84, 85.

3. Scholars such as Robert Stam and Caryl Emerson have deployed Bakhtin's concept of "chronotope" as a useful tool to examine adaptations in film and literary studies. See, for instance, Robert Stam's *Subversive Pleasures: Bakhtin, Cultural Criticism, and Film* (Baltimore: Johns Hopkins University Press, 1989); and Caryl Emerson's *Boris Godunov: Transpositions of a Russian Theme*. More recent scholarly work has focused on the central importance of the chronotope in the study of adaptation. For instance, in "The Chronotope and the Study of Literary Adaptation: The Case of *Robinson Crusoe*," in *Bakhtin's Theory of the Literary Chronotope: Reflections, Applications, Perspectives*, ed. Nele Bemong, Pieter Borghart, M. De Dobbeleer, Kristoffel Demoen, Koen De Temmerman, and Bart Keunen (Ghent, Belgium: Academia Press, 2010), Tara Collington provides analyses of three different rewritings of the Robinson Crusoe story, each showcasing a Crusoe in a different temporal/spatial setting, and demonstrating significant differences in the story that are caused by chronotopic changes.

4. Bakhtin, *Dialogic Imagination*, 154.

5. Ibid., 155.

6. Wu Cheng'en, *The Journey to the West*, trans. Yu (1977–83), 1:429

7. Carlos Rojas calls the five-hundred-year gap a "temporal interregnum" in which the adaptations he discussed, including *The Lost Empire*, *A Chinese Odyssey*, and *Journey to the Max*, grapple with identity problems represented via the temporal dislocation (see Rojas, "Western Journeys of *Journey to the West*," in *Sinographies: Writing China*, ed. Eric Hayot, Haun Saussy, and Steven G. Yao, 333–54 (Minneapolis: University of Minnesota Press, 2007).

8. Bakhtin, *Dialogic Imagination*, 248.

9. Ibid., 90.

10. Ibid., 91.

11. When Nick meets the Monkey King for the first time, he is informed that he is in the China that was rebuilt within "Emperor Huangdi's tomb," while at the beginning of the miniseries Nick himself speaks of the miniature of China that is contained in one of Emperor Qin Shihuangdi's tombs. Since Nick and his company were talking about the tombs of Qin Shihuang and his terra-cotta warriors, one must take the film to mean that the mythical China is located within Emperor Qin Shihuang's tomb.

12. See Hwang interview in "It's OK to Be Wrong and/or It's OK to Be Hwang," http://usasians-articles.tripod.com/davidhenryhwang-screenwriter.html.

CHAPTER 6

1. Elizabeth Ammons and Annette White Parks, *Tricksterism in Turn-of-the-Century American Literature: A Multicultural Perspective* (Hanover, NH: University Press of New England, 1994), xi, "Tricksters and trickster energy [of writers at the margins] articulate a whole other, independent, cultural reality and positive way of negotiating multiple cultural systems." Essays in the collection that Ammons coedited with White-Parks deal with the relationship between trickster strategies and energies on one hand and hegemonic white patriarchal power in the United States on the other.

2. Ibid. The introduction expresses belief that trickster strategies of writers in marginal social positions are capable of creating a space "located and constantly reinvented in cultural borderlands or even in a space totally outside white patriarchal authority."

3. This expansion is seen, for instance, in the work of anthropologist Victor Turner, *The Anthropology of Performance* (Baltimore: PAJ, 1988).

4. See Judith Butler, *Gender Trouble Feminism and the Subversion of Identity* (New York: Routledge, 1990); and Judith Butler, *Bodies That Matter: On the Discursive Limits of "Sex"* (New York: Routledge, 1993).

5. Dorinne Kondo, for instance, writes about the ways Japanese fashion and Asian American theater illuminate the performance of race (see Kondo, *About Face: Performing Race in Fashion and Theatre* (New York: Routledge, 1997).

6. A non-profit theater company, based in New York, whose stated mission is the promotion of traditional Chinese art and bridging of Eastern and Western aesthetics and forms. Other Monkey King plays that CTW produced include *The Birth of Monkey King, Monkey King in New York,* and *Monkey King and the Mountain of Fiery Tongues* (for more information, see www.chinesetheatreworks.org).

7. *Day Jobs, Opera Dreams* premiered in 2003. It was recently performed in the 25th Ko Festival of Performance held at Amherst College, Amherst, Massachusetts, July–August, 2016.

8. For more about *Journey beyond the West*, see Arthur J. Sabatini, "Fred Ho's Operatic Journey," in *Yellow Power, Yellow Soul: The Radical Art of Fred Ho*, ed. Roger N. Buckley and Tamara Roberts, 63–94 (Champaign: University of Illinois Press, 2013), 71–74; and Bill Mullen "Making Monkey Signify: Fred Ho's Revolutionary Vision Quest," in *Afro-Orientalism*, 163–206 (Minneapolis: University of Minnesota Press, 2004), 184–89.

9. Fred Ho, *Monkey: Part Two*, The Monkey Orchestra (Koch Jazz, 1997), liner notes.

10. Ibid.

11. Mullen, "Making Monkey Signify," 184–89.

12. The epilogue of *Monkey: Part Two* states that although "there have been many interpretations of the world [of Monkey], the point, however, is to change it."

13. For a discussion of Wittman's imagination of a panethnic Asian American community, see Karen Har-Yen Chow, "Imagining Panethnic Community and Performing Identity in Maxine Hong Kingston's *Tripmaster Monkey: His Fake Book*," in *Contemporary Asian American Communities: Intersections and Divergences*, ed. Linda Trinh Võ and Rick Bonus, 177–90 (Philadelphia: Temple University Press, 2002.

14. Homi Bhabha, *The Location of Culture* (New York: Routledge, 1994), 66.

15. Ibid., 67, emphasis original.

16. See Gene Yang's comment on the origins of *American Born Chinese* at www.firstsecondbooks.com/authors/geneYangBlogMain.html. Yang has made it clear in various interviews that his version of the Monkey King story is about his own experience as an Asian American. See, for another instance, the December 2006 interview of Gene Yang by Jonathan Baylis at www.the-trades.com/article.php?id=5053.

17. The Chinese translation of "I am who I am" in Exodus 3:13–15 in the Studium Biblicum Version of the Bible in Chinese used by Chinese Catholics.

18. June 2007 interview with Gene Yang, http://writingya.blogspot.com/2007/06/summer-blog-blast-tour-kick-off-gene.html.

19. Wu Cheng'en, *The Journey to the West*, trans. Yu (1977–83), 166–79.

20. Ibid., 171–72.

21. Ibid., 172.

22. Ibid., 173.

23. Gene Leun Yang, *American Born Chinese* (New York: First Second, 2006), 15.

24. Wu Cheng'en, *The Journey to the West*, trans. Yu (1977–83), chap. 4.

25. Yang, *American Born Chinese*, 60.

26. Ibid., 69–70.

27. Ibid., 84.

28. Ibid., 67.

29. Ibid., 78.

30. Ibid., 79.

31. Ibid., 80–81.

32. Ibid., 67. See the description of four "living creatures" in Revelation 4:7; four "living beings" in Ezekiel 1:4–28; and "cherubim" with four faces in Ezekiel 10:1–22.

33. Yang, *American Born Chinese*, 215.

34. Ibid.

35. See Lisa Lowe, *Immigrant Acts: On Asian American Cultural Politics* (Durham, NC: Duke University Press, 1996), for discussions of the representation of Asians as perpetual immigrants by American culture.

36. Philip P. Choy, Lorraine Dong, and Marlon K. Hom, eds., *The Coming Man: 19th Century American Perceptions of the Chinese* (Seattle: University of Washington Press, 1994), 147.

37. See Gene Yang's comment on stereotypes at http://firstsecondbooks.typepad.com/mainblog/2007/05/gene_yang_on_st.html, May 2007.

38. Ibid. See also Yang, *American Born Chinese,* 48, for the referenced image.

39. See Gene Yang's comment on origins of *American Born Chinese* at www.firstsecondbooks.com/authors/geneYangBlogMain.html.

40. Ibid.

41. Yang, *American Born Chinese*, 221.

42. Ibid., 212–13.

43. Edward Said, *Orientalism* (New York: Pantheon, 1978), 72.

44. Bhabha, *The Location of Culture,* 101.

45. Gene Yang has admitted that the Monkey King story is a reflection of his own experience and that "Jin's story is based on [his] own" (www.firstsecondbooks.com/authors/geneYangBlogMain.html).

46. Yang, *American Born Chinese*, 145.

47. Homi Bhabha, "The Other Question," *Screen* 24, no. 6 (1983): 18–36, reprinted in *The Location of Culture*, by Bhabha, 66–84 (New York: Routledge, 1994), 77.

48. Ibid., 80, emphasis original.

49. Shirley Geok-lin Lim, "The Ambivalent American: Asian American Literature on the Cusp," in *Reading the Literatures of Asian America*, ed. Lim and Amy Ling (Philadelphia: Temple University Press, 1992), 18–19.

50. Ibid., 19.

51. Ibid., 22.

52. David Palumbo-Liu, *Asian/American Historical Crossings of a Racial Frontier* (Stanford, CA.: Stanford University Press, 1999), 1.

53. Chuh, *Imagine Otherwise: On Asian Americanist Critique* (Durham, NC: Duke University Press, 2003), 9.

54. Ibid., 10.

55. Qtd. ibid., 82.

56. Jin/Danny is associated with buck teeth twice in the book. The first time is when little Jin has just transferred to a new school and is called a "Bucktooth" by a group of non-Asian schoolkids, one of whom really has bucked-out teeth. The second time is when, after Chin-Kee's visit, Danny's friend Melanie realized that his teeth "buck out a little" and therefore

referred him to her uncle, an orthodontist (see Yang, *American Born Chinese*, 33, 124).

57. Chuh has suggested that we might "think in terms of 'Asian American' *unification* rather than identity to frame the cultural and political collectivity" (see Chuh, *Imagine Otherwise*, 82).

CONCLUSION

1. Wagner, *The Contemporary Chinese Historical Drama*, 139.

2. A bulletin board system site started in 1997 at bbs.mit.edu but later moved to the current domain at www.mitbbs.com.

SELECTED BIBLIOGRAPHY

Abbas, Ackbar. *Hong Kong: Culture and the Politics of Disappearance*. Minneapolis: University of Minnesota Press, 1997.

Ahmad, Aijaz. "Jameson's Rhetoric of Otherness and the 'National Allegory.'" *Social Text* 17 (1987): 3–25.

Althusser, Louis. "Ideology and Ideological State Apparatuses (Notes towards an Investigation)." *Lenin and Philosophie and Other Essays*, translated by Ben Brewster, 127–88. New York: Monthly Review Press, 1971.

Ammons, Elizabeth, and Annette White Parks, eds. *Tricksterism in Turn-of-the-Century American Literature: A Multicultural Perspective*. Hanover, NH: University Press of New England, 1994.

Anderson, Benedict. *Imagined Communities: Reflections on the Origin and Spread of Nationalism*. London: Verso, 1983.

Anonymous. *Antian hui* 安天会 (Tranquilizing heaven). Hand-copied transcript, produced by Baiben Zhang 百本张 bookshop, ca. 1850. Rare Book Division, National Library of China, Beijing.

———. "Antian hui" 安天会 (Tranquilizing heaven). *Wenming dagu shuci* 文明大鼓书词. Printed by Beiping Damochang Xuegutang 北平打磨厂学古堂, ca. 1900.

———. "Da'nao tiangong" 大闹天宫 (Havoc in heaven). Damochang Zhiwentang 打磨厂致文堂, ca. 1900.

Bakhtin, M. M. *The Dialogic Imagination*. Translated by Caryl Emerson and Michael Holquist. Austin: University of Texas Press, 1981.

———. "Discourse Typology in Prose." In *Readings in Russian Poetics: Formalist and Structuralist Views*, edited by Ladislav Matejka and Krystyna Pomorska. Cambridge: MIT Press, 1971.

———. "Toward a Reworking of the Dostoevsky Book." In *Critical Essays on Dostoevsky*, edited by Robin Feuer Miller, 247–64. Boston: G. K. Hall, 1986.

Balibar, Etienne, and Immanuel Wallerstein. *Race, Nation, Class: Ambiguous Identities*. New York: Verso, 1991.

Bantly, Francisca Cho. "Buddhist Allegory in the *Journey to the West*." *Journal of Asian Studies* 48, no. 3 (1989): 512–24.

Barthes, Roland. *Mythologies*. Paris: Éditions du Seuil, 1957.

Bassnett, Susan, and André Lefevere, eds. *Constructing Cultures: Essays on Literary Translation*. Clevedon, United Kingdom: Multilingual Matters, 1998.

———. *Post-colonial Translation: Theory and Practice*. London: Routledge, 1999.

———. *Translation, History and Culture*. London: Pinter, 1990.

Beal, Samuel. *Si-yu-ki: Buddhist Records of the Western World. Translated from the Chinese of Hiuen Tsiang (A.D. 629)*. 1884. Reprint, New York: Paragon, 1968.

Bell, Duncan. "Mythscapes: Memory, Mythology, and National Identity." *British Journal of Sociology* 54, no. 1 (2003): 63–81.

Bemong, Nele, Pieter Borghart, M. De Dobbeleer, and Kristoffel Demoen, eds. *Bakhtin's Theory of the Literary Chronotope: Reflections, Applications, Perspectives*. Ghent, Belgium: Academia Press, 2010.

Berry, Chris. *Perspectives on Chinese Cinema*. Conference on Chinese Oral and Performing Literature. Ithaca, NY: China-Japan Program, Cornell University, 1985.

———. *Postsocialist Cinema in Post-Mao China: The Cultural Revolution after the Cultural Revolution*. New York: Routledge, 2004.

Bhabha, Homi. *The Location of Culture*. New York: Routledge, 1994.

———. "Of Mimicry and Man: The Ambivalence of Colonial Discourse." *October* 28 (1984): 125–33.

———. "The Other Question." *Screen* 24, no. 6 (1983): 18–36, reprinted in *The Location of Culture*, 66-84. New York: Routledge, 1994.

———. "Signs Taken for Wonders: Questions of Ambivalence and Authority under a Tree outside Delhi, May 1817." *Critical Inquiry* 12, no. 1 (1985): 144–65.

———. "Sly Civility." *October* 34 (1985): 71–80.

Butler, Judith. *Bodies That Matter: On the Discursive Limits of "Sex."* New York: Routledge, 1993.

———. *Gender Trouble: Feminism and the Subversion of Identity*. New York: Routledge, 1990.

Cai Tieying 蔡铁鹰. *Xiyou Ji de dansheng*《西游记》的诞生 (The birth of *Xiyou ji*). Beijing: Zhonghua Shuju, 2007.

———. *Xiyou Ji ziliao huibian* 西游记资料汇编 (A collection of materials on *Xiyou ji*). Beijing: Zhonghua Shuju, 2010.

Cai Zhizhong 蔡志忠. *Xiyou ji 38 bian* 西游记38变 (Thirty-eight transformations of *Xiyou ji*). Taipei: Shibao Wenhua Chubanshe, 1987.

Campany, Robert. "Demons, Gods, and Pilgrims: The Demonology of the *Hsi-yu Chi*." *Chinese Literature: Essays, Articles, Reviews* 7, no. 1/2 (1985): 95–115.

Cardwell, Sarah. *Adaptation Revisited: Television and the Classic*. Manchester, United Kingdom: Manchester University Press, 2002.

Chan, Leo Tak-hung. "Text and Talk: Classical Literary Tales in Traditional China and the Context of Casual Oral Storytelling." *Asian Folklore Studies* 56, no. 1 (1997): 33–63.

Chao, Patricia. *Monkey King*. New York: HarperCollins, 1997.

Cheang, Pou-Soi, dir. *Xiyou ji: Danao tiangong* 西游记: 大闹天宫 (*The Monkey King*). Hong Kong: Global Star Productions et al., 2014.

———, dir. *Xiyou ji zhi Sun Wukong sanda Baigu Jing*, 西游记之孙悟空三打白骨精 (*The Monkey King 2)*. Hong Kong: Filmko Films Production Limited, 2016.

Chen Dakang 陈大康. *Mingdai xiaoshuo shi* 明代小说史 (A history of the Ming novel). Shanghai: Shanghai wenyi chubanshe, 2000.

———. *Tongsu xiaoshuo de lishi guiji* 通俗小说的历史轨迹 (The historical route of popular fiction). Changsha: Hunan chubanshe, 1993.

Chen Pingyuan 陈平原. "Dangdai Zhongguo daxue de bulv yu shengji" 当代中国大学公平发展的步履与生机 (Chinese universities: Development and prospect). *Tansuo yu zhengming* 探索与争鸣 (Exploration and free views) 5 (2015): 17–19.

———. *Ershi shiji zhongguo xiaoshuo shi* 二十世纪中国小说史 (A history of the twentieth-century Chinese novel). Beijing: Beijing daxue chubanshe, 1989.

———. *Xiaoshuo shi: Lilun yu shijian* 小说史: 理论与实践 (History of the novel: Theory and practice). Beijing: Beijing daxue chubanshe, 1993.

———. *Zhongguo xiaoshuo xushi moshi de gaibian* 中国小说叙事模式的转变 (Transformation of the narrative model of the Chinese novel). Shanghai: Shanghai Renmin chubanshe, 1988.

Chen Yinchi 陈引驰, "*Datang Sanzang qujing shihua* shidaixing zaiyi: yi yunwen tizhi de kaocha wei zhongxin" 大唐三藏取经诗话时代性再议: 以韵文体制的考察为中心 (A Revisit of the Time of *Monk Xuanzang of the Tang Dynasty on a Pilgrimage for Buddhist Scriptures:* Focus on Rhyme Style), Fudan Journal (Social Sciences) 5 (2014): 69–80.

Cheng, Christina Miu Bing. "Colonial Stereotyping and Cultural Anthropophagy."

In *Colonizer and Colonized*, edited by Theo D'haen and Patricia Krüs, 135–50. Amsterdam: Rodopi, 2000.

Cheung, King-Kok. "The Woman Warrior versus the Chinaman Pacific: Must a Chinese-American Critic Choose between Feminism and Heroism?" In *Conflicts in Feminism*, edited by Marianne Hirsch and Evelyn Fox Keller, 234–51. New York: Routledge, 1990.

Chow, Karen Har-Yen. "Imagining Panethnic Community and Performing Identity in Maxine Hong Kingston's *Tripmaster Monkey: His Fake Book*." In *Contemporary Asian American Communities: Intersections and Divergences*, edited by Linda Trinh Võ and Rick Bonus, 177–90. Philadelphia: Temple University Press, 2002.

Chow, Rey. *The Protestant Ethnic and the Spirit of Capitalism*. New York: Columbia University Press, 2002

———. *Writing Diaspora: Tactics of Intervention in Contemporary Cultural Studies*. Bloomington: Indiana University Press, 1993.

Choy, Philip P., Lorraine Dong, and Marlon K. Hom, eds. *The Coming Man: 19th Century American Perceptions of the Chinese*. Seattle: University of Washington Press, 1994.

Chuh, Kandice. *Imagine Otherwise: On Asian Americanist Critique*. Durham, NC: Duke University Press, 2003.

Chun, Mei. *The Novel and Theatrical Imagination in Early Modern China*. Leiden, Netherlands: Brill, 2011.

Collington, Tara. "The Chronotope and the Study of Literary Adaptation: The Case of *Robinson Crusoe*." In *Bakhtin's Theory of the Literary Chronotope: Reflections, Applications, Perspectives*, edited by Nele Bemong, Pieter Borghart, M. De Dobbeleer, Kristoffel Demoen, Koen De Temmerman, and Bart Keunen. Ghent, Belgium: Academia Press, 2010.

Cooksey, Thomas L. "Hero of the Margin: The Trickster as Deterritorialized Animal." *Thalia: Studies in Literary Humor* 18 (1998): 50–61.

Crump, J. I. *Chinese Theater in the Days of Kublai Khan*. Ann Arbor: Center for Chinese Studies, University of Michigan, 1990.

Da Cuo, ed. "Nao tiangong" 闹天宫. *Xi kao*. Vol. 28. Shanghai: Zhonghua Tushuguan, 1924.

Dai Quan 戴荃. "Wukong" 悟空. *Zhongguo hao gequ* (Sing my song). Season 2, episode 5. CCTV-3.

Dagut, M. B. "Can 'Metaphor' Be Translated?" *Babel* 22 (1976): 21–33.

Davies, J. M. Q. "Allegoresis, Hybridity and Mo's the Monkey King." *Mattoid* 52–53 (1998): 278–87.

Deeney, John J. "Of Monkeys and Butterflies: Transformation in M. H. Kingston's *Tripmaster Monkey* and D. H. Hwang's *M. Butterfly*." *MELUS* 18 (1993): 21–39.

Deppman, Hsiu-Chuang. *Adapted for the Screen: The Cultural Politics of Modern Chinese Fiction and Film*. Honolulu: University of Hawai'i Press, 2010.

Dirlik, Arif. "Postsocialism? Reflections on 'Socialism with Chinese Characteristics.'" In *Marxism and the Chinese Experience*, edited by Dirlik and Maurice Meisner, 362–84. Armonk, NY: M. E. Sharpe, 1989.

Dong, Lan. *Mulan's Legend and Legacy in China and the United States*. Philadelphia: Temple University Press, 2011.

Dudbridge, Glen. *The Hsi-yu chi: A Study of Antecedents to the Sixteenth-Century Chinese Novel*. Cambridge: Cambridge University Press, 1970.

Edison, Victoria, and James Edison. *Cultural Revolution: Posters & Memorabilia*. Atglen, PA: Schiffer, 2005.

Ellwood, Robert S. "A Japanese Mythic Trickster Figure: Susa-No-O." In *Mythical Trickster Figures: Contours, Contexts, and Criticisms*, edited by William J. Hynes and William G. Doty, 141–58. Tuscaloosa: University of Alabama Press, 1993.

Emerson, Caryl. *Boris Godunov: Transpositions of a Russian Theme*. Bloomington: Indiana University Press, 1986.

Eperjesi, John R. *The Imperialist Imaginary: Visions of Asia and the Pacific in American Culture*. Hanover, NH: Dartmouth College Press, 2005.

Esherick, Joseph W., Paul G. Pickowicz, and Andrew G. Walder. *The Chinese Cultural Revolution as History*. Stanford, CA: Stanford University Press, 2006.

Evans, Harriet, and Stephanie Donald, eds. *Picturing Power in the People's Republic of China: Posters of the Cultural Revolution*. Lanham, MD: Rowman and Littlefield, 1999.

Even-Zohar, Itamar. "Polysystem Studies." *Poetics Today* 11, no. 1 (Spring 1990): 9–26.

Fang, Hong. "The Ethnic Trickster in Maxine Hong Kingston's *Tripmaster Monkey: His Fake Book*." PhD diss., University of Hong Kong, 2003.

Fong, Kuang-Yu, dir. *Day Jobs, Opera Dreams*. Long Island, NY: Chinese Theatre Works Ensemble, 2003.

Foucault, Michel. "Nietzsche, Genealogy, History." In *Language, Counter-Memory, Practice: Selected Essays and Interviews*, edited by D. F. Bouchar, 139–64. Ithaca, NY: Cornell University Press, 1977.

———. *This Is Not a Pipe*. Translated by James Harkness. Berkeley: University of California Press, 1983.

Fu Chengzhou 傅承洲. "*Xiyou bu* zuozhe Dong Sizhang kao" 西游补作者董斯张考 (On Dong Sizhang, author of *Xiyou bu*). *Wenxue yichan* 文学遗产 3 (1989): 120–22.

Fulbrook, M. "Myth-Making and National Identity: The Case of the GDR."

In *Myths and Nationhood*, edited by G. Hosking and G. Schopflin, 72–87. New York: Routledge, 1997.

Gao, Yan. *The Art of Parody: Maxine Hong Kingston's Use of Chinese Sources.* New York: Peter Lang, 1996.

Gao Hongjun 高洪钧. "*Xiyou bu* zuozhe shi shei" 西游补作者是谁 (Who is the author of *Xiyou bu*?). *Tianjin shida xuebao* 天津师大学报 6 (1985): 81–84.

Gates, Henry Louis, Jr. "Preface: Talking Books." In *The Norton Anthology of African American Literature*, edited by Gates et al. New York: Norton, 1997.

———. *The Signifying Monkey: A Theory of African-American Literary Criticism.* New York: Oxford University Press, 1988.

Ge Ben 葛卉. "Yiyi de zhuixun he jiazhi chidu de xiaojie: cong *Xiyou ji* dao *Dahua Xiyou*" 意义的追寻与价值尺度的消解——从西游记到大话西游 (Pursuit of meaning, deconstruction of value: From *Journey to the West* to *A Chinese Odyssey*). *Dianying wenxue* 10 (2006): 17–18.

Ge Meihong 葛美宏. "*Xiyou ji* xiaoshuo de gaibian yu yingxiang yanjiu shuping"《西游记》小说的改编与影响研究述评 (Review of adaptation and influence study of the novel *Journey to the West*). In *Jiujiang xueyuan xuebao* (shehui kexue ban) 178, no. 3 (2015): 37–41.

Genette, Gérard. *Palimpsests: Literature in the Second Degree.* Lincoln: University of Nebraska Press, 1997.

Gentzler, Edwin. *Contemporary Translation Theories.* London: Routledge, 1993.

———. *Translation and Identity in the Americas: New Directions in Translation Theory.* New York: Routledge, 2007.

———. *Translation and Rewriting in the Age of Post-Translation Studies.* New York: Routledge, 2017.

———. "Translation Metaphor: Beyond the Western Tradition." *Translation Perspectives* 11 (2000): 3–22.

Gulik, Robert Hans van. *The Gibbon in China: An Essay in Chinese Animal Lore.* Leiden, Netherlands: E. J. Brill, 1967.

Hagedorn, Jessica Tarahata. *Charlie Chan Is Dead: An Anthology of Contemporary Asian American Fiction.* New York: Penguin, 1993.

Hanan, Patrick, et al. *Writing and Materiality in China: Essays in Honor of Patrick Hanan.* Cambridge: Harvard University Asia Center for Harvard-Yenching Institute. Distributed by Harvard University Press, 2003.

Hayot, Eric, Haun Saussy, and Steven G. Yao. *Sinographies: Writing China.* Minneapolis: University of Minnesota Press. 2008.

Hegel, Robert E. *The Novel in Seventeenth-Century China.* New York: Columbia University Press, 1981.

———. "Picturing the Monkey King: Illustrations and Readings of the 1641 Novel *Xiyou bu*." In *The Art of the Book in China*, 175–91. London: London University School of Oriental and African Studies, 2006.

———. "Traditional Chinese Fiction—The State of the Field." *Journal of Asian Studies* 53, no. 2 (May 1994): 394–425.

Helstern, Linda Luzut. "Griever: An American Monkey King in China: A Cross-Cultural Re-Membering." In *Loosening the Seams: Interpretations of Gerald Vizenor*, 136–54. Bowling Green, OH: Popular, 2000.

Hermans, Theo, ed. *The Manipulation of Literature: Studies in Literary Translation*. London: Croom Helm, 1985.

Hills, Matt. *Fan Cultures*. London: Routledge, 2002.

Hinton, Carma, et al. dirs. *Morning Sun* 八九点钟的太阳 (Ba jiu dian zhong de taiyang). Brookline, MA: Long Bow Group, 2003.

Ho, Fred. *Monkey: Part One*. The Monkey Orchestra. Port Washington, NY: Koch International, 1996.

———. *Monkey: Part Two*. The Monkey Orchestra. Port Washington, NY: Koch International, 1997.

Ho Menghua, dir. *Cave of the Silken Web* 盘丝洞. Produced by Run Run Shaw邵逸夫. Hong Kong: Shaw Brothers, 1967.

———, dir. *The Land of Many Perfumes* 女儿国. Produced by Runme Shaw 邵仁枚. Hong Kong: Shaw Brothers, 1968.

———, dir. *Monkey Goes West* 西游记. Produced by Run Run Shaw 邵逸夫. Hong Kong: Shaw Brothers, 1966.

———, dir. *Princess Iron Fan* 铁扇公主. Produced by Runme Shaw 邵仁枚. Hong Kong: Shaw Brothers, 1966.

Hockx, Michel. *Internet Literature in China*. New York: Columbia University Press, 2015.

Hou Zhenwei 侯振威. "Wangluo + xiaoyuan + daoban: Nairen xunwei de Dahua Xiyou xianxiang" 网络+校园+盗版: 耐人寻味的大话西游现象 (Internet + campus + bootleg: The intriguing *Dahua Xiyou* phenomenon). *Bejing wanbao*, August 24, 2000.

Hsia, C. T. "Comedy and the Myth in the *Hsi yu chi*." In *Wen-lin: Studies in the Chinese Humanities*, edited by Chow Tse-tsung, 229–45. Madison: University of Wisconsin Press, 1968.

———. "Journey to the West." In *The Classical Chinese Novel: A Critical Introduction*, 115–64. New York: Columbia University Press, 1968.

Hu Shih 胡适 (1891–1962). "*Xiyou ji* kaozheng" 西游记考证 (Textual criticism of *Xiyou ji*). In *Hu Shih gudian wenxue yanjiu lunji* 胡适古典文学研究论集 (Selected essays of Hu Shih on classical literature). Shanghai: Shanghai Guji Chubanshe, 1988.

Huang Zhouxing 黄周星 (1611–1680). *Xiyou zhengdaoshu* 西游证道书 (The way to enlightenment through *Journey to the West*). Beijing: Zhonghua Shuju, 1998.

Huoji火鸡. *Tianpeng zhuan* 天蓬传 (Story of Tianpeng). Beijing: Guangming Ribao Chubanshe, 2002.

Hutcheon, Linda. *A Theory of Adaptation*. London: Routledge, 2013.

Hwang, David Henry. *M. Butterfly*. New York: Penguin, 1989.

Hyde, Lewis. *Trickster Makes This World: Mischief, Myth, and Art*. New York: North Point Press, 1988.

Hynes, William J. "Mapping the Characteristics of Mythic Tricksters: A Heuristic Guide." In *Mythical Trickster Figures: Contours, Contexts, and Criticisms*, edited by Hynes and William G. Doty, 33–45. Tuscaloosa: University of Alabama Press, 1993.

Hynes, William J., and William G. Doty. "Introducing the Fascinating and Perplexing Trickster Figure." In *Mythical Trickster Figures: Contours, Contexts, and Criticisms*, edited by Hynes and Doty, 1–12. Tuscaloosa: University of Alabama Press, 1993.

Jameson, Frederic. "Third-World Literature in the Era of Multinational Capitalism." *Social Text* 15 (Fall 1986): 65–88.

Jameson, R. D. "The Chinese Art of Shifting Shape." *Journal of American Folklore* 64, no. 253 (1951): 275–80.

Jenkins, Henry. *Convergence Culture: Where Old and New Media Collide*. New York: New York University Press, 2006.

Ji Xianlin 季羡林, "*Luomo yanna* zai Zhongguo" «罗摩衍那»在中国 (*Ramayana* in China). *Zhongguo bijiao wenxue* 3 (1988): 13–22.

Jin Hezai 今何在. *Wukong zhuan* 悟空传 (Story of Wukong). Beijing: Guangming Ribao Chubanshe, 2001.

Kaplan, Amy, and Donald E. Pease, eds. *Cultures of United States Imperialism*. Durham, NC: Duke University Press, 1993.

Karcher, Stephen. "Journey to the West: C. G. Jung and the I Ching." *Spring: A Journal of Archetype and Culture* 66 (1999): 1–28.

Kidnie, Margaret Jane. *Shakespeare and the Problem of Adaptation*. London: Routledge, 2009.

Kim, Elaine H. Foreword to *Reading the Literatures of Asian America*, edited by Shirley Geok-lin Lira and Amy Ling. Philadelphia: Temple University Press, 1992.

———. Preface to *Charlie Chan Is Dead: An Anthology of Contemporary Asian American Fiction*, edited by Jessica Hagedorn. New York: Penguin, 1993.

Kingston, Maxine Hong. *China Men*. 1977. New York: Knopf, 1980.

———. *Tripmaster Monkey: His Fake Book*. New York: Knopf, 1989.

———. *The Woman Warrior: A Girlhood among Ghosts*. 1976. New York: Vintage, 1989.

Kondo, Dorinne. *About Face: Performing Race in Fashion and Theatre*. New York: Routledge, 1997.

Lai, Linda Chiu-han. "Film and Enigmatization: Nostalgia, Nonsense, and Remembering." In *At Full Speed: Hong Kong Cinema in a Borderless World*, edited by Esther C. M. Yau. Minneapolis: University of Minnesota Press, 2001.

Lau, Jeffrey 刘镇伟, dir. *Dahua Xiyou* 3 大话西游 3 (*A Chinese Odyssey: Part Three*). Beijing: Chunqiu Time Co., 2016.

———, dir. *Qing dian dasheng* 情癫大圣 (*A Chinese Tall Story*). Hong Kong: Asia Premium Investment, 2005.

———, dir. *Xiyou ji di yibai ling yi hui zhi Yueguang baohe* 西游记第一百零一回之月光宝盒 (*A Chinese Odyssey: Part One, Pandora's Box*). Hong Kong: Xi'an Film Studio, Choi Sing Film Company, 1995.

———, dir. *Xiyou ji di yibai ling yi hui zhi Xianlü qiyuan* 西游记第一百零一回之仙履奇缘 (*A Chinese Odyssey: Part Two, Cinderella*). Hong Kong: Xi'an Film Studio, Choi Sing Film Company, 1995.

Lefevere, André. *Translation, Rewriting and the Manipulation of Literary Fame*. London: Routledge, 1992.

Lemke, T. "'The Birth of Bio-Politics': Michel Foucault' s Lecture at the Collège De France on Neo-Liberal Governmentality." *Economy and Society* 30, no. 2 (2001): 190–207.

Lévi-Strauss, Claude. "The Structural Study of Myth." In *Structural Anthropology*, translated by C. Jacobson and B. Schoepf. Garden City, NY: Anchor, 1967.

Li, Qiancheng. *Fictions of Enlightenment: "Journey to the West," "Tower of Myriad Mirrors," and "Dream of the Red Chamber."* Honolulu: University of Hawaii Press, 2004.

———. trans. "Hu Shi's Rewriting of Chapter 99 of *The Journey to the West: An Introduction and Translation*." *Renditions* 67 (Spring 2007): 28–45.

———. "Transformations of Monkey: *Xiyou ji* Sequels and the Inward Turn." In *Snakes' Legs: Sequels, Continuations, Rewritings, and Chinese Fiction*, edited by Martin W. Huang, 46–74. Honolulu: University of Hawai'i Press, 2004.

———. "*Xiyou bu* de zuozhe ji Ming Qing banben"《西遊补》的作者及明清版本 (On the authorship of *Xiyou bu* and its Ming and Qing editions). *Chuantong Zhongguo yanjiu jikan* 7 (2009): 306–21.

Li Feng 李冯. "Ling yizhong shengyin" 另一种声音 (Another voice). In *Jinye wuren rushui* 今夜无人入睡 (No one sleeps tonight), 45–71. Wuhan: Hubei Jiaoyu Chubanshe, 2002.

Li Shiren 李时人and Jinghao Cai 蔡镜浩. *Datang Sanzang qujing shihua jiaozhu* 大唐三藏取经诗话校注 (Collation and annotation of *Datang Sanzang qujing shihua*). Beijing: Zhonghua Shuju, 1997.

———. "*Datang Sanzang qujing shihua* chengshu shijian kaobian" «大唐三藏取经诗话»成书时间考辩 (Investigation on the composition date of *Datang Sanzang qujing shihua*). *Xuzhou shifan xueyuan xuebao* 3 (1982): 22–30.

Liang, Yan. "When High Culture Embraces the Low: Reading *Xiyou ji* as Popular Fiction in Chinese Society." PhD diss., University of California, Santa Barbara, 2008.

Liang Jinhua 梁建华, ed. *Zhou Xingchi ying zhuan* 周星驰影传 (Stephen Chow and his films). Wuhan: Hubei Renmin Chubanshe, 2006.

Liang Shi 良士, and Chen Guangyi 陈光镒. *Da'nao tiangong* 大闹天宫 (Havoc in heaven). Shanghai: Xinmeishu Chubanshe, 1954.

Lim, Shirley Geok-lin, "The Ambivalent American: Asian American Literature on the Cusp." In *Reading the Literatures of Asian America*, edited by Lim and Amy Ling. Philadelphia: Temple University Press, 1992.

Lin, Patricia. "Clashing Constructs of Reality: Reading Maxine Hong Kingston's *Tripmaster Monkey: His Fake Book* as Indigenous Ethnography." In *Reading the Literatures of Asian America*, edited by Shirley Geok-lin Lim and Amy Ling, 333–48. Philadelphia: Temple UP, 1992.

Lin Changzhi 林长治. Shaseng riji 沙僧日记 (Sand Monk's diary). Changsha: Hunan Wenyi Chubanshe, 2002.

Lin Geng 林庚 (1910–2006). *Xiyou ji manhua* 西游记漫话 (On *Journey to the West*). Beijing: Beijing Chubanshe, 2004.

Liu, Lydia H. *The Clash of Empires: The Invention of China in Modern World Making*. Cambridge: Harvard University Press, 2004.

———. *Translingual Practice: Literature, National Culture, and Translated Modernity—China,* 1900–1937. Stanford: Stanford University Press, 1995.

———. *Yuji shuxie: Xiandai sixiangshi xiezuo gangyao* 语际书写: 现代思想史写作批评纲要. Shanghai: Sanlian shudian, 1999.

Liu Fu 刘复and Jiarui Li 李家瑞, eds. *Zhongguo suqu zongmu gao* 中国俗曲总目稿 (Annotated bibliography of Chinese folk songs). Institute of History and Philology, Academia Sinica, 1932.

Liu Jiyou 刘继卣 (1918–1983). *Nao tiangong* 大闹天宫 (Havoc in heaven). Shanghai: Shanghai Renmin Meishu Chubanshe, 1956.

Lowe, John. "Monkey Kings and Mojo: Postmodern Ethnic Humor in Kingston, Reed, and Vizenor." *MELUS: The Journal of the Society for the Study of the Multi-Ethnic Literature of the United States* 21, no. 4 (1996): 103–26.

Lowe, Lisa. *Immigrant Acts: On Asian American Cultural Politics*. Durham, NC: Duke University Press, 1996.

Lu, James. "Enacting Asian American Transformations: An Inter-Ethnic Perspective." In "Theory, Culture, and Criticism," special issue, *MELUS* 23, no. 4 (1998): 85–99.

Lu, Sheldon H. "Postscript: Answering the Question, What is Chinese Postsocialism?" In *Chinese Modernity and Global Biopolitics: Studies in Literature and Visual Culture*, 204–10. Honolulu: University of Hawaii Press, 2007.

Lu Xun 鲁迅 (1881–1936). *Zhongguo xiaoshuo de lishi bianqian* 中国小说的历史变迁 (Historical transformations of the Chinese novels). Hong Kong: Xiang Gang Jindai Tushu Gongsi, 1968.

———. *Zhongguo xiaoshuo shilue* 中国小说史略 (A brief history of the Chinese novel). Beijing: Renmin Wenxue Chubanshe, 1973.

Lu Yunting 路云亭. "Yihetuan yu Sun Wukong" 义和团与孙悟空 (The Boxers and Sun Wukong). *Journal of Jiangnan University* (Humanities & Social Sciences) 8, no. 6 (2009): 75–80, 95.

Luo, Manling. *Literati Storytelling in Late Medieval China*. Seattle: University of Washington Press, 2015.

Lutgendorf, Philip. "Evolving a Monkey: Hanuman, Poster Art, and Postcolonial Anxiety." In *Beyond Appearances? Visual Practices and Ideologies in Modern India*, 71–112. London: Sage, 2003.

———. "Five Heads and No Tale: Hanuman and the Popularization of Tantra." *International Journal of Hindu Studies* 5, no. 3 (2001): 269–96.

———. *Hanuman's Tale: The Messages of a Divine Monkey*. Oxford: Oxford University Press, 2007.

Ma, Sheng-mei. "Amy Tan's the Chinese Siamese Cat: Chinoiserie and Ethnic Stereotypes." *Lion and the Unicorn* 23, no. 2 (1999): 202–18.

———. *The Deathly Embrace: Orientalism and Asian American Identity*. Minneapolis: University of Minnesota Press, 2000.

———. *East-West Montage: Reflections on Asian Bodies in Diaspora*. Honolulu: University of Hawai'i Press, 2007.

———. *Immigrant Subjectivities in Asian American and Asian Diaspora Literatures*. Albany: State University of New York Press, 1998.

MacDonald, Peter, dir. *The Lost Empire*. Written by David Henry Hwang. Los Angeles, CA: Hall Mark Entertainment et al., 2001.

Mair, Victor H. *China and Beyond: A Collection of Essays*. Amherst, NY: Cambria, 2013.

———. *Painting and Performance: Chinese Picture Recitation and its Indian Genesis*. Honolulu: University of Hawaii Press, 1988.

———. "Suen Wu-Kung = Hanumat?: The Progress of a Scholarly Debate." In *Proceedings of the Second International Conference on Sinology*, 659–752. Taipei: Academia Sinica, 1989.

———. *T'ang Transformation Texts: A Study of the Buddhist Contribution to the Rise of Vernacular Fiction and Drama in China*. Cambridge: Harvard University Press, 1989.

Makarius, Laura. "The Myth of the Trickster: The Necessary Breaker of Taboos." In *Mythical Trickster Figures: Contours, Contexts, and Criticisms*, edited by William J. Hynes and William G. Doty, 66–86. Tuscaloosa: University of Alabama Press, 1993.

Masson, J. Moussaieff. "Hanuman as an Imaginary Companion." *Journal of the American Oriental Society* 101, no. 3 (1981): 355–60.

Mao Zedong 毛泽东 (1893–1976). *Mao Tsetung Poems*. Beijing: Foreign Languages Press, 1976.

———. *Mao Zedong xuanji* 毛泽东选集 (Selected works of Mao Zedong). Beijing: Renmin chubanshe, 1977.

———. *The Poems of Mao Tse-tung*. Translated by Willis Barnestone and Ko Ching-po. New York: Harper and Row, 1972.

———. *Selected Works of Mao Tse-Tung*. Beijing: Foreign Language Press, 1975.

———. "Talks at the Yan'an Forum on Literature and Art" 在延安文艺座谈会上的讲话. In *Modern Chinese Literary Thought: Writings on Literature, 1893–1945*, edited by Kirk A. Denton, 458–84. Stanford, CA: Stanford University Press, 1996.

McCloud, Scott. *Understanding Comics*. Northampton, MA: Kitchen Sink, 1993.

McGrath, James. *Postsocialist Modernity: Chinese Cinema, Literature, and Criticism in the Market Age*. Stanford, CA: Stanford University Press, 2008.

McLaren, Anne E. "Constructing New Reading Publics in Late Ming China." In *Printing and Book Culture in Late Imperial China*, edited by Cynthia J. Brokaw and Kai-Wing Chow, 152–83. Berkeley: University of California Press, 2005.

Miller, Stuart Creighton. *The Unwelcome Immigrant: The American Image of the Chinese, 1785–1882*. Berkeley: University of California Press, 1969.

Mingbai Ren 明白人. *Tangseng zhuan* 唐僧传 (Story of Tangseng). Chengdu: Bashu shushe, 2001.

Minkoff, Rob, dir. *The Forbidden Kingdom*. Santa Monica, CA: Lions Gate Films et al., 2008.

Mitchell, W. J. T. *Iconology: Image, Text, Ideology.* Chicago: University of Chicago Press, 1986.

———. "Metapictures." In *Picture Theory: Essays on Verbal and Visual Representation*, by Mitchell. Chicago: University of Chicago Press, 1995.

Mo, Timothy. *The Monkey King.* 1st Morrow ed. New York: Morrow, 1987.

Mo Nianjing 莫念经. *Xiyou Tangseng zhuan* 西游唐僧传 (Xiyou—Story of Tripitaka). www.qidian.com.Moore, Steven. *The Novel: An Alternative History* 1600–1800. London: Bloomsbury Academic, 2013.

Mullen, Bill. "Making Monkey Signify: Fred Ho's Revolutionary Vision Quest." In *Afro-Orientalism,* 163–206. Minneapolis: University of Minnesota Press, 2004.

Murong Xuecun 慕容雪村. *Tangseng qingshi* 唐僧情史 (Love story of Tripitaka). Tianjing: Tianjin Renmin Chubanshe, 2003.

Nakano, Miyoko 中野美代子. *Sun Wukong de dansheng: Hou de minjian wenxue yu Xiyou ji* 孙悟空的诞生——猴的民间文学与西游记 (The birth of Sun Wukong—Monkey folklore and *Xiyou ji*). *Xiyou ji de mimi* 西游记的秘密 (Secrets of *Xiyou ji*). Translated by Wang, Xiuwen. Beijing: Zhonghua shu ju, 2002.

———. *Yu Sun Wukong de duihua /Xi you ji de mimi*与孙悟空的对话/西游记的秘密 (Conversations with Sun Wukong/ Secrets of *Xiyou ji*). Translated by Wang, Xiuwen. Beijing: Zhonghua shu ju, 2002.

Narula, Joginder. *Hanuman, God and Epic Hero: The Origin and Growth of Hanuman in Indian Literary and Folk Tradition.* New Delhi: Manohar, 1991.

Nergaard, Siri, and Stefano Arduini. "Translation: A New Paradigm." *Translation*, inaugural issue (December 2011): 8–17.

Nguyen, Viet Thanh. "The Remasculinization of Chinese America: Race, Violence, and the Novel." *American Literary History* 12, no. 1/2 (2000): 130–57.

Ong, Aihua. *Flexible Citizenship: The Cultural Logics of Transnationality.* Durham, NC: Duke University Press, 1999.

Palumbo-Liu, David. *Asian/American Historical Crossings of a Racial Frontier.* Stanford, CA: Stanford University Press, 1999.

Parker, A., and E. K. Sedgwick. *Performativity and Performance.* New York: Routledge, 1995.

Pelton, Robert D. *The Trickster in West Africa: A Study of Mythic Irony and Sacred Delight.* Los Angeles: University of California Press, 1980.

———. "West African Tricksters: Web of Purpose, Dance of Delight." In *Mythical Trickster Figures: Contours, Contexts, and Criticisms,* edited by William J. Hynes and William G. Doty, 122–40. Tuscaloosa: University of Alabama Press, 1993.

Pickowicz, Paul G. "Huang Jianxin and the Notion of Postsocialism." In *New Chinese Cinemas: Forms, Identities, Politics,* edited by Nick Browne, Pickowicz, Vivian Sobchack, and Esther Yau, 57–87. Cambridge: Cambridge University Press, 1994.

Plaks, Andrew H. "After the Fall: Hsing-shih yin-yüan chuan and the Seventeenth-Century Chinese Novel." *Harvard Journal of Asiatic Studies* 45, no. 2 (1985): 543–80.

———. "Allegory in Hsi-Yu Chi and Hung-Lou Meng." In *Chinese Narrative: Critical and Thearetical Essays*, edited by Plaks, 163–202. Princeton, NJ: Princeton University Press, 1977.

———. *The Four Masterworks of the Ming Novel.* Princeton, NJ: Princeton University Press, 1987.

Qian Zhongshu 钱钟书 (1910–1998). *Guanzhui bian* 管锥编 (Compilations of tubes and awls). Shanghai: Zhonghua shuju, 1979.

Qingtian shangxian 青天上仙. *Xiyou Shaseng zhuan* 西游沙僧传 (Xiyou—Story of Sand Monk). www.qidian.com

Qitiandasheng Sun Wukonog 齐天大圣孙悟空 (aka *The Monkey King*). Hong Kong: Television Broadcasting Limited, 2002.

Quiquemelle, Marie-Claire. "The Wan Brothers and Sixty Years of Animated Film in China." Translated by Claire Beliard. In *Perspectives on Chinese Cinema*, edited by Chris Berry, 175–86. London: BFI, 1991.

Reinelt, Janelle G. "The Politics of Discourse: Performativity Meets Theatricality." *SubStance* 31, no. 2 (2002): 201–15.

Renmin Ribao dianzi ban 1946–2006 人民日报电子版 1946–2006 (The People's Daily Newspaper: 1946–2006 electronic edition).

Robertson, Carl Albert. "Reading the False Attribution in Xiyou zhengdao shu (The Book to Enlightenment of the *Journey to the West*)." PhD diss., University of Oregon, 2002.

Rojas, Carlos. *The Great Wall: A Cultural History.* Cambridge: Harvard University Press, 2010.

———. "Western Journeys of *Journey to the West.*" In *Sinographies: Writing China*, edited by Eric Hayot, Haun Saussy, and Steven G. Yao, 333–54. Minneapolis: University of Minnesota Press, 2007.

Rolston, David L. *How to Read the Chinese Novel.* Princeton, NJ: Princeton University Press, 1990.

———. *Traditional Chinese Fiction and Commentary: Reading and Writing between the Lines.* Stanford, CA: Stanford University Press, 1997.

Rothfork, John. "Confucianism in Timothy Mo's The Monkey King." *World Literature Written in English* 29, no. 2 (1989): 50–61.

Ruoff, A., LaVonne Brown, and Gerald Vizenor. "Woodland Word Warrior:

An Introduction to the Works of Gerald Vizenor." In "Genre, Theme and Form," special issue, *MELUS* 13, no. 1/2 (1986): 13–43.

Sa Mengwu 萨孟武. *Xiyou ji yu zhongguo gudai zhengzhi* 西游记与中国古代政治 (*Journey to the West* and politics in premodern China). Taibei: Sanmin Shuju, 1969.

Sabatini, Arthur J. "Fred Ho's Operatic Journey." In *Yellow Power, Yellow Soul: The Radical Art of Fred Ho*, edited by Roger N. Buckley and Tamara Roberts, 63–94. Champaign: University of Illinois Press, 2013.

Said, Edward. *Orientalism*. New York: Pantheon, 1978.

Saiyuki 西遊記 (aka *Alakazam the Great*). Japan: Osamu Tezuka and Toei Company, 1960.

Saiyuuki 西遊記 (aka *Monkey!*). 52 episodes. Japan: Nippon Television, International Television Films, and Japanese Broadcasting Corporation, 1978.

Saiyuuki 西遊記. Japan: Fuji TV, 2006.

Saiyuuki 西遊記. Japan: Fuji TV and Taho, 2007.

Sanders, Julie. *Adaptation and Appropriation*. London: Routledge, 2016.

Schueller, Malini Johar. "Theorizing Ethnicity and Subjectivity: Maxine Hong Kingston's *Tripmaster Monkey* and Amy Tan's *The Joy Luck Club*." *Genders* 15 (1992): 72–85.

Scott, John W. "The Uses of the Grotesque in *Gulliver's Travels* and the *Journey to the West*." *Tamkang Review: A Quarterly of Comparative Studies between Chinese and Foreign Literatures* 19, no. 1–4 (1988): 785–802.

Shahar, Meir. "The Lingyin Si Monkey Disciples and the Origins of Sun Wukong." *Harvard Journal of Asiatic Studies* 52, no. 1 (1992): 193–224.

Shao, Ping. "Huineng, Subhūti, and Monkey's Religion in *Xiyou ji*." *Journal of Asian Studies*, 65, no. 4 (November 2006): 713–40.

———. "Monkey and Chinese Scriptural Tradition: A Rereading of the Novel *Xiyou ji*." PhD diss., Washington University in St. Louis, 1997.

Shapiro, Elliott H. "Authentic Watermelon: Maxine Hong Kingston's American Novel." *MELUS* 26, no. 1 (2001): 5–28.

Simon, Sherry. *Translating Montreal: Episodes in the Life of a Divided City*. Montreal, Quebec: McGill-Queen's University Press, 2006.

Smith, A. D. "National Identity and Myths of Ethnic Descent." *Nationalism: Critical Concepts in Political Science*. London: Routledge, 2000.

Sohn, Stephen Hong. "Introduction: Alien/Asian: Imagining the Racialized Future." *MELUS* 33, no. 4 (2008): 5–22.

Sollors, Werner, ed. *Theories of Ethnicity: A Classical Reader*. New York: New York University Press, 1996.

Spence, Jonathan D. *Mao Zedong*. New York: Viking, 1999.

Spivak, Gayatri Chakravorty. "Can the Subaltern Speak?" In *The Translation Studies Reader*, edited by Lawrence Venuti. London: Routledge, 2000.

———. *A Critique of Postcolonial Reason: Toward a History of the Vanishing Present.* Cambridge: Harvard University Press, 1999.

———. *Death of a Discipline.* New York: Columbia University Press, 2003.

———. *In Other Worlds: Essays in Cultural Politics.* New York: Methuen, 1987.

———. "The Politics of Translation." In *Outside the Teaching Machine.* New York: Routledge, 1993.

———. "Three Women's Texts and a Critique of Imperialism." *Critical Inquiry* 12, no. 1 (1985): 243–61.

Subbaraman, Ramnath. "Beyond the Question of the Monkey Imposter: Indian Influence on the Chinese Novel, *The Journey to the West.*" *Sino-Platonic Papers* 114 (March 2002): 1–35.

Sui Shusen 隋树森 and Zang Maoxun 臧懋循, eds. *Yuanqu Xuan Waibian* 元曲选外编 (Additional selected works of the Yuan qu). Beijing: Zhonghua Shuju, 1959.

Tian Xiaopeng 田晓鹏. *Xiyou ji zhi dasheng guilai* 西游记之大圣归来 (Monkey King: Hero is back). Beijing: Beijing Weiying Shidai, 2015.

Tsai Chih Chung 蔡志忠. *Journey to the West: A Humorous Interpretation of the Historical Chinese Classic.* Translated by Alan Chong. Singapore: Asiapac, 1993.

Turner, Victor Witter. *The Anthropology of Performance.* Baltimore: PAJ, 1988.

Tymoczko, Maria. Introduction to *Translation and Power*, edited by Tymoczko and Edwin Gentzler. Amherst: University of Massachusetts Press, 2002.

———. *Translation in a Postcolonial Context: Early Irish Literature in English Translation.* Manchester, United Kingdom: St. Jerome, 1999.

Venuti, Lawrence. *The Scandals of Translation: Towards an Ethics of Difference.* London: Routledge, 1998.

———."Translation and the Formation of Cultural Identities." In *Cultural Functions of Translation*, edited by Christian Schaffner and Helen Kelly-Holmes. Philadelphia: Multilingual Matters, 1995.

———. *The Translator's Invisibility: A History of Translation.* London: Routledge, 1995.

Vizenor, Gerald Robert. *Griever: An American Monkey King in China.* Normal: Illinois State University, 1987.

Wagner, Rudolf G. *The Contemporary Chinese Historical Drama: Four Studies.* Berkeley: University of California Press, 1990.

Walker, Hera S. "Indigenous or Foreign: A Look at the Origins of the Monkey Hero Sun Wukong." *Sino-Platonic Papers* 81 (1998): 1–110.

Wan Laiming 万籁鸣 and Tang Cheng 唐澄, dirs. *Da'nao tiangong* 大闹天宫 (Havoc in heaven). Shanghai: Shanghai meishu dianying zhipian chang, 1961–64.

Wan Laiming 万籁鸣 and Wan Guchan 万古蟾, dirs. *Tieshan gongzhu* 铁扇公主 (Princess Iron Fan). Shanghai: Zhongguo Lianhe Yingye Gongsi, 1941.

Wan Laiming 万籁鸣 and Wan Guohun 万国魂, dirs. *Wo Yu Sun Wukong* 我与孙悟空 (Sun Wukong and I). Taiyuan: Beiyue Wenyi Chubanshe, 1986.

Wang, Jing. *The Story of Stone: Intertextuality, Ancient Chinese Stone Lore, and the Stone Symbolism in "Dream of the Red Chamber," "Water Margin," and "The Journey to the West."* Durham, NC: Duke University Press, 1992.

Wang Dewei 王德威. "Xianggang: Yizuo chengshi de gushi" 香港——一座城市的故事 (Hong Kong: A story of a city). In *Ruhe xiandai, zenyang wenxue: 19–20 shiji zhongwen xiaoshuo xinlun* 如何现代，怎样文学：十九、二十世纪中文小说新论 (The making of the modern, the making of a literature: New perspectives on 19th and 20th century Chinese fiction), 279–306. Taipei: Rye Field, 1998.

Wang Guowei 王国维. *Song Yuan xiqu shi* 宋元戏曲史 (A history of the drama of Song and Yuan). Shanghai: Shanghai Guji Chubanshe, 1998.

Wang Hecheng 王贺成, ed. *Xinzhu Sun Houzi nao tiangong quanqu* 新著孙猴子闹天宫全曲 (Monkey creates uproar in heaven, new complete script). Printed by Zhuyou zhai, 1880. Copy in National Library of China, Beijing.

Wangtian Yaomingyue 望天邀明月. *Xiyou Bajie zhuan* 西游八戒传 (Xiyou—story of Bajie). www.anzhuowang.net.

Weng Ouhong 翁偶虹 (1908–1994). "Da'nao tiangong" 大闹天宫 (Havoc in heaven), 1977. In *Zhongguo jingju xikao*, www.xikao.com.

———. *Weng Ouhong Bianju Shengya* 翁偶虹编剧生涯 (Weng Ouhong as a playwright). Beijing: Zhongguo Xiju Chubanshe, 1986.

———. *Weng Ouhong Ju Zuo Xuan* 翁偶虹剧作选 (Selected plays of Weng Ouhong). Beijing: Zhongguo Xiju, 1994.

Williams, A. Noelle. "Parody and Pacifist Transformations in Maxine Hong Kingston's *Tripmaster Monkey: His Fake Book*." *MELUS* 20, no. 1 (1995): 83–100.

Winkler, Martin M., ed. *Classical Myth and Culture in the Cinema*. New York: Oxford University Press, 2001.

Wong, Sau-ling Cynthia. *Reading Asian American Literature: From Necessity to Extravagance*. Princeton, NJ: Princeton University Press, 1993.

Wong, Sau-ling C., and Jeffrey J. Santa Ana. "Gender and Sexuality in Asian American Literature." *Signs* 25, no. 1 (1999): 171–226.

Wriggins, Sally Hovey. *The Silk Road Journey with Xuanzang.* Oxford: Westview, 2004.

Wu Cheng'en 吴承恩 (ca. 1500–ca. 1582). *Havoc in Heaven: Adventures of the Monkey King.* Translated by W. J. F. Jenner. Beijing: Foreign Languages Press, 1979.

———. *The Journey to the West.* Translated by Anthony C. Yu. Chicago: University of Chicago Press, 1977–83.

———. *The Journey to the West.* Translated by W. J. F. Jenner. Beijing: Foreign Languages Press, 1982–84.

———. *The Journey to the West.* Translated by Anthony C. Yu. Chicago: University of Chicago Press, 2012.

———. *The Monkey and the Monk: An Abridgment of "The Journey to the West."* Translated by Anthony C. Yu. Chicago: University of Chicago Press, 2006.

———. *Xiyou ji* 西游记 (The journey to the West). Beijing: Renmin Wenxue Chubanshe, 1988.

Wu Junchao 吴俊超. *Bajie riji* 八戒日记 (Diary of Bajie). Guangzhou: Huacheng Chubanshe, 2003.

Wu Xiaoru 吴小如. "Guanyu Sun Wukong de wutai xingxiang" 关于孙悟空的舞台形象 (Onstage image of Sun Wukong). In *Wu Xiaoru xiqu suibi ji* 吴小如戏曲随笔集 (Essays on drama by Wu Xiaoru), 34–36. Tianjin: Tianjin Guji Chubanshe, 2005.

———. "Huiyi Hao Zhenji" 回忆郝振基 (Remembering Hao Zhenji). In *Wu Xiaoru xiqu suibi ji* 吴小如戏曲随笔集 (Essays on drama by Wu Xiaoru), 94–95. Tianjin: Tianjin Guji Chubanshe, 2005.

Xiyou ji 西游记 (Journey to the West). Directed by Yang Jie. 25 episodes. Beijing: China Central Television 1986.

Xiyou ji 西游记 (Journey to the West). Directed by Yang Jie. 16 episodes. Beijing: China Central Television, 1998.

Xiyou ji 西游记 (Journey to the West). Directed by Zhang Jianya. Produced by Zhang, Jizhong, et al. Beijing: Ciwen chuanmei youxian gongsi, 2011.

Xu Hongda 徐宏达. *Nao tiangong* 闹天宫 (Havoc in heaven). *Lianhuan huabao* 连环画报 11, no. 121 (1956). Beijing: Renmin Meishu Press.

Xu Zhengkang 许正康. *Shaseng zhuan* 沙僧传 (Story of Sand Monk). www.qidian.com

Xuanzang 玄奘 (ca 596–664). *Datang xiyu ji* 大唐西域记. Taibei: Taiwan Shangwu Yinshuguan, 1968.

Yan Dunyi 严敦易. "*Xiyou ji* he gudian xiqu de guanxi" 西游记和古典戏曲的关系 (The relationship between *Journey to the West* and classical drama). In *"Xiyou ji" Yanjiu lunwen ji* 西游记研究论文集 (Collected essays on the study of *Xiyou ji*). Beijing: Zuojia Chubanshe, 1957.

Yang, Gene Leun. *American Born Chinese*. New York: First Second, 2006.

Yang Jingxian 杨景贤. *Yang Donglai xiansheng piping "Xiyou ji"* 杨东来先生批评西游记 (*Xiyou ji*: Annotated by Yang Donglai). Tokyo, Japan: Shibun, 1928.

Yau, Esther C. M. "Hong Kong Cinema in a Borderless World." In *At Full Speed: Hong Kong Cinema in a Borderless World*, edited by Yau, 1–28. Minneapolis: University of Minnesota Press, 2001.

Yeh, Alfred Kuang-yao. "The Evolution of a Rebel: An Interpretation of Wu Cheng-En's Journey to the West." *Fu Jen Studies* 10 (1977): 17–23.

Yen, Alsace. "A Technique of Chinese Fiction: Adaptation in the "Hsi-Yu Chi" with Focus on Chapter Nine." *Chinese Literature: Essays, Articles, Reviews* 1, no. 2 (1979): 197–213.

Yim Ho 严浩, dir. *Floating City* 浮城 (Fu cheng). Hong Kong: Mandarin Films Distribution, Well Go USA Entertainment, and Uzumasa, 2012.

Young, Ed. *Monkey King*. New York: HarperCollins, 2001.

Yu, Anthony C. *Comparative Journeys: Essays on Literature and Religion East and West*. New York: Columbia University Press, 2009.

———. "Heroic Verse and Heroic Mission: Dimensions of the Epic in the Hsi-Yu Chi." *Journal of Asian Studies* 31, no. 4 (1972): 879–97.

———. Introduction to *The Journey to the West*, translated by Yu, 10–96. Chicago: University of Chicago Press, 2012.

———. "Narrative Structure and the Problem of Chapter Nine in the 'Hsi-Yu Chi.'" *Journal of Asian Studies* 34, no. 2 (1975): 295–311.

———. "Religion and Literature in China: The 'Obscure Way' of the *Journey to the West*." In *Tradition and Creativity: Essays on East Asian Civilization*, 109–54. New Brunswick, NJ: Transaction, 1987.

Yu, Hongmei. "Visual Spectacular, Revolutionary Epic, and Personal Voice: The Narration of History in Chinese Main Melody Films." *Modern Chinese Literature and Culture* 25, no. 2 (Spring 2013): 168–218.

Xi Xi 西西. "Fucheng zhiyi" 浮城志异 (Marvels of a floating city and other stories). In *Fucheng zhiyi: Xianggang xiaoshuo xinxuan* 《浮城志异——香港小说新选 (New selected Hong Kong stories), edited by Ai Xiaoming, 24–36. Beijing: Zhongguo Renmin Daxue Chubanshe, 1991.

Zeng, Li. "Adaptation as an Open Process: *Dahua* Fandom and the Reception of *A Chinese Odyssey*." *Adaptation* 6, no. 2 (2012): 187–201.

Zhang, Xudong. *Postsocialism and Cultural Politics: China in the Last Decade of the Twentieth Century*. Durham, NC: Duke University Press, 2008.

Zhang Chengjian 张乘健. *Gudai wenxue yu zongjiao lunji* 古代文学与宗教论集 (Collected essays on premodern literature and religion). Changchun: Jilin Renmin Chubanshe, 2001.

Zhang Jinchi 张锦池. "*Datang Sanzang qujing shihua* chengshu niandai kaolun" 大唐三藏取经诗话成书年代考论 (A discussion of the date of *Tale of the Grand Tang Sanzang Seeking Buddhist Sutra*), *Xueshu jiaoliu* 4 (1990): 108–14, 67.

Zhang Jing'er 张静二. *Xiyou ji renwu yanjiu* 西游记人物研究 (Studies on characters in *Journey to the West*). Taibei: Taiwan Xuesheng Shuju, 1984.

Zhang Lixian 张立宪, Liu Chun 刘春, Ma Xiongying 马雄鹰, Zhong Lu 钟鹭, and Chen Jianxing 陈键兴, eds. *Dahua Xiyou baodian* 大话西游宝典 (Bible for *A Chinese Odyssey*). Beijing: Xiandai Chubanshe, 2000.

Zhao Hongben 赵宏本, Qian Xiaodai 钱笑呆, ill., Wang Xingbei 王星北, ed. *Sun Wukong sanda Baigu jing* 孙悟空三打白骨精 (Monkey subdues the White Bone Demon). Shanghai: Shanghai Renmin Chubanshe, 1962.

Zheng Faxiang 郑法祥. "Jingju 'Wukong xi' de biaoyan jifa" 京剧"悟空戏"的表演技法 (Techniques for performing Wukong in Peking Opera). *Shanghai Xiju* 3, no. 29 (1963): 29.

Zheng Xiaolong 郑晓龙, dir. *Guasha* 刮痧 (*The Guasha Treatment*). Beijing: Beijing Forbidden City Film Co., 2001.

Zheng Zhenduo 郑振铎. "Xiyou ji de yanhua" 西游记的演化 (Evolution of *Journey to the West*). In *Zhongguo wenxue yanjiu xinbian*中国文学研究新编 (Chinese literary studies new edition), 263–99. Taibei: Wenguang, 1973.

Zhongguo Xiju Chubanshe. *Guben Yuan Ming Zaju* 孤本元明杂剧 (Transcripts of unique copy *zaju* operas of Yuan and Ming). Beijing: Zhongguo xiju, 1958.

Zhu Hongbo竺洪波. "Cong Xiyou xi dao *Xiyou ji*—dui *Xiyou ji* xiqu jieduan de zai renshi" 从"西游戏"到<西游记>——对<西游记>戏曲阶段的再认识 (From drama to novel: Rethinking the drama stage of the *Journey to the West*). *Xiqu Yanjiu* 2 (2010): 194–206.

———. *Sibainian Xiyou ji xueshu shi* 四百年西游记学术史 (History of *Xiyou ji* study of the past four hundred years). Shanghai: Fudan Daxue Chubanshe, 2006.

Zhu Yixuan 朱一玄 and Liu Yucheng 刘毓忱, eds. *Xiyou ji ziliao huibian* 西游记资料汇编 (Research materials for *Xiyou ji* study). Henan: Zhongzhou Shuhua She, 1983.

INDEX

www.ingramcontent.com/pod-product-compliance
Lightning Source LLC
LaVergne TN
LVHW050152080826
844660LV00002B/174

* 9 7 8 0 2 9 5 7 4 3 1 8 9 *